MW01620797

The CARE Method Series

The CARE Method

Based on the Risk-Need-Responsivity Model, a Manual for Counselors

Nil Buckley
MA, LPC, LAC, DVCS

Offering **C**ompassion, **A**ccountability, **R**eflection, and **E**mpathy for Lasting Behavioral Change

The CARE Method
Based on the Risk-Need-Responsivity Model, a Manual for Counselors
Nil Buckley © 2024

Softcover ISBN: 978-1-61206-328-7

To purchase this book at quantity discounts, go to CAREmethodBook.com

Published by:

AlohaPublishing.com

Printed in the United States of America

Contents

A Message to Counselors Providing the CARE Method 9
Client's Testimonials 11
The Author's Story....................13
Introduction to the Care Method 15
Five Reasons Why Treating Court-Mandated Clients Can Be Challenging and Why Some Mental Health Professionals Struggle 17
Five Mistakes to Avoid 19
What Is the RNR Model? 21
Evaluating Clients and Developing a Treatment Plan 23
Why the CARE Method Is So Effective 27
Chapter 1: Understanding Intimate Partner Violence....................29
Chapter 2: Core Values 63
Chapter 3: Intergenerational Trauma 81
Chapter 4: Resiliency 99
Chapter 5: Behavioral Change 117
Chapter 6: Mind-Altering Substances and Their Impact on Relationships....................131
Chapter 7: The Amygdala Hijack 145
Chapter 8: Emotional Intelligence 159
Chapter 9: Triggers....................177
Chapter 10: Habits and the Mind....................193
Chapter 11: Attachment Theory and Attachment Styles....................207
Chapter 12: What Makes a Relationship Healthy? 223
Chapter 13: Codependency and Trauma Bonding in Relationships....................239
Chapter 14: Understanding Cognitive Distortions and Their Connection to Behavioral Responses....255
Chapter 15: The Four Horsemen of the Relationship Apocalypse and Their Antidotes............269
Chapter 16: The Four Styles of Communication 283

Chapter 17: Responsible Parenting 297
Chapter 18: Healthy Conflict Resolution 313
Chapter 19: Neuroplasticity and Relationships 327
Chapter 20: Becoming Accountable 339
Chapter 21: My Personal Change Plan 353
Appendix A: Required Presentations 365
Appendix B: Financial Accountability Presentation 369
Appendix C: Genogram 373
Appendix D: Time-Out Contract 375
Appendix E: Cycle of Abuse Presentation 379
Appendix F: Apology Letter to My Child(ren) Template 381
The Evaluation and Intake Process 385
About The Colorado DVOMB 389
Acknowledgments 393
Additional Resources 395
Notes 397

To every counselor working with clients who have participated in domestic violence, your unwavering compassion and dedication do not go unnoticed. Your commitment to fostering change, understanding, and healing in those you serve is truly inspiring. This manual is dedicated to you and the incredible impact you have on countless lives. Thank you for your tireless work, empathy, and resilience in the face of challenges. You are making a profound difference, one client at a time.

Nil Buckley

A Message to Counselors Providing the CARE Method

Dear Counselor/Colleague,

When I first began my journey as a counselor, I often found myself grappling with self-doubt and a lack of experience. Despite graduating from a top-rated master's program, I quickly realized that no formal education could fully prepare me for the unique challenges of working with the forensic population. I discovered that the key to effective counseling in this field lay not just in knowledge, but in the resilience to learn from my own mistakes, the determination to earn my clients' trust, and the courage to find my own confidence.

This manual is the culmination of my journey and the lessons I've learned along the way. My hope is that it serves as a guiding light for you, offering practical insights and effective strategies to navigate each chapter. May it empower you to connect deeply with your clients, inspire positive change, and bolster your own confidence as a counselor. Remember, every step you take with your clients is a step toward transformation, not just for them, but for you as well. Embrace this journey with an open heart and a determined spirit. Together, we can make a profound impact.

With warm regards and best wishes for your success,

Nil Buckley

How to Use This Book

This manual includes sections specifically designed to equip you, the counselor, with the tools and guidance needed to effectively teach the material. Each section is followed by images of the individual pages from the workbook your clients have, making it easy to follow along and support your clients as they work through the exercises and activities. This structure is intended to facilitate a seamless teaching and learning experience, ensuring that you are well prepared to guide your clients toward meaningful change.

A Note About Reliatrax Integration

The homework and individual presentations in this curriculum are available electronically through Reliatrax's Client Portal if *The Care Method* book for counselors is purchased. For counselors using Reliatrax, access is granted only with the author's consent. Reliatrax, an electronic health record system that I have used for many years, has been highly supportive in integrating the homework assignments from *The Care Method* directly into the client portal. This integration allows for efficient management and tracking of client compliance with homework tasks.

Client Testimonials

These statements come from my clients who have completed the CARE Method treatment.

"The CARE method was a life-changing experience, providing invaluable insight into my behaviors and triggers. The curriculum's comprehensive approach and supportive group setting helped me gain confidence and understand myself better. This method has given me the tools to maintain my happiness and sobriety."

"Attending programs and classes written and developed by Nil Buckley was transformative. The service's knowledge and education provided profoundly changed my life for the better. The step-by-step program taught me about communication and attachment styles, along with accountability, healthy relationships, and effective communication. The comprehensive support helped me understand my behavior, fostering lifelong changes and a commitment to personal growth. The CARE Method truly empowers individuals to rebuild their lives positively."

"Ms. Buckley's thoughtful, comprehensive curriculum comes together with her compassionate yet no-nonsense approach to create an incredibly impactful and invaluable treatment program. I am thrilled to see it become available to a wider audience, as I wholeheartedly believe in its ability to affect countless lives for the better. I cannot overstate my gratitude for the time I spent in treatment; the CARE Method has helped me to heal, grow, and take accountability in new and truly transformative ways!"

"Before beginning the program, I just wanted to get through it as fast as I could. However, it didn't take long to realize how wrong I was and how the program offered so much more than I ever thought possible. Through my time and experience with the CARE Method, I not only learned how to have healthy relationships and break toxic behaviors in relationships, I also had so much time to look within. I learned about myself and gained peace of mind—which I never thought was possible. I found closure with trauma that I didn't know I could overcome and found my way to a healthier self. Because of this process, I became the best version of myself and have no doubt that anyone else who uses the curriculum will find the same peace I've gained."

"The CARE Method classes are both challenging and rewarding for anyone seeking to understand themselves and others. In the field of self-betterment and mental health treatment, the process of this scientifically based and backed curriculum is excellent. I recommend it for everyone who wants to grow emotionally and become more self-aware."

"When I found this curriculum, I was addicted, angry, and hopeless. In one year, it transformed my life, helping me overcome my struggles with dignity and respect. Today, I'm a better father and person, with self-esteem, confidence, and a renewed ability to face life's challenges. This curriculum gave me the tools to rebuild my life, and for that, I am forever grateful."

The Author's Story

I immigrated to the United States in 2007 with approximately $50 in my pocket and a determination to build a new life. Leaving behind my family was a bold decision. I left a promising career at the second-largest mining company in the world and the familiarity of my home in Santa Inês, a small town in northeast Brazil. Despite the fear and doubts of my community, I arrived safely in the United States where I was welcomed by my host family. Driven by a desire to help others, I pursued a career in mental health counseling. In 2014, I was accepted into the Clinical Mental Health Counseling Program at the University of Colorado, Colorado Springs. My initial focus was on working with veterans experiencing trauma. However, during my internship that same year, I was matched with an outpatient practice, which led me to work with men and women who were on probation for domestic violence.

This experience sparked a passion within me to address the root causes of domestic violence so I could create positive change in my community. Following my internship, I gained valuable experience working with families involved in the criminal justice system and the Department of Human Services at Savio House, where I witnessed the struggles of families and children living in poverty and abusive or neglectful environments. This experience solidified my commitment to serve marginalized communities.

My desire to make a deeper impact led me to the Colorado Department of Corrections. My role at Centennial Correctional Facility was to provide mental health counseling to a diverse population of inmates, including domestic violence offenders, sex offenders, murderers, and serial killers. This is when I truly began to believe in the power of compassionate counseling. Regardless of their crimes, I found a way to empathize and connect with my clients, believing fervently in the healing potential of understanding and empathy—even in the most challenging criminal cases. While working there, I pursued approval from the Colorado Offender Management Board to specialize in working with domestic violence offenders. However, a subsequent internship at a private practice left me deeply troubled by the outdated methods and a lackluster approach to genuine healing, which propelled me to establish Vivus Counseling Services. At Vivus, I dedicate myself to delivering a meaningful and contemporary approach to counseling services that is client-centered.

The CARE Method is the result of significant independent research, professional training, and also learning from the mistakes I made in the beginning of my career. It is a unique and effective approach to helping clients with interpersonal relationship issues heal and build healthy relationships. I firmly believe in the transformational power of care and empathy, provided that we approach healing with open hearts and minds.

Introduction to the Care Method

I take great pride in my role as an approved DVOMB Provider of domestic violence (DV) treatment within the State of Colorado. Colorado stands at the forefront of this field, with our initiatives and practices serving as a model for other states across the nation. The Colorado Domestic Violence Offender Management Board (DVOMB) and its staff, research, and leadership team have made a tremendous impact on the evolution of domestic violence treatment in our state. Probation departments all over the country look up to Colorado and its DVOMB as a leading example in the field of domestic violence, recognizing the revolutionary changes and advancements made over the past decade. I am proud to be part of a system that is dedicated to setting the highest standards and driving progress in domestic violence treatment.

The CARE Method was born out of a deep desire to offer something truly impactful to my clients. When I first began providing court-ordered treatment, I often felt scattered despite having somewhat of a plan for each session. Also, my sessions lacked an internal connection, and I realized that a cohesive, comprehensive approach was essential for meaningful progress.

As I mentioned, in Colorado, we have a dedicated board (DVOMB) that oversees the treatment of domestic violence offenders. In 2020, I had the honor of being appointed as a board member and invited to serve on the Standards Revision Committee (SRC). I am privileged to have been asked to continue serving for another four years and remain deeply committed to contributing to the vital work of the Domestic Violence Offender Management Board (DVOMB) in this field. As a member of the Standards Revision Committee for the past four years, I have been privileged to help write and review the standards for the evaluation and treatment of offenders. It was during this time that I began to develop my own curriculum, the CARE Method, which is rooted in the competencies outlined in our standards.

Over the past several years, I have received an overwhelming amount of positive feedback from my clients. Comments like, "Why don't they teach us this in high school? If I had known this before, I would have never gotten arrested," and "This treatment has changed my life and my marriage" have been incredibly encouraging. Additionally, I have received positive feedback from my staff and the professionals I have supervised at my practice.

It was during this time that I realized my approach and curriculum needed to be shared with others. My hope is that the CARE Method will serve as a powerful tool in your counseling practice, enabling you to guide your clients with confidence and compassion. By fostering a deeper understanding and addressing core issues, we can facilitate lasting change and growth. In the next page, I will address why working with the court-mandated population can be so challenging and why many mental health professionals get burned out quickly and fail.

Five Reasons Why Treating Court-Mandated Clients Can Be Challenging and Why Some Mental Health Professionals Struggle

1. Resistance to treatment: Court-mandated clients often enter treatment with skepticism or reluctance, viewing the process as a formality rather than a personal goal. This resistance can hinder engagement and progress, making it challenging for therapists to foster meaningful change.

2. Extrinsic motivation: Many court-mandated clients are driven by external motivations, such as avoiding legal consequences, rather than intrinsic desires for personal growth. This extrinsic motivation can limit their commitment to treatment, affecting the effectiveness of therapeutic interventions.

3. Stigma and shame: Clients in this population frequently experience stigma and shame related to their legal issues and perceived failures. This can create significant barriers to open communication and self-disclosure, as clients may fear judgment or further legal repercussions. The resulting discomfort can impede their willingness to fully engage in the therapeutic process.

4. Barriers to building trust and rapport: Establishing a therapeutic relationship can be difficult when clients are distrustful of the process or view the therapist as an extension of the legal system. Successful treatment relies on building trust and rapport, which can be compromised if clients see the therapist as an enforcer rather than a supportive ally.

5. Complex legal, social, and interpersonal issues: Court-mandated clients often face a range of interconnected legal and social challenges, including ongoing legal battles, family conflicts, and financial instability. They often present with co-occurring needs such as mental health issues, trauma, and substance abuse issues. Addressing these multifaceted issues and needs requires a holistic approach and coordination with other service providers. Professionals may struggle with the added complexity if they lack the skills or resources to manage these challenges effectively.

How the CARE Method Addresses the Challenges

The difficulties associated with treating court-mandated clients—such as resistance to treatment, extrinsic motivation, building trust, navigating complex legal and social issues, and inconsistent compliance—highlighted the need for a more effective approach. In response to these challenges, I developed the CARE Method, which integrates techniques from motivational interviewing and person-centered therapy. Motivational interviewing helps to reduce resistance and enhance client engagement by focusing on their intrinsic motivations and fostering a collaborative relationship. Meanwhile, the person-centered approach ensures that clients are treated with empathy and respect, allowing them to feel valued and understood. By addressing the unique barriers faced by court-mandated clients, *The Care Method* book describes the process and offers a structured, supportive framework that promotes genuine change and increases the likelihood of successful treatment outcomes. This method not only facilitates deeper client buy-in but also equips counselors with practical tools to navigate and overcome these common obstacles.

Five Mistakes to Avoid

1. Not knowing how to challenge clients in a clinically effective way: Challenging clients is a crucial part of therapy, but it must be done thoughtfully and strategically. When I started, I sometimes pushed clients too hard, too soon, which led to resistance and setbacks. Effective challenging involves understanding each client's readiness for change, using motivational interviewing techniques, and fostering a supportive environment where clients feel safe to explore difficult issues. The goal is to strike a balance between providing a comfortable space for clients and encouraging them to step out of their comfort zones in a way that promotes growth and self-awareness. Remember this: the forensic population is prone to struggle with a sense of mistrust, so if the environment does not feel safe, they will not open up.

2. Placing clients in treatment without treatment plans: Early in my career, I made the mistake of starting treatment without a clear, individualized plan for each client. This approach can lead to unfocused sessions, unclear goals, and ineffective outcomes. A treatment plan serves as a road map for therapy, outlining specific objectives, strategies, and timelines. It ensures that both the therapist and client are aligned in their efforts and can measure progress over time. In Colorado, we measure the client's progress on a continuous basis and also during their treatment plan reviews (TPR). Developing a treatment plan requires a thorough assessment of the client's needs and strengths. Additionally creating an effective DV risk assessment is essential. In Colorado we utilize the DVRNA, which has been validated.[1]

3. Disregarding clients' buy-in: One of my significant early mistakes was not prioritizing client buy-in for the treatment process. Without the client's active participation and agreement, even the

---

1. Domestic Violence Offender Management Board (DVOMB). (2016). *Domestic violence risk and needs assessment (DVRNA) scoring manual* (5th ed.). Division of Criminal Justice, Colorado Department of Public Safety.

most well-crafted treatment plans can fail. Clients need to understand the purpose of their therapy, believe in its value, and be committed to the process. This requires clear communication, setting collaborative goals, and regularly checking in with clients to ensure they feel heard and engaged. Building a therapeutic alliance based on trust, respect, and unconditional regard is essential for effective treatment and to obtain client buy-in.

4. Not structuring group sessions: In my early attempts at facilitating group therapy, I often lacked a clear structure, leading to sessions that felt chaotic and unfocused. Structured group sessions provide a framework that helps manage time, ensures all participants have an opportunity to contribute, and keeps the group on track with its objectives. A structured session typically includes a clear agenda, time for each participant to speak, planned activities or discussions, and a wrap-up that summarizes key points and sets goals for the next meeting. Structure provides a sense of safety and predictability, which is crucial for effective group therapy.

This is where I began to notice that my curriculum, the CARE Method, was proving its effectiveness. By implementing structured sessions, I saw a significant improvement in group dynamics and participant engagement. The CARE Method provided a clear and consistent framework that not only kept sessions organized but also fostered a supportive and productive environment. Clients were more engaged, and we achieved more meaningful progress toward their goals.

5. Not taking care of myself—compassion fatigue and burnout: In the beginning, I underestimated the importance of self-care and experienced compassion fatigue and burnout as a result. Constantly dealing with clients' trauma and emotional pain without adequate self-care can lead to physical and emotional exhaustion, reduced empathy, and decreased effectiveness as a therapist. It's crucial to recognize the signs of burnout and prioritize self-care by setting aside time for rest, seeking supervision or peer support, and engaging in activities that rejuvenate you. Taking care of yourself is not only essential for your well-being but also for providing the best care to your clients.

What Is the RNR Model?

The risk-need-responsivity (RNR) model is a widely recognized approach to offender rehabilitation and treatment within the criminal justice system. It is based on three (3) key principles:

1. **Risk principle**: This principle focuses on targeting interventions to individuals who present a higher risk of reoffending. By identifying and prioritizing those with a higher risk, resources can be allocated more effectively, leading to better outcomes in reducing recidivism.
2. **Need principle**: The need principle emphasizes addressing criminogenic needs, which are dynamic factors that contribute to criminal behavior. These needs may include issues such as substance abuse, lack of education or employment, antisocial attitudes, and poor impulse control. By targeting these needs through evidence-based interventions, the likelihood of reoffending can be significantly reduced.
3. **Responsivity principle**: The responsivity principle highlights the importance of delivering interventions in a manner that is responsive to the individual's learning style, abilities, and motivation. This involves tailoring treatment approaches to match the cognitive abilities, personality traits, cultural background, and other characteristics of the offender, thereby maximizing the effectiveness of the intervention.

The CARE Method is designed with the understanding that each client has unique needs and risks, a principle strongly supported by the risk-need-responsivity model. The RNR model emphasizes the importance of addressing individual risks, criminogenic needs, and personal responsivity factors. By focusing on these key elements, the CARE Method aims to provide tailored interventions that effectively reduce recidivism. This approach ensures that higher-risk individuals receive the necessary support, dynamic factors contributing to problematic behavior are addressed, and treatment is delivered in a way that resonates with the individual's learning style and motivation. By integrating these evidence-based principles, the CARE Method aspires to foster meaningful change, reduce future incidents, and ultimately transform lives.

Evaluating Clients and Developing a Treatment Plan

In Colorado, every individual arrested for domestic violence and placed on probation is required to complete a post-sentence domestic violence evaluation. As DVOMB providers, we may handle the evaluation and treatment plan in one session or separate them into different appointments. Either way, we know that a treatment plan is crucial not only for the client's success in treatment but also because the DVOMB standards mandate that every evaluation must result in an individualized treatment plan.

Evaluating court-ordered clients is challenging, and developing a treatment plan adds another layer of complexity. As a DVOMB provider, you must align each client's treatment plan with the risk factors identified during the evaluation. For example, you should include a treatment goal for substance abuse if your client has a history of substance use or is currently struggling with addiction.

Below are essential tips to help create an effective treatment plan.

1. **Engage your defensive client**: When conducting the evaluation, which comes before the treatment plan, be mindful of your professional attitude. Many clients view us as extensions of the court system, positioned as authority figures. If you want to build rapport, avoid presenting yourself in an intimidating manner. Draw from person-centered therapy to create a sense of safety for your client.

Once you've completed the disclosure statement, ask if they understand the purpose of the evaluation. If they respond with "risk factors" or "needs," acknowledge their insight with a "Good job," then proceed to explain the remainder of the evaluation.

One mistake I made early on was starting with, "What happened? Why were you arrested?" Today, I begin by saying, "To make the best recommendations on your behalf, I need to get to know you better. Let's start by discussing your childhood."

Maintain a calm, empathetic presence—this is where trauma may surface. Make eye contact, thank them for sharing, and show empathy. Building this rapport makes it easier to gather essential information on substance abuse, mental health, and relationship history.

2. **Use a structured approach when learning about relationship history.** Ask questions like these:

    - How long did you date before moving in together?
    - What is the reason for most of your conflicts?
    - How do you resolve conflict?
    - What conflict happened that brought you to treatment?
    - Why did the relationship end (if applicable)?

These questions help identify whether the client has insight into their actions or is blaming the partner for everything. A client lacking insight will often start answers with, "My wife/girlfriend . . ." or "She . . ." instead of taking personal responsibility. Statements you want to hear start with "I."

Save the discussion about the incident leading to their arrest (if applicable) for one of the last steps. Compare their account with the police report, but here's an important tip: **don't read the police report before interviewing your client**. I've learned that letting the client know you haven't read the report builds trust immediately. I tell clients, "I have the discovery for your case, but I haven't read it yet because I want to prevent any bias before evaluating you." This transparency has led to greater honesty and self-disclosure from clients.

3. **Collaborate with clients on their treatment plans**: Once the first half of the interview is complete, take a moment to review the police report. Review the report before the second meeting if you're scheduling the treatment plan for a later session. The evaluation form includes questions about strengths and weaknesses. One easy way to start a conversation about treatment goals is to ask the client to expand on a weakness they've already identified.

If clients struggle to pinpoint areas for growth, I often say, "Reflect on yourself as a partner in both current and past relationships. What are some things you could improve to become a healthier partner?" This approach rarely fails. However, those deeply in denial or still in the pre-contemplation stage might not be ready for treatment. In such cases, pre-treatment to enhance insight and accountability might be necessary, though it's worth noting that pre-treatment is not yet formally part of the Colorado DVOMB standards. I anticipate it will be in the near future.

When your client identifies areas they want to work on, praise them sincerely. Then, refer back to the risk factors identified in the evaluation. As an example, I might say, "In reviewing the risk factors associated with your arrest, it's clear that substance use played a significant role in the violation of the protection orders. Would you agree that staying sober is crucial to your success?" When the client agrees, affirm their insight: "I agree, and we will include a treatment plan goal that addresses this risk factor."

Be creative when developing treatment plan goals: You most likely won't create seven different treatment goals (the average number of risk factors for high-risk clients) for every case. Think critically—if a client has violated a protection order or stalked their victim, this signals issues with respecting boundaries. In that case, *respecting boundaries* should be a goal in their treatment plan.

Overall, your treatment plans shouldn't be overly difficult to create or engage the client in. It comes down to how we approach the interview. Use motivational interviewing techniques, coming from a place of curiosity and compassion. Understand that many clients may have limited insight, and the evaluation process is not the time for confrontation. Your goal is to gather information, assess their amenability to treatment, and evaluate their risks and needs.

*For information about how Colorado performs the evaluation and intake process to lay a foundation for individualized treatment, see The Evaluation and Intake Process section on page 385.

Why the CARE Method Is So Effective

What makes the CARE Method stand out? I won't claim to have invented any of the concepts in this book. In fact, all the chapters in *The CARE Method* are derived from evidenced-based theories, such as an attachment theory (Bowlby), etc. When I first began creating the CARE Method curriculum, I drew heavily on the Colorado DVOMB standards and required competencies to shape the material. Colorado leads the way in domestic violence treatment, with tremendous progress made—particularly under the leadership of Acting Program Manager Jesse Hansen, MPA, and Implementation Specialist Caroleena Frane, LPC, LAC, ADS. They are forward-thinking professionals who truly care about impacting our state. One of the benefits of being a DVOMB provider is the discretion and autonomy the standards grant us to develop our own curriculum. While we have the freedom to tailor our approach, one key requirement is that we must incorporate evidence-based practices to ensure effective treatment.

But back to the real question: it's not that I am the only one to teach clients about trauma, attachment styles, communication techniques, or the cycle of abuse. You're likely covering similar topics if you're a DVOMB provider or DV counselor. What sets my approach apart is how I deliver these sessions—the method I follow.

When I first began practicing as a DV counselor, I relied on Excel spreadsheets to track topics, with folders scattered on my computer. While this worked, it lacked the cohesive flow that defines the CARE Method today. Here's what I believe will make a significant difference in your client's success:

1. **Structure your sessions by alternating between psychoeducation week and group processing week**. During psychoeducation weeks, engage your clients by doing some reading together. If you prefer, use a dry-erase board to explain concepts—just make sure the clients are involved in the discussion. In this way, each chapter takes at least two sessions to cover.

2. **Set clear expectations for homework**. At the end of each chapter, inform your clients that the following week will focus solely on reviewing their homework and providing feedback. This gives them a clear goal to work toward.

3. **Challenge the client to be intentional**. If a client arrives unprepared or with minimal effort in their homework, acknowledge their effort by saying, "I appreciate that you completed the homework. However, I'm not convinced that you allocated enough time to be intentional with your answers. Moving forward, I expect you to be better prepared and more thoughtful in your responses." Deliver this message kindly, respectfully, but above all—firmly.

4. **Work through the curriculum chronologically**. The CARE Method is also unique because each chapter builds upon the last. For example, after learning about the Four Horsemen (chapter 15), it becomes clear that understanding the four styles of communication (chapter 16) is essential for eliminating destructive behaviors. I often tell my clients, "Don't miss next week's session, or you might find yourself lost in what we're learning."

5. **Finally, follow this method consistently**. Feel free to adjust how you deliver each session, but don't change the structure: psychoeducation followed by group processing. I promise you'll see tremendous growth in your clients as they learn to approach each homework assignment with intention and sincerity. They will understand that if they fall short in either area, you'll challenge them to rise to the occasion.

This method has proven to be highly effective. I frequently hear from probation officers that my clients can articulate the lessons they're learning in their treatment group with clarity and insight.

1

Understanding Intimate Partner Violence

"Between stimulus and response, there is a space. In that space is our power to choose our response. In our response lies our growth and our freedom."

—Viktor E. Frankl

Understanding intimate partner violence (IPV) is crucial for recognizing the many forms abuse can take. In chapter 1, clients are introduced to the foundational concepts of IPV, starting with a comprehensive definition that goes beyond physical violence to include emotional, psychological, and financial abuse. The chapter aims to expand clients' awareness of abusive behaviors, challenging the common misconception that abuse is limited to physical acts. By broadening their perspective, clients can gain a deeper understanding of the complexities of IPV and begin to identify harmful patterns in their own relationships.

Be aware that because of the amount of information this chapter covers, it will probably take more than two sessions to cover everything.

As a counselor, your role is to help clients recognize and confront any initial resistance or denial they may have regarding their own behaviors. Many clients may minimize their actions or fail to see the emotional and psychological impact of their behavior on others. This chapter is designed to guide clients through an exploration of these behaviors and their underlying causes, paving the way for deeper self-awareness.

You will need to facilitate discussions that help clients identify patterns of control and power that may have influenced their relationships. This chapter encourages clients to begin reflecting on how their beliefs and values may have contributed to their actions. The exercises included are aimed at increasing self-awareness, with the intention of setting the stage for the transformative work that will follow in subsequent chapters.

As you guide clients through this chapter, focus on fostering an environment of empathy and honesty. Encourage them to engage fully with the material, as this chapter is crucial for establishing a foundation for the change process. Be prepared to address common challenges, such as denial or minimization of abusive behavior, and use this opportunity to start building trust and open communication in the therapeutic relationship.

This chapter not only introduces the critical concepts of IPV but also sets the tone for the rest of the program, encouraging clients to approach the material with openness and a willingness to engage in honest self-examination.

Goals of This Chapter

The goal of this chapter is designed to help clients develop a deep and meaningful insight into the dynamics of intimate partner violence (IPV). Understanding these dynamics is critical for fostering empathy, which is a cornerstone of promoting healthier relationships. By gaining insight, clients are better equipped to recognize harmful patterns in their own behaviors and relationships, which is essential for informed intervention and meaningful change. This chapter is one of the longest in the CARE Method, reflecting the complexity and importance of the topics covered. The depth of material ensures that clients have ample opportunity to explore these dynamics thoroughly, making it one of the most pivotal chapters in the entire program.

Colorado DVOMB Standards Competencies

This chapter aligns closely with specific Colorado Domestic Violence Offender Management Board (DVOMB) standards, particularly those focusing on **domestic violence history**, **accountability/responsibility for behaviors**, and **pro-criminal attitudes and behaviors**. The DVOMB stresses the importance of understanding the history of domestic violence, recognizing patterns that contribute to abusive dynamics. Additionally, this chapter challenges clients to confront and take full accountability for their actions. By acknowledging their behaviors and the impact they have had on others, clients can initiate the process of making amends and transitioning toward healthier, nonviolent ways of interacting in relationships.

The integration of pro-criminal attitudes and behaviors into this chapter is crucial as well, as it addresses the underlying beliefs and thought patterns that may have justified or rationalized abusive actions. Clients are encouraged to critically examine these attitudes, understanding how they have perpetuated harmful behaviors and impeded their growth. By actively working to shift these pro-criminal mindsets, clients can align their actions with principles of respect, empathy, and nonviolence.

These standards are fundamental to the therapeutic goals of the CARE Method, ensuring that clients not only gain a deeper understanding of the dynamics of intimate partner violence (IPV) but also take concrete steps toward accountability, dismantling harmful attitudes, and fostering positive change.

Important Things to Know

In this first chapter, it's crucial for clients to **fully understand what intimate partner violence (IPV)** is. Many clients may come into this program with misconceptions, often believing that IPV is limited to physical violence. However, this chapter helps expand their awareness to include emotional, psychological, and financial abuse.

By gaining a comprehensive understanding of what IPV looks like, clients will be better equipped to examine their own behaviors and begin to recognize patterns they may not have seen before. This foundational knowledge sets the stage for the work ahead, as clients will soon move on to explore how their **core values** and **beliefs** shape these behaviors. Understanding the dynamics of IPV is the first step toward taking responsibility and making meaningful changes.

Key Concepts and Terminology

Intimate partner violence (IPV): A pattern of behavior in a relationship that is used to gain or maintain power and control over an intimate partner. It includes physical, emotional, psychological, and financial abuse.

Physical abuse: The use of physical force against another person that results in bodily injury, pain, or impairment. Examples include hitting, slapping, pushing, and other forms of physical harm.

Emotional abuse: Nonphysical behaviors that aim to control, isolate, or frighten someone. This can include verbal abuse, manipulation, humiliation, and intimidation.

Psychological abuse: A form of abuse where the abuser uses threats, fear, and mental manipulation to control the victim. This often overlaps with emotional abuse.

Financial abuse: Controlling a person's ability to acquire, use, and maintain financial resources. It often includes withholding money, limiting access to funds, or forcing a partner to be financially dependent.

Coercive control: A pattern of behavior that seeks to take away the victim's liberty or freedom and to strip away their sense of self. This can involve manipulation, isolation, and control over every aspect of the victim's life.

Accountability: The act of taking responsibility for one's actions, particularly in acknowledging and accepting the harm caused by abusive behaviors.

Responsibility: The obligation to act correctly and to make amends for any harm done to others. In the context of IPV, it involves recognizing one's role in the abuse and working toward change.

Empathy: The ability to understand and share the feelings of another person. In the context of IPV, developing empathy is crucial for understanding the impact of one's actions on others.

Intervention: Actions taken to prevent further abuse, which can include therapeutic strategies, legal measures, or other forms of support designed to stop the cycle of violence and promote healthier behaviors.

Discussion Prompts

Chapter 1 lays the groundwork for understanding intimate partner violence (IPV) and the various forms it can take. As you guide your clients through this material, the following discussion prompts can help facilitate meaningful conversations, encourage self-reflection, and deepen their understanding of the concepts introduced.

Defining abuse:

- Ask clients how they define abuse and what behaviors they associate with it.
- **Discussion prompt**: "When you hear the word 'abuse,' what comes to mind? How do you differentiate between physical and nonphysical forms of abuse?"

Personal reflection on past relationships:

- Encourage clients to reflect on their past relationships and identify any patterns of behavior that may have been abusive.
- **Discussion prompt**: "Think about your past relationships. Can you identify any behaviors that, in hindsight, could be considered abusive? How did those behaviors affect you and the other person involved?"

Recognizing emotional and psychological abuse:

- Help clients understand that abuse is not limited to physical acts. Emotional and psychological abuses are equally harmful.
- **Discussion prompt**: "Have you ever experienced or engaged in behaviors that might be considered emotionally or psychologically abusive? What were the impacts of those behaviors on the relationship?"

Understanding coercive control:

- Discuss the concept of coercive control and how it might manifest in a relationship.
- **Discussion prompt**: "Coercive control involves manipulating and dominating another person. Can you recall instances in your relationships where you or your partner may have exercised such control? What was the outcome?"

Accountability and responsibility:

- Encourage clients to take responsibility for their actions and to recognize the importance of accountability in the process of change.
- **Discussion prompt**: "Reflect on your actions in your relationships. Are there behaviors you need to take responsibility for? How can acknowledging these actions help you move toward positive change?"

Impact on others:

- Discuss the ripple effects of abusive behavior on partners, children, and others.
- **Discussion prompt**: "Abusive behaviors often have a far-reaching impact. How do you think your actions have affected others in your life? What steps can you take to repair the harm done?"

Empathy development:

- Encourage clients to develop empathy by considering how their actions might feel if they were on the receiving end.
- **Discussion prompt**: "Imagine being in your partner's shoes during a time when you exhibited abusive behavior. How do you think they felt? How does this perspective change your view of your actions?"

Intervention and change:

- Explore the importance of seeking help and making changes to stop abusive patterns.
- **Discussion prompt**: "What steps can you take to change abusive patterns in your relationships? How can intervention, whether through therapy, education, or other means, support your journey toward healthier relationships?"

Contents

Chapter 1: Understanding Intimate Partner Violence
Extended Language for the Definition of Domestic Violence
Where Do Abusive Behaviors Come From?
How Many Forms of Abuse Are There?
The Cycle of Abuse
Understanding Strangulation as a Lethality Risk Factor
Understanding Weapons as a Lethality Risk Factor
Can an Abusive Person Change?
Signs an Abusive Person Is Changing
Homework

1

Understanding Intimate Partner Violence

"Anything can be taken from a man but one thing; the last of the human freedoms, to choose one's attitude in any given set of circumstances, to choose one's own way."

—Victor E. Frankl

What is domestic violence? When you hear "domestic violence" what is the first thing that comes to mind?

In the space below, please draw or write what comes to your mind.

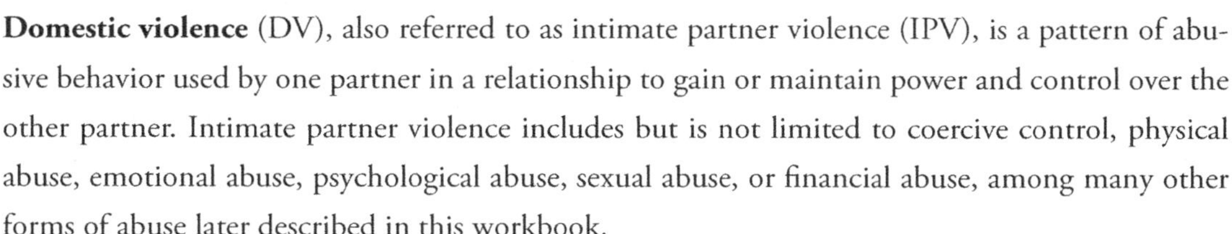

Domestic violence (DV), also referred to as intimate partner violence (IPV), is a pattern of abusive behavior used by one partner in a relationship to gain or maintain power and control over the other partner. Intimate partner violence includes but is not limited to coercive control, physical abuse, emotional abuse, psychological abuse, sexual abuse, or financial abuse, among many other forms of abuse later described in this workbook.

THE CARE METHOD

Domestic violence can occur within intimate relationships, such as those between spouses or partners, or within families. Domestic violence can affect anyone regardless of age, gender, sexual orientation, race, religion, or socioeconomic status.

The history of domestic violence is complex and multifaceted, with its roots extending back centuries. Here's a brief overview of some key points:

Early history: Domestic violence has likely existed for as long as human societies have formed intimate relationships. In many historical societies, it was often considered acceptable for a husband to discipline his wife or children through physical means. Women and children were often regarded as property of the husband and father, and their rights were limited. The modern understanding of domestic violence began to emerge in the late 20th century as advocacy groups, feminists, and researchers shed light on the prevalence and impact of abuse within intimate relationships. In many countries, laws were enacted to criminalize domestic violence and provide legal protections for victims.

There has been a gradual shift in public perception regarding domestic violence. It is no longer seen as a private matter to be dealt with within the confines of the family, but rather as a serious social issue that requires intervention and support for victims. The rise of advocacy groups, shelters, hotlines, and support services has provided resources for victims of domestic violence to seek help and escape abusive situations. These organizations also work to raise awareness, educate the public, and advocate for policy changes to address the root causes of domestic violence. Despite progress, domestic violence remains a pervasive problem worldwide. Many victims still face barriers to seeking help, such as fear of retaliation, economic dependence, cultural norms, and lack of awareness about available resources. Efforts to combat domestic violence continue through prevention programs, education campaigns, and initiatives to hold perpetrators accountable for their actions.

Extended Language for Definition of Domestic Violence

The criminal definition for domestic violence serves as the legal basis upon which a court determines if an underlying factual basis of domestic violence exists. The following definition of domestic violence is a more comprehensive definition of domestic violence that shall be used for the purposes of evaluation, assessment, and treatment of those who participate in domestic violence as defined by the Colorado DVOMB Standards.

UNDERSTANDING INTIMATE PARTNER VIOLENCE

Caution should be exercised when applying this definition and list of abuse types in circumstances that have not been identified through the legal system. **It is important to note that not all domestic violence behaviors are illegal, but they are abusive or harmful to the person who has experienced the behavior.**

Extended Definition of DV

Domestic violence is an emerging or established pattern of attitudes and behaviors that are abusive, controlling, harmful, or predatory against a person. Such domestic violence behaviors are choices that attempt to cause a specific outcome rooted in power and control and often intersect with multiple forms of abuse. Domestic violence offenders can present with multiple areas of risk to reoffend (i.e., domestic violence reoffending, lethality, non-domestic violence reoffending). A domestic violence offender is a person who engages in a pattern of one or more of the following abuse categories: **dominance**, **dependence**, **dissonance**, **vengeance**, **surveillance**, and **violence**. This list is not exhaustive regarding the forms of abuse related to domestic violence and should be considered and used for clinical purposes.[1]

Where Do Abusive Behaviors Come From?

Where do you think abusive behaviors come from? Write your answers in the space below.

1. Colorado DVOMB Standards, 2024

THE CARE METHOD

Domestic violence stems from a desire to gain and maintain power and control over an intimate partner. Perpetrators of abuse harbor a belief in their entitlement to dictate and constrain their partner's lives, either due to a conviction that their own feelings and needs should take precedence within the relationship or because they derive satisfaction from the dominance afforded by such abuse. Employing various tactics, abusers aim to undermine equality in the relationship, thereby fostering a climate where their partners feel devalued and deprived of respect.

Note: As a counselor specializing in domestic violence (DV), I firmly advocate for the importance of comprehending the underlying causes of behaviors, a principle that my clients consistently value. Understanding the roots of our thoughts and actions is essential for fostering meaningful change. Without this understanding, it becomes challenging to address and modify problematic behaviors effectively.

Empowering individuals with insights into the etiology, or cause, of their behavior not only facilitates personal growth but also equips them with the tools necessary for navigating healthier patterns of thought and action. Below are some key factors that can contribute to the development of abusive behaviors:

Individual Factors:

a. **Personal history of abuse**: Individuals who have experienced abuse or trauma themselves, particularly during childhood, may be more likely to perpetrate abuse in their own relationships. This can be due to learned behaviors and coping mechanisms acquired from their past experiences.
b. **Personality traits**: Certain personality traits, such as narcissism, low empathy, aggression, and a need for control, can predispose individuals to engage in abusive behaviors.
c. **Mental health issues**: Some mental health conditions, such as antisocial personality disorder, borderline personality disorder, substance abuse disorders, or untreated depression and anxiety, can contribute to abusive behavior if left untreated. It's important to understand that these conditions do not cause intimate partner violence, but instead, they can contribute to or exacerbate abusive behavior.

Relational Factors:

d. **Power imbalance**: Abuse often occurs in relationships where there is a significant power imbalance, with one partner exerting control over the other.

UNDERSTANDING INTIMATE PARTNER VIOLENCE

e. **Poor communication skills**: Inadequate communication skills and conflict resolution strategies can lead to escalating tensions and resorting to abusive behaviors as a means of asserting dominance or resolving conflicts. The four styles of communication are taught in chapter 16 of this workbook, and conflict resolution is taught in chapter 18 of this workbook.

f. **Cycle of violence**: In some cases, abusive behavior can become cyclical, with periods of tension building, followed by an explosive incident, and then reconciliation (honeymoon) or a period of calm before the cycle begins again. It is important to understand that not all violence is the same, and the cycle of abuse is different for every relationship.

Societal and Cultural Factors:

g. **Gender norms and expectations**: Traditional gender roles and societal norms that condone or excuse male aggression and dominance over women can contribute to the perpetuation of abusive behaviors.

h. **Socialization**: Individuals may learn abusive behaviors from their family, peers, or cultural influences, further perpetuating a cycle of violence.

i. **Lack of support services**: Inadequate access to support services, such as shelters, counseling, and legal resources, can leave victims trapped in abusive relationships and enable perpetrators to continue their behavior unchecked.

It's important to recognize that while these factors may contribute to the development of abusive behaviors, they do not excuse or justify them. Ultimately, individuals are responsible for their own actions, and interventions should focus on holding perpetrators accountable, providing support and resources for victims, and addressing the underlying causes of abuse.

How Many Forms of Abuse Are There?

How many forms of abuse do you think exist? Write your answer below.

THE CARE METHOD

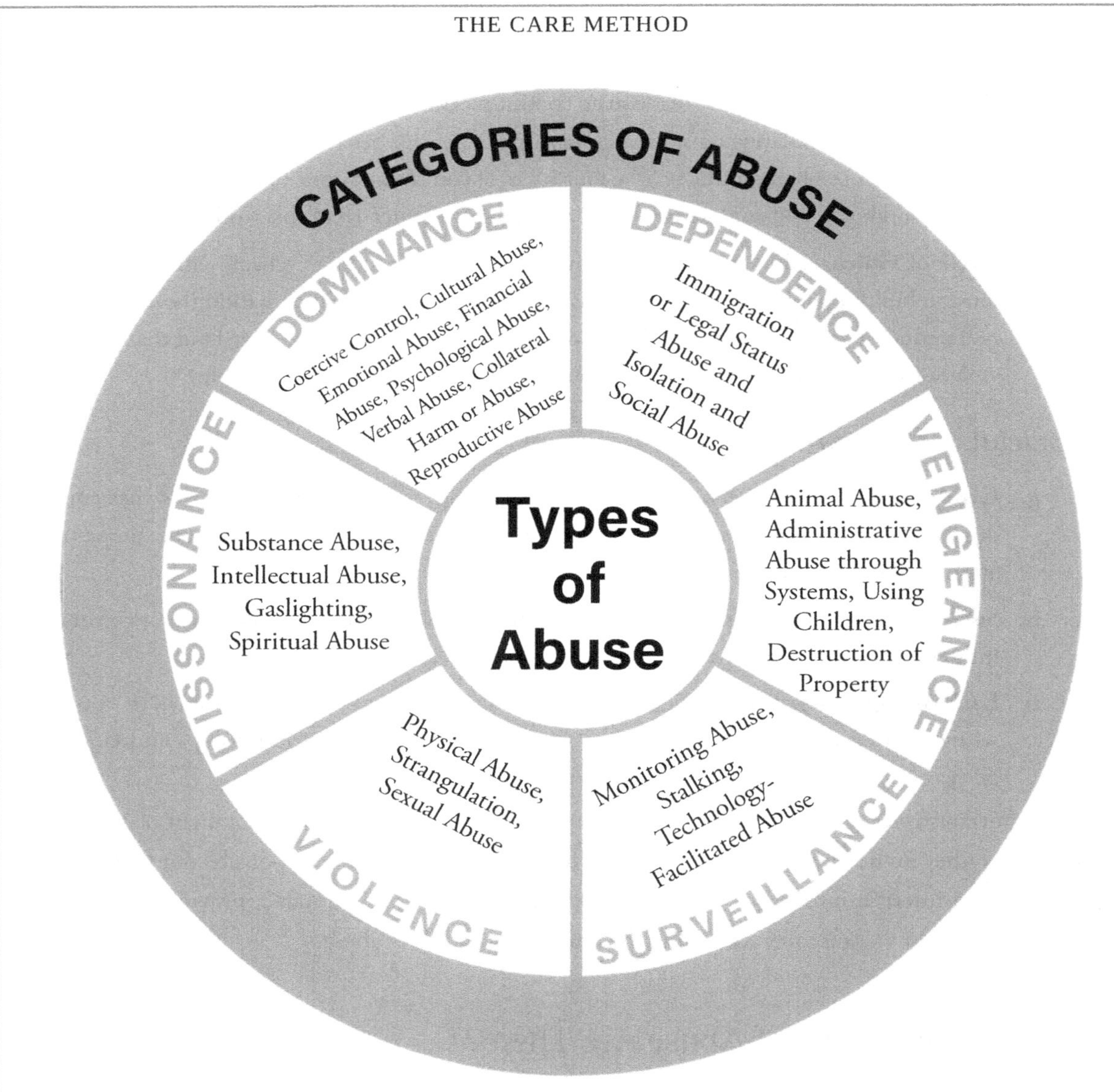

The Types of Abuse Wheel was created by Eronilde Buckley and is based on the latest research defining the 24 types of domestic abuse. This wheel has been adapted from the Duluth Model using the Colorado DVOMB Standards.

UNDERSTANDING INTIMATE PARTNER VIOLENCE

DOMINANCE

Coercive control: Engaging in a pattern of behaviors to gain control and power by eroding a victim's autonomy, self-efficacy, and self-esteem, marked by domination and entrapment that extends across the spectrum of violent tactics.

Does this reflect your behavior? If yes, please provide an example below:

Cultural abuse: Using culture as a means to excuse, minimize, or otherwise justify abusive behavior. This may include disparaging the victim's culture, forcing a victim to embrace the offender's culture, isolating a victim from mainstream culture, using culture to silence a victim, using a language barrier to isolate a victim, using other language to shut a victim out, etc.

Does this reflect your behavior? If yes, please provide an example below:

THE CARE METHOD

Emotional abuse: Using nonphysical behaviors that may be subtle or more obvious which are meant to control, isolate, or frighten the victim. This type of abuse may present as threats, insults, yelling, constant monitoring, excessive jealousy, manipulation, humiliation, intimidation, or dismissiveness. While these emotionally abusive behaviors do not leave physical marks, they do cause harm, disempower, and traumatize the victim who is experiencing the abuse.

Does this reflect your behavior? If yes, please provide an example below:

Financial abuse: Controlling the victim's access to economic assets or resources for the purpose of exploiting and limiting the victim's capacity to support themselves independent of the offender.

Does this reflect your behavior? If yes, please provide an example below:

UNDERSTANDING INTIMATE PARTNER VIOLENCE

Psychological abuse: Intense or repeated patterns of confusing or doubt-inducing behavior that creates psychological stress, confusion, or doubt in the victim. Threatening of suicide or homicide, threatening gestures or actions, denying abuse, gaslighting, or stalking.

Does this reflect your behavior? If yes, please provide an example below:

Verbal abuse: Using words or verbal iterations to control, coerce, manipulate, intimidate, ridicule, or degrade the victim and negatively impact their psychological health or otherwise cause harm. Verbal abuse may overlap with other forms of abuse.

Does this reflect your behavior? If yes, please provide an example below:

THE CARE METHOD

Collateral harm or abuse: Causing harm to secondary victims whether directly or indirectly to manipulate, intimidate, or coerce in an abusive or controlling manner.

Does this reflect your behavior? If yes, please provide an example below:

Reproductive abuse: Using coercion, control, deceit, manipulation, or threats to impact pregnancy, sabotage of contraceptives, use of contraceptives, restrict access to contraceptives, and unilaterally decide reproductive choices as a method to gain power and control over another person(s).

Does this reflect your behavior? If yes, please provide an example below:

UNDERSTANDING INTIMATE PARTNER VIOLENCE

DEPENDENCE

Immigration or legal status abuse: Using or exploiting a victim or their family's lack of documentation, legal or illegal status, or citizenship as a means to threaten, control, or coerce the victim.

Does this reflect your behavior? If yes, please provide an example below:

Isolation and social abuse: Attempting to foster conditions that aim to isolate a victim from their friends, family, or community. These behaviors cause harm by cutting off healthy relationships, limiting social engagement, interfering with social networks, disrupting social interactions, or attempting to cause reputational harm.

Does this reflect your behavior? If yes, please provide an example below:

THE CARE METHOD

DISSONANCE

Substance abuse: Attitudes or behaviors displayed while under the influence that are directed at enabling, threatening, or coercing a victim. Mood-altering substances can be used in a manner by the offender to perpetuate coercive control against the victim. The use of mood-altering substances by an offender does not cause domestic violence nor is it an excuse for abuse.

Does this reflect your behavior? If yes, please provide an example below:

Intellectual abuse: Disrespecting another's learning style, ability, ways of thinking, or intellectual interests. This can involve ridiculing a victim's ideas, devaluing a victim's opinions, or controlling the victim's access to educational or other learning opportunities.

Does this reflect your behavior? If yes, please provide an example below:

30

UNDERSTANDING INTIMATE PARTNER VIOLENCE

Gaslighting: Attempting to create self-doubt and confusion in the victim's mind by distorting reality and forcing the victim to question their own judgment and intuition.

Does this reflect your behavior? If yes, please provide an example below:

Spiritual abuse: Using faith, spirituality, religion, or the lack thereof as a means to intimidate, hurt, or control the victim.

Does this reflect your behavior? If yes, please provide an example below:

THE CARE METHOD

VENGEANCE

Animal abuse: Mistreating, threatening, or killing any pet or animal, such as torturing, tormenting, mutilating, maiming, poisoning, or abandoning to emotionally manipulate or coerce the victim.

Does this reflect your behavior? If yes, please provide an example below:

Administrative abuse through systems: Utilizing systems intended to provide safety for a victim to harass, threaten, intimidate, and control the victim instead.

Does this reflect your behavior? If yes, please provide an example below:

UNDERSTANDING INTIMATE PARTNER VIOLENCE

Using children: Using or manipulating children as a means to control, coerce, manipulate, or otherwise cause harm to a victim.

Does this reflect your behavior? If yes, please provide an example below:

Destruction of property: Damaging, destroying, devaluing, or taking possession of the tangible property of the victim as an act to harm, retaliate, or intimidate the victim.

Does this reflect your behavior? If yes, please provide an example below:

THE CARE METHOD

SURVEILLANCE

Monitoring abuse: Using or manipulating the environment physically or virtually to gain access and gather information about a victim regarding their schedule, activities, whereabouts, and interactions. These behaviors are a violation of the victim's expectation of and right to privacy regardless of consent, awareness, or knowledge. These behaviors can undermine a victim's sense of safety, sanity, and security. This definition may include unwanted advances by the domestic violence offender in the pursuit of the identified victim.

Does this reflect your behavior? If yes, please provide an example below:

Stalking: Engaging in a pattern of behavior directed at a specific person that attempts to develop, expand, or maintain a relationship with the victim. These behaviors can cause substantial emotional distress or fear for the victim's safety or the safety of others. Victims may or may not be aware of these behaviors.

Does this reflect your behavior? If yes, please provide an example below:

UNDERSTANDING INTIMATE PARTNER VIOLENCE

Technology-facilitated abuse: Using technology such as social media and social networking to bully, harass, stalk, or intimidate. This behavior can also take the form of verbal or emotional abuse perpetrated online. Offenders may use overlapping tactics to surveil their intimate partners.

Does this reflect your behavior? If yes, please provide an example below:

VIOLENCE

Physical abuse: Using any physical act or object (including weapons) with the potential for causing harm, injury, disability, or death to exert power and control over the victim. Such physical acts can include targeting anyone or anything the victim may have an attachment to. Physical abuse can include coercing other people to commit any physical acts against the victim.

Does this reflect your behavior? If yes, please provide an example below:

THE CARE METHOD

Strangulation: Impeding or restricting the airway or circulation of the blood of a victim by applying pressure to the neck or chest, or by blocking the nose or mouth.

Does this reflect your behavior? If yes, please provide an example below:

Sexual abuse: Using any physical act, behavior, or exploitation that is sexual in nature and causes harm to the victim without consent.

Does this reflect your behavior? If yes, please provide an example below:

UNDERSTANDING INTIMATE PARTNER VIOLENCE

The Cycle of Abuse

The cycle of abuse is a pattern commonly observed in abusive relationships, characterized by distinct phases that perpetrators and victims may cycle through. This model was initially conceptualized by psychologist Lenore Walker in 1979,[2] based on her work with survivors of domestic violence. The cycle typically consists of three (3) main phases:

1. **Tension-building phase**: In this initial phase, tension begins to mount within the relationship due to various stressors, conflicts, or triggers. Communication may become strained, and minor incidents of verbal or emotional abuse may occur. The victim may attempt to placate the abuser or avoid confrontation in an effort to de-escalate the tension.
2. **Explosion or acute violence phase**: This phase is marked by a sudden and intense outburst of abusive behavior from the perpetrator. It may involve physical, emotional, or sexual violence, as the abuser seeks to assert control and dominance over the victim. The abuse can be severe and may result in significant harm to the victim.
3. **Honeymoon or reconciliation phase**: Following the explosion phase, the abuser may express remorse, apologize, and make promises to change their behavior. This phase is characterized by a period of relative calm and reconciliation, during which the abuser may shower the victim with affection, gifts, or acts of kindness. The victim may hope that the abuse will not recur and may believe the abuser's promises of change.

The cycle of abuse is often described as a repeating pattern, with the phases escalating in intensity. Victims may become trapped in this cycle, experiencing a sense of hopelessness and confusion as they oscillate between periods of abuse and reconciliation. It's important to note that not all abusive relationships follow this exact pattern, and variations may occur based on individual circumstances. Dr. Lenore Walker's research and conceptualization of the cycle of abuse have been instrumental in understanding the dynamics of domestic violence and informing interventions and support services for survivors. Her work has contributed significantly to the field of psychology and the broader efforts to address and prevent domestic violence.

2. Fisher, Bonnie S., and Lab, Steven P. (2 February 2010). *Encyclopedia of Victimology and Crime Prevention*. SAGE Publications. ISBN 978-1-4129-6047-2. p. 257.

THE CARE METHOD

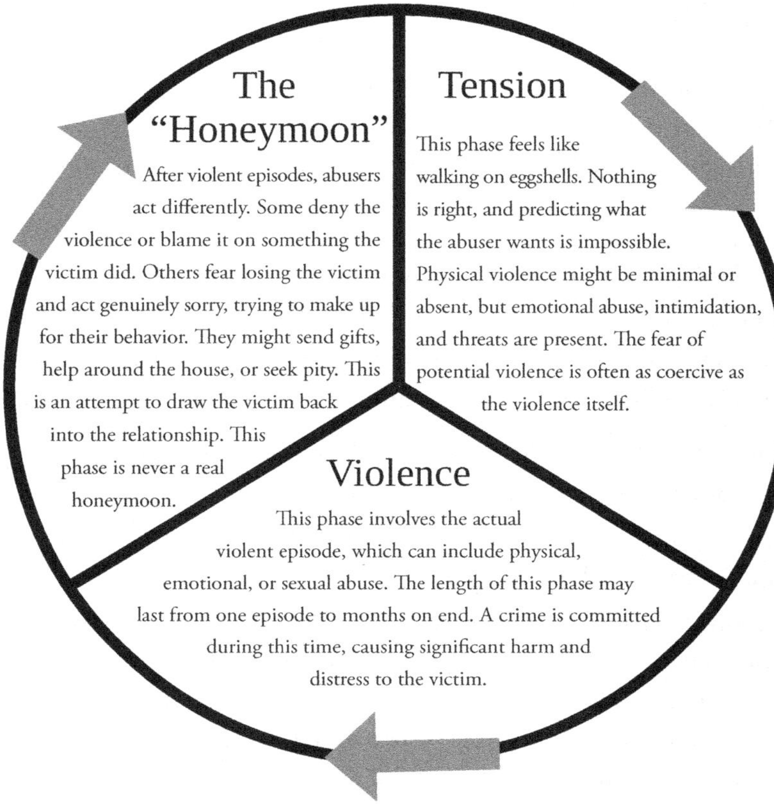

The "Honeymoon"

After violent episodes, abusers act differently. Some deny the violence or blame it on something the victim did. Others fear losing the victim and act genuinely sorry, trying to make up for their behavior. They might send gifts, help around the house, or seek pity. This is an attempt to draw the victim back into the relationship. This phase is never a real honeymoon.

Tension

This phase feels like walking on eggshells. Nothing is right, and predicting what the abuser wants is impossible. Physical violence might be minimal or absent, but emotional abuse, intimidation, and threats are present. The fear of potential violence is often as coercive as the violence itself.

Violence

This phase involves the actual violent episode, which can include physical, emotional, or sexual abuse. The length of this phase may last from one episode to months on end. A crime is committed during this time, causing significant harm and distress to the victim.

Cycle of Abuse based on D. Lenore Walker's research

Understanding Strangulation as a Lethality Risk Factor

Strangulation is one of the most lethal forms of violence. It can take only seconds for someone to lose consciousness from strangulation, and death can occur within minutes if oxygen supply to the brain is cut off. Even if strangulation does not result in death, it can cause serious long-term health problems, including brain damage, cognitive impairment, and speech difficulties. Psychologically, the impact of being strangled by an intimate partner can be profound.[3] Victims may experience severe anxiety, depression, post-traumatic stress disorder (PTSD), and a pervasive

3. Logan, T. Examining Relationship and Abuse Tactics Associated with Nonfatal Strangulation Experiences Before and After a Protective Order. *Violence and Gender, 8*(2), 95–103 (2021, June 14). doi: 10.1089/vio.2020.0012

UNDERSTANDING INTIMATE PARTNER VIOLENCE

sense of vulnerability. Strangulation is a significant risk factor for homicide. Studies have shown that a victim of strangulation is at a much higher risk of being killed by their intimate partner in the future. This is because strangulation is often a sign of an escalation of violence in an abusive relationship.

The signs and symptoms of strangulation can vary depending on the severity of the attack. Some common signs and symptoms include:[4]

a. Difficulty breathing
b. Hoarseness
c. Wheezing
d. Loss of consciousness
e. Dizziness
f. Headache
g. Neck pain
h. Bruising on the neck
i. Redness of the face and eyes
j. Incontinence

Can you think of some examples of an escalation of violence? This can be anything from grabbing, shoving, shouting, etc. Write them below.

4. National Domestic Violence Hotline. (2024). The Dangers of Strangulation. Retrieved from *National Domestic Violence Hotline*: https://www.thehotline.org/resources/the-dangers-of-strangulation/

THE CARE METHOD

Understanding Weapons as a Lethality Risk Factor

Research consistently shows that the presence of a firearm in domestic violence situations increases the risk of homicide for women by a substantial margin. Firearms in the hands of abusers not only pose a direct threat to the lives of victims but also to children, family members, law enforcement responders, and the community at large. The accessibility of the weapon, combined with threats or previous uses of the weapon, escalates the situation's urgency and the potential for lethal violence.

In a study conducted by Sorenson & Wiebe, 2004,[5] they assessed weapon use in intimate partner violence and perspectives on hypothetical firearm policies. The researchers conducted structured in-person interviews with 417 women in 67 battered women's shelters. They found that words, hands or fists, and feet were the most common weapons used against battered women. About one-third (1/3) of the battered women had a firearm in the home. In two-thirds (2/3) of these households, the intimate partner used the gun(s) against the woman, usually threatening to shoot/kill her (71.4%) or to shoot at her (5.1%). Most battered women thought spousal notification or consultation regarding gun purchase would be useful and that a personalized firearm ("smart gun") in the home would make things worse. The researchers concluded that a wide range of objects are used as weapons against intimate partners. Firearms, especially handguns, are more common in the homes of battered women than in households in the general population.

Can an Abusive Person Change?

Do you think an abusive person can change? Why or why not? Write your answer below.

5. Sorenson, S.B., and Wiebe, D.J. Weapons in the Lives of Battered Women. *Am. J. Public Health*, 94(8), 1412–1417 (2004, August). doi: 10.2105/ajph.94.8.1412

UNDERSTANDING INTIMATE PARTNER VIOLENCE

Signs an Abusive Person Is Changing

Write down some signs that you believe are evidence of an abusive person changing.

The truth is that abusive people can change their ways. Of course, this does not happen by mere conviction or just because they "feel bad." There has to be a genuine acceptance of their fault and a willingness to seek the right kind of help. Here are a few signs that an abusive person is changing:

a. Admitting fully to what they have done
b. Stopping excuse-making
c. Making amends
d. Accepting responsibility and recognizing that abuse is a choice
e. Not declaring themselves "cured," but rather accepting that overcoming abusiveness is a decades-long process
f. Demonstrating respectful, kind, and supportive behaviors
g. Not blaming their partner or children for the consequences of their actions
h. Changing how they respond to their partner or former partner's anger and grievances
i. Not demanding credit for improvements they've made

THE CARE METHOD

Homework

Self-Reflection on Abusive Behaviors

1. Reflect on the different forms of abuse discussed (physical, emotional, psychological, coercive control, financial, etc.). Can you identify any behaviors you have engaged in that align with these forms of abuse?

____

____

____

2. Have you ever used intimidation, threats, or coercion to control your partner?

____

____

____

3. How do you feel about the behaviors you've identified? Do you recognize them as abusive?

____

____

____

Understanding the Cycle of Abuse

4. Describe your understanding of the cycle of abuse. How do you recognize when you're in the tension-building phase, explosion phase, or honeymoon phase?

____

____

____

UNDERSTANDING INTIMATE PARTNER VIOLENCE

5. Reflect on a specific incident where you may have been in the explosive or honeymoon phase of the cycle. What were your thoughts and emotions during each phase?

____

____

____

____

Accountability and Choice

6. Do you believe that abuse is a choice? Why or why not?

____

____

____

7. Reflect on a time when you chose not to engage in abusive behavior. What factors influenced this decision?

____

____

____

Impact on the Victim(s)

8. How do you think your abusive behaviors have affected your partner/former partner? Consider both the immediate and long-term impacts.

____

____

____

____

THE CARE METHOD

9. Reflect on any patterns you've noticed in your partner's responses to your abusive behaviors. How do you feel about these patterns?

____

____

____

____

____

____

Empathy and Responsibility

10. Put yourself in your partner's shoes. How would you feel if you were on the receiving end of the behaviors you've identified?

____

____

____

____

____

11. What steps are you willing to take in order to take responsibility for your actions and work toward change?

____

____

____

____

____

UNDERSTANDING INTIMATE PARTNER VIOLENCE

Recognizing Healthy Relationships

12. Describe what a healthy, non-abusive relationship looks like to you.

13. Reflect on any role models or positive examples of relationships you've observed. What can you learn from them?

Creating a Plan for Change

14. What steps can you take to break the cycle of abuse in your relationship?

2

Core Values

"Values are like fingerprints. Nobody's are the same, but you leave them all over everything you do.

—Elvis Presley

The beliefs we hold at our core drive the way we act and relate to others. In chapter 2, clients explore the concept of core values—fundamental beliefs that influence their behavior, choices, and relationships. Whether positive or negative, these values significantly impact how individuals navigate intimate partner relationships, including instances of intimate partner violence (IPV). This chapter helps clients identify their own core values and reflect on how these beliefs may have contributed to abusive behaviors or unhealthy patterns in relationships.

You will guide clients in recognizing that early influences—such as family upbringing, peer interactions, and media exposure—have shaped their core values and, consequently, their behavior. For example, clients who prioritize control or dominance might be more prone to engage in IPV, while those rooted in empathy and equality are less likely to exhibit such behaviors.

As a counselor, your role is to support clients as they explore how core values evolve over time. Help them reflect on harmful or outdated beliefs that may no longer serve them, facilitating their recognition that change is possible and necessary. Encourage them to engage fully with the exercises and discussions aimed at increasing self-awareness. This chapter sets the stage for clients to align their behaviors with healthier, more constructive values, leading to improved relationships and a reduction in abusive tendencies.

As you work through this material with clients, focus on creating an open and empathetic environment. Address potential resistance or reluctance, and guide them toward honest self-examination. The exercises in this chapter are designed to pave the way for deeper self-reflection and are critical for the transformative work that follows in subsequent sessions.

Goals of This Chapter

Understanding the foundation of one's core values is essential for fostering healthier relationships. By recognizing the influence of these values on their behavior, clients can begin to align their actions with healthier relationship dynamics. The chapter encourages clients to reflect on their life experiences, particularly any past trauma, and consider how these moments have molded the beliefs and values that guide their behaviors, especially in relationships.

By examining these connections, clients can begin to identify harmful or negative core values that may have contributed to abusive behaviors. The goal is to provide clients with the tools and self-awareness needed to shift toward healthier values that promote empathy, respect, and nonviolence in relationships. This chapter serves as an essential part of the overall CARE Method, as it equips clients with the insight needed for long-term change and personal growth.

Colorado DVOMB Standards Competencies

Chapter 2 aligns with the Colorado Domestic Violence Offender Management Board (DVOMB) Standards, particularly those that focus on **past experiences/trauma** and **intergenerational patterns**. The DVOMB highlights the significance of recognizing how past trauma can shape current behaviors and influence the dynamics of intimate partner violence. This chapter encourages clients to explore their own trauma history, helping them recognize how these experiences have impacted their actions and relationships.

By confronting these patterns, clients can gain insights into the roots of their behaviors, understanding how past experiences may have contributed to abusive dynamics. This is a crucial step in fostering empathy and breaking free from harmful cycles. Integrating past experiences and intergenerational patterns into this chapter equips clients with the tools to examine how these factors have shaped their beliefs and actions, ultimately promoting respect, empathy, and nonviolence in their relationships.

Important Things to Know

Last week, we focused on understanding **intimate partner violence (IPV)** and its various forms. In this chapter, as we dive into **core values**, you'll help clients make the connection between those behaviors and the deeply ingrained beliefs they've carried since childhood. Core values often shape how individuals approach relationships, and in this chapter, we'll explore how those values can influence unhealthy or abusive patterns.

Next week, we'll build on this by looking at **intergenerational trauma**, helping clients understand how the values and beliefs they carry may be passed down through generations. This chapter on core values is key in helping them begin to understand the roots of their behaviors and start the process of meaningful change.

Key Concepts and Terminology

Core values: The deeply held beliefs that guide a person's decisions, behaviors, and understanding of the world. Core values influence how individuals act in relationships, particularly in matters of respect, trust, and communication.

Belief systems: The set of principles that a person holds to be true, often shaping their perceptions and actions. In the context of intimate partner violence (IPV), belief systems can include views on power, control, and gender roles.

Cognitive distortions: Inaccurate or biased ways of thinking that can contribute to negative behaviors, including justifying abusive actions or blaming others for one's own shortcomings.

Self-awareness: The ability to recognize one's own emotions, values, and behaviors and how they impact relationships. Developing self-awareness is crucial for identifying patterns of unhealthy or abusive behavior.

Responsivity: The idea of how well one can respond to emotional cues and adapt behaviors in a relationship. Responsivity helps individuals understand the needs of their partner and respond in healthy ways rather than controlling or abusive actions.

Trauma history: The experiences from a person's past, especially during childhood, that may shape their beliefs and behaviors in relationships. Trauma history can influence how someone views control, power, and emotional connection.

Discussion Prompts

These prompts below will help facilitate thoughtful discussions that encourage self-reflection, allowing clients to identify how their values may have shaped their past actions. These conversations are crucial for understanding the deeper roots of abusive or unhealthy behaviors, while also fostering personal growth and change.

Identifying core values:

- Ask clients to think about their most deeply held values and how these values guide their behavior.
- **Discussion prompt**: "What are your core values? How do you think these values influence your behavior in relationships, both positively and negatively?"

Influence of past experiences:

- Encourage clients to reflect on how their past experiences, including trauma, may have shaped their core values.
- **Discussion prompt**: "Think about your past experiences, especially those that were challenging or painful. How do you believe these experiences have shaped your core values and how you engage in relationships?"

Impact of core values on relationships:

- Discuss how certain values can positively or negatively affect intimate relationships.
- **Discussion prompt**: "How have your core values influenced the way you interact in relationships? Can you identify any values that may have contributed to unhealthy behaviors or conflict?"

Challenging unhealthy core values:

- Help clients recognize when certain core values might need to be reassessed or changed to foster healthier relationships.
- **Discussion prompt**: "Are there any core values you hold that may not be serving you well in your relationships? How might these values contribute to harmful behaviors, and what could you change to promote healthier interactions?"

Shifting core values toward growth:

- Encourage clients to think about how they can align their values with healthier relationship dynamics.
- **Discussion prompt**: "What steps can you take to shift your core values toward promoting respect, empathy, and nonviolence in your relationships? How can these changes influence your future interactions?"

Self-reflection on core beliefs:

- Prompt clients to examine whether their current beliefs about power, control, or respect align with their values.
- **Discussion prompt**: "Are your beliefs about control, power, and respect in line with the core values you want to live by? How can adjusting these beliefs lead to healthier, more respectful relationships?"

Trauma's role in shaping core values:

- Explore the connection between past trauma and the development of certain core values.
- **Discussion prompt**: "How has past trauma shaped your values? Do you notice any patterns of behavior that stem from unhealed trauma, and how might you work toward healing and change?"

Empathy and growth:

- Encourage clients to consider how cultivating empathy and awareness of others' feelings can shape their core values moving forward.
- **Discussion prompt**: "How does developing empathy for others change the way you approach relationships? How can empathy help you reshape your core values to support healthier, more positive interactions?"

Contents

Chapter 2: Core Values
What Are Core Values?
Where Do Core Values Come From?
Do Your Behaviors Align With Your Core Values?
Can Core Values Change?
Negative Core Values
Why Are Core Values Important in Intimate Relationships?
Homework

2

Core Values

"Whatever things you go through, you stay true to who you are and your core values."

—Sophie Gregoire Trudeau

Every human being has a set of fundamental beliefs or guiding principles that dictate who they are and how they behave. We call these your core values. In chapter 1, we learned about intimate partner violence and the various types of abuse. In this chapter, I want you to learn how IPV and core values are connected.

What Are Core Values?

Core values are the essence of your being, the principles you hold as sacrosanct, often reflecting your deepest convictions and priorities. While they can be encapsulated in single words like integrity, compassion, or resilience, they embody vast, multifaceted concepts that influence your actions and shape your relationships. In other words, core values define who you are as a person and guide your decision-making in your daily life.

THE CARE METHOD

As seen in chapter 1, intimate partner violence (IPV) is a complex issue that often has deep connections to an individual's core values and beliefs. These core values and beliefs can shape behaviors, attitudes, and interactions within relationships. Below are several ways in which IPV can be connected to core values and beliefs:

1. Beliefs About Gender Roles

Traditional gender roles: Individuals who hold traditional beliefs about gender roles may be more likely to engage in or tolerate IPV. For example, a belief that men should be dominant and women submissive can create a power imbalance that fosters abusive behavior.

Equality and respect: Conversely, those who value gender equality and mutual respect are less likely to engage in or tolerate IPV. Promoting these values can be a protective factor against IPV.

2. Cultural and Societal Norms

Cultural acceptance of violence: In some cultures, violence is seen as an acceptable way to resolve conflicts or assert authority. These cultural norms can perpetuate IPV.

Societal change and awareness: Societies that actively challenge and change these norms through education and legal reforms can reduce the prevalence of IPV.

3. Personal Beliefs About Control and Power

Need for control: IPV often stems from a desire to control one's partner. This need for control can be rooted in personal insecurities, past traumas, or a fundamental belief in one's right to dominate another person.

Healthy relationship values: Beliefs in partnership, mutual support, and shared decision-making can counteract tendencies toward control and abuse.

4. Emotional Regulation and Conflict Resolution

Negative beliefs about emotions: Individuals who believe that expressing emotions is a sign of weakness or who lack healthy ways to manage stress and anger may resort to violence.

Positive emotional coping strategies: Beliefs in the importance of healthy emotional expression and conflict resolution skills can reduce the likelihood of IPV.

CORE VALUES

5. Attitudes Toward Abuse and Accountability

Denial and justification: Some individuals believe that abuse is justified or that it is not their fault, often externalizing blame onto their partner or circumstances.

Responsibility and change: Beliefs in personal accountability and the possibility of change can lead individuals to seek help.

Where Do Core Values Come From?

Parents and Caregivers

Without question, your parents/caregivers have been the most important influence on your core values. Much of who you are was developed during the years between birth to age 5. Your parents or adult caregivers were the people you spent the most time with during this era. You were greatly influenced by what you heard them say and saw them do.

Did you know that some of the core values we learned from our parents have served us well, and some of the core values that we adopted have NOT served us well in any capacity?

In the space below, write down some of the core values that served you well, and some that have not.

Significant Other Adults

Throughout life, you're influenced by adults other than your parents. Think about the impact of significant other adults in your life—grandparents, schoolteachers, coaches, Sunday school teachers, youth group leaders, and pastors. You were impacted by their words and behavior, and unconsciously modeled yourself after them.

THE CARE METHOD

In the space below, name some of the individuals who have impacted you positively by demonstrating healthy core values that you have adopted.

Friends and Peers

When you entered school, your friends and peer group became vitally important to the development of your core values. As a teenager, you wanted to fit in and therefore conformed to the core values of this group. So, it's critical for teenagers to choose their friends carefully because they tend to become like their peer group.

Did you know that friends and peers can contribute to a shift in your core values as early as in early adolescent years?

Were you ever in trouble as a teenager as a result of peer pressure or influence?

Write down a few core values you learned from friends, as well as where and when the incident that birthed these values happened:

CORE VALUES

The Media

The development of your core values is greatly affected by the media. You are influenced by the music you listen to, websites you visit, print media you read, TV shows you watch, and movies you attend. It's easy to assimilate unhealthy core values (perfectionism, materialism, superficiality) unless you intentionally screen your media intake.

In what ways do you believe media is influencing yourself, your family, and your children?

Life Experiences

What happens in your life impacts your core values—whether the experiences are positive or negative. How you handle life experiences shapes your core values.

Write down three (3) significant experiences that created new core values in your life or changed some of your core values.

THE CARE METHOD

Do Your Behaviors Align With Your Core Values?

All of us have experienced those moments where we said or did something that made us want to dig a hole and hide. Maybe it was blurting out a secret by mistake or not honoring a commitment that broke some of your boundaries.

Has there ever been a time when you did or said something you felt great shame for? Why do you think you felt that way?

You felt shame because the behavior or action you took or engaged in did NOT align with your core values. We don't always act in accordance with the things we truly believe in. Often, this is due to the influences we surround ourselves with, as well as a lack of awareness or care for others.

To identify whether your behaviors are in alignment with your core values, you have to ask yourself if you are living or acting in a genuine way and in accordance with what would make you feel proud and fulfilled as an individual.

Are you living in a way that honors your core values? Write your answer below.

CORE VALUES

Can Core Values Change?

Do you think your core values can change? Why or why not? Write your answer below.

The answer to this very important question is yes! Your core values are constantly being shaped by the experiences you have as an adult, and we are all fully capable of developing new core values and also letting go of those that do not serve us well.

A destructive core value can have a harmful or detrimental impact on an individual's thoughts, feelings, behaviors, and relationships with others. It can contribute to negative self-talk, low self-esteem, and self-sabotaging behaviors, and can foster attitudes of hostility, intolerance, or apathy toward others.[6]

Negative Core Values

Superiority: A belief that one is inherently better or superior to others can lead to arrogance, condescension, and mistreatment of those who are perceived as inferior.

Control: A belief that one must have complete control over oneself and others can lead to manipulative and coercive behaviors and can damage relationships.

Intoxication: Many people value the feeling—or lack of it—when they are drunk or high. While intoxication may temporarily relieve suffering, it can lead to addiction if positive life changes are not made.

6. Ahmed, A. (2021, February 23). A History of Research into Core Values. Retrieved from *Start With Values* website: https://startwithvalues.com/a-history-of-research-into-core-values/

THE CARE METHOD

Perfectionism: A belief that one must be perfect or flawless can lead to unrealistic expectations, self-criticism, and anxiety.

Riches: Financial well-being is essential but becoming rich for the sake of it often leads individuals to feel unfulfilled. A life spent focused entirely on the acquisition of materials may lead to negative consequences in terms of relationships and other dimensions of well-being.

Approval-seeking: A belief that one must constantly seek approval or validation from others can lead to people-pleasing behaviors and a lack of authentic self-expression.

Victimhood: A belief that one is constantly being victimized or persecuted can lead to a victim mentality, a lack of personal responsibility, and a tendency to blame others for one's problems.

Reflect on the negative core values mentioned above. What are the ones you identify with or have identified with in the past? Share your examples in the box below:

CORE VALUES

Why Are Core Values Important in Intimate Relationships?

Now that you have a good understanding of core values, why do you think they are important in intimate relationships specifically?

Write your answer here:

Core values in a relationship are the guiding beliefs that direct your words and actions. Knowing your core values will help you know when another individual's core values do not align with yours. If you are not aware of your core values, it will be difficult to find a partner with whom you are truly compatible.

Core values represent what's truly important to you in life. When your core values align with your partner's, it creates a strong foundation for the relationship. You'll naturally share similar goals, priorities, and outlooks on life, making decision-making and navigating challenges easier. Imagine both of you valuing honesty and open communication. This fosters trust and a safe space for sharing true feelings. On the other hand, when core values clash, disagreements can become more intense and difficult to resolve. For example, if one partner values financial security highly and the other prioritizes adventure and travel, it can lead to friction when discussing finances. Having a shared understanding of core values allows for more empathetic communication during conflicts. You can approach disagreements with a focus on finding solutions that respect each other's core beliefs.[7]

7. Fuller, K. (2021, August 9). Why It's So Important for Couples to Talk About Their Values. Retrieved from *Psychology Today*: https://www.psychologytoday.com/za/blog/happiness-is-state-mind/202108/why-its-so-important-couples-talk-about-their-values

THE CARE METHOD

Homework

1. Reflecting on Positive Core Values

Think back to your childhood and upbringing. What are three (3) core values that you learned during this time that have had a positive impact on your life?

Describe each value and how it has influenced your beliefs, attitudes, and behaviors.

____

____

____

2. Positive Role Models and Influence

Reflect on individuals in your life who have served as positive role models and influenced the development of your healthy core values. Who are these individuals, and what qualities or behaviors do they embody that you admire and seek to emulate?

____

____

____

3. Exploring Negative Core Values

a. Are there any core values that you learned while growing up that have not positively impacted your life? Identify at least two (2) of these values and describe them in detail. Are these values still relevant to you today, or have they evolved or become less significant over time?

____

____

____

____

56

CORE VALUES

b. Reflect on how these negative core values have influenced your beliefs and behaviors in adulthood and in your relationships. Have they contributed to any challenges or conflicts in your relationships or personal growth?

4. Impact of Negative Core Values on Relationships

Reflect on your adult relationships and consider how your negative core values may have impacted them. In what ways have these values influenced your communication patterns, decision-making processes, or emotional responses within intimate relationships?

5. Assessing Compatibility and Red Flags in Future Relationships

a. When entering into new relationships, what signs or behaviors might indicate a mismatch in values or potential red flags for conflict or violence?

b. Describe how you can proactively address concerns regarding values compatibility to prevent future conflicts from escalating.

3

Intergenerational Trauma

"Trauma creates change you don't choose.
Healing is about creating change you do choose."

—Michelle Rosenthal

The lasting impact of trauma can stretch across generations, shaping behaviors and relationships in ways we might not even realize. In this chapter, clients are introduced to the concept of intergenerational trauma—the process by which unresolved trauma is passed down through families, often influencing present-day actions and relationship dynamics. The goal is to help clients understand how their family history, particularly past trauma, may be affecting their actions and beliefs, especially in intimate partner relationships.

As a counselor, your role is to guide clients in identifying patterns of trauma that may have originated in their family systems and to help them understand how these patterns affect their current relationships. Many clients may not have previously considered how deeply ingrained family trauma affects their emotional responses, such as anger, control, or withdrawal. For example, a client who grew up witnessing or experiencing violence may have internalized the idea that aggression or control is a necessary tool in relationships.

This chapter is designed to help clients reflect on these patterns, making connections between their past and their present behaviors. Encourage clients to begin the process of breaking these cycles of trauma. By recognizing the legacy of their family's trauma, they can start developing healthier, more productive ways of interacting in relationships, fostering empathy and self-awareness.

Be mindful that this material may evoke strong emotions and memories. Your role is to provide a supportive and empathetic environment where clients feel safe to reflect on painful realizations. As you guide them through this process, focus on fostering self-awareness and encouraging them to embrace positive change. This chapter is a critical part of the healing process, helping clients move forward by acknowledging and addressing the trauma they carry from previous generations.

Goals of This Chapter

Breaking the cycle of trauma starts with understanding where it begins. Clients are encouraged to explore how unresolved trauma in their family history may be affecting their current behaviors and relationships. Recognizing these patterns is crucial for clients to begin disrupting the cycle and fostering healthier, more constructive relationship dynamics.

The chapter invites clients to reflect on their own family history and consider how past trauma may have influenced their emotional responses, relationship dynamics, and behaviors. By examining these connections, clients can begin to identify unhealthy patterns that have been passed down through generations, which may have contributed to abusive behaviors or unhealthy coping mechanisms.

The goal of this chapter is to provide clients with the tools and insight needed to break these cycles of trauma, fostering personal healing and growth. By developing self-awareness and empathy, clients can learn to change the patterns of behavior that have negatively impacted their relationships, creating a foundation for healthier, nonviolent interactions.

Colorado DVOMB Standards Competencies

Chapter 3 aligns with specific Colorado Domestic Violence Offender Management Board (DVOMB) standards, particularly focusing on **past experience/trauma** and **intergenerational patterns**. The DVOMB underscores the significance of understanding how trauma and behaviors are passed down across generations, affecting current actions and relational dynamics. This chapter helps clients recognize how unresolved trauma from previous generations can manifest in their behaviors and relationships.

By exploring family history and identifying patterns of trauma, clients gain insight into how these experiences have shaped their responses to conflict and stress. Recognizing intergenerational trauma is a crucial step in breaking harmful cycles, allowing clients to understand the deeper roots of their behaviors. This understanding enables them to make positive changes, promoting healthier relationships and nonviolence.

Integrating these intergenerational patterns into the therapeutic process fosters empathy, self-awareness, and a commitment to creating more positive interactions. Clients are encouraged to reflect on how their family's legacy of trauma may have influenced their attitudes, beliefs, and actions, particularly in intimate partner relationships.

Important Things to Know

Now that clients have explored **core values** and how these beliefs influence their behaviors, this chapter introduces the concept of **intergenerational trauma.** It's important for clients to understand how patterns of trauma, learned behaviors, and emotional responses can be passed down through generations.

By recognizing how their family history and past traumas may have shaped their current actions, clients can begin to see how deeply rooted these patterns are. This understanding will allow them to start breaking free from harmful cycles and take steps toward healthier relationships. In the next chapter, we'll focus on building **resilience**, helping clients develop the strength to overcome these past influences and continue on their path to personal growth.

Key Concepts and Terminology

Intergenerational trauma: The psychological and emotional consequences of trauma experienced by one generation that are passed down to subsequent generations. This can manifest in the form of behavioral patterns, emotional responses, or coping mechanisms that individuals adopt based on the unresolved trauma of their ancestors.

Trauma transmission: The process by which trauma is passed from one generation to the next. Trauma transmission can occur through parenting styles, family dynamics, and unspoken beliefs or attitudes, often perpetuating cycles of abuse or dysfunction.

Emotional inheritance: The ways in which emotions, particularly those related to unresolved trauma or pain, are handed down from one generation to another. Emotional inheritance can affect an individual's relationships, sense of self, and emotional regulation.

Breaking the cycle: The act of consciously recognizing and stopping patterns of behavior that have been passed down through generations. Breaking the cycle requires self-awareness, a commitment to change, and often external support through counseling or therapy.

Family systems theory: A therapeutic framework that views the family as an interconnected system where the behaviors of one member affect the whole. In the context of intergenerational trauma, family systems theory helps explain how trauma within a family affects each member and how patterns of behavior are transmitted across generations.

Discussion Prompts

The following prompts are designed to facilitate meaningful discussions that help clients explore how trauma from previous generations may influence their current behaviors and beliefs. These conversations can foster awareness, encourage self-reflection, and help clients begin the process of breaking harmful cycles.

Identifying patterns of trauma:

- Ask clients to think about patterns of trauma within their family and how these patterns have influenced their beliefs and actions.
- **Discussion prompt**: "What patterns of trauma do you recognize in your family? How do you think these experiences have shaped your behavior in your own relationships?"

Impact of family history:

- Encourage clients to reflect on how their family history and upbringing have shaped their emotional responses and relationship dynamics.
- **Discussion prompt**: "How has your family history, particularly unresolved trauma, influenced your relationships? Are there any behaviors or emotional responses you notice that may have been passed down through generations?"

Breaking the cycle of trauma:

- Help clients identify ways in which they can start to break the cycle of trauma transmission.
- **Discussion prompt**: "What steps can you take to break the cycle of trauma in your family? How can you ensure that you do not pass on unhealthy behaviors to future generations?"

Self-reflection on generational trauma:

- Prompt clients to reflect on their own role in perpetuating or addressing trauma within their family dynamic.
- **Discussion prompt**: "What role do you play in either continuing or stopping the trauma patterns that have been passed down in your family? How can recognizing this role help you make positive changes?"

Recognizing emotional inheritance:

- Discuss the concept of emotional inheritance, where feelings such as fear, anger, or grief are handed down from one generation to the next.
- **Discussion prompt**: "What emotions do you think have been inherited from previous generations in your family? How have these emotions influenced your actions or interactions with others?"

Responsibility for change:

- Encourage clients to take responsibility for breaking harmful patterns, emphasizing personal growth and healing.
- **Discussion prompt**: "How can taking responsibility for your own healing contribute to breaking the cycle of trauma? What actions can you take to ensure you are moving toward healthier relationship dynamics?"

Cultural and societal expectations:

- Explore the role of cultural and societal norms in perpetuating trauma within families and how clients can challenge these expectations.
- **Discussion prompt**: "How have cultural or societal expectations played a role in the transmission of trauma within your family? How can you challenge or reshape these expectations to promote healthier behaviors?"

Empathy and generational healing:

- Discuss the importance of developing empathy for past generations while working toward personal growth and change.
- **Discussion prompt**: "How can cultivating empathy for previous generations help you in your own healing process? How does this empathy contribute to breaking the cycle of trauma in your life?"

Contents

Chapter 3: Intergenerational Trauma
What Is Intergenerational Trauma?
Examples of Intergenerational Trauma.
How Does Intergenerational Trauma Impact Us?
Who Is Affected the Most?
Historical Trauma and Marginalized Groups
How Do We Pass It on to Our Children?
Epigenetics
The Impact of Intergenerational Trauma on Your Family
Additional Negative Effects
Healing From Intergenerational Trauma
Homework

3

Intergenerational Trauma

"Our brains are wired for connection, but trauma rewires them for protection. That's why healthy relationships are difficult for wounded people."

—Ryan North

In chapter 2, you explored how intimate partner violence can be connected to an individual's core values. This chapter will help you start noticing how each session in the CARE Method is intentionally designed to address these connections. Intimate partner violence and core values are not innate; they are learned behaviors often transmitted through generations. As you progress through this chapter, you will develop profound insights into yourself and uncover the roots of your behaviors, laying the foundation for meaningful change.

What Is Intergenerational Trauma?

Intergenerational trauma is a concept that sheds light on the recurring challenges faced by families across generations. It is the transmission (or passing down) of the oppressive or traumatic effects of historical events to younger generations.[8]

For example, imagine a great-grandmother who endured the horrors of a concentration camp in Germany. As a coping mechanism, she might have learned to suppress her emotions or cut them

8. Keenan, W., Sanchez, C.E., Kellogg, E., and Tracey, S.M. (2019, February 13). Addressing Historical, Intergenerational, and Chronic Trauma: Impacts on Children, Families, and Communities. Retrieved from National Library of Medicine: https://www.ncbi.nlm.nih.gov/books/NBK540764/

THE CARE METHOD

off entirely. This, in turn, could lead her to interact with her family in a detached and emotionally distant way, creating a strained and complex family dynamic.

The impact of this type of historical trauma can then ripple through generations. The grandchildren, never having known a different family dynamic, might inherit this emotional distance and develop defensive behaviors around expressing their own emotions. This cycle of denial and emotional suppression could potentially continue to negatively affect future generations.

Although the reality of intergenerational trauma has been present since the beginning of time, it is still relatively new in the realm of psychology. In fact, the formal term wasn't coined until the 1980s. Let me give you brief timeline of this concept within the confines of psychology:

Early observations in the 1960s: The concept of intergenerational trauma gained traction in the field of psychology in 1966. A groundbreaking study by Dr. Vivian M. Rakoff and colleagues in Canada documented high levels of emotional distress in children of Holocaust survivors.[9] This research sparked a wave of investigations into the transmission of trauma across generations, heavily focused on anxiety, depression, and PTSD in both trauma survivors and their offspring.[10]

Formalization of the concept in the 1980s: The term "intergenerational trauma" or "historical trauma" is credited to Maria Yellow Horse Brave Heart and her work with the Hutterite community, a religious group that had experienced persecution.[11] Around the same time, psychologists studying Holocaust survivors observed a higher prevalence of mental health issues in their children. This groundbreaking research highlighted the possibility of trauma transmission across generations.

2000s: While it was not explicitly called intergenerational trauma at the time, scholars like Marianne Hirsch began exploring the concept of "post memory," where descendants carry the emotional weight of their ancestors' experiences, even if they haven't lived through them themselves.[12]

---

9. Rakoff, V., Sigal, J.J., and Epstein, N.B. Children and families of concentration camp survivors. *Can. Ment. Hlth.*, 14, 24-26 (1967); Sigal, J.J., Ph.D., and Rakoff, V., M.D. Concentration Camp Survival: A Pilot Study of Effects on Second Generation. *The Canadian Journal of Psychiatry*, 16:5, (1971). https://doi.org/10.1177/070674377101600503

10. DeAngelis, T. The legacy of trauma. *Monitor on Psychology*, 50(2), 36 (2019, February 1). https://www.apa.org/monitor/2019/02/legacy-trauma. Retrieved from American Psychology Association: https://www.apa.org/monitor/2019/02/legacy-trauma#:~:text=One%20of%20the%20first%20articles,(Canada's%20Mental%20Health%2C%20Vol.

11. Keenan, W., Sanchez, C.E., Kellogg, E., and Tracey, S.M. (2019, February 13). Addressing Historical, Intergenerational, and Chronic Trauma: Impacts on Children, Families, and Communities. Retrieved from National Library of Medicine: https://www.ncbi.nlm.nih.gov/books/NBK540764/

12. Hirsch, M. (2008). The Generation of Postmemory. Retrieved from University of Warwick: https://warwick.ac.uk/fac/arts/history/research/centres/ehrc/research/current_research/memory/poetics_today-2008-hirsch-103-28.pdf

INTERGENERATIONAL TRAUMA

Growing recognition: Since the 2000s, research on intergenerational trauma has expanded to explore its impact on various populations, including those who have experienced slavery, war, genocide, and other forms of collective trauma.[13]

Focus Areas

Continued study on intergenerational trauma has focused in two areas:[14]

Biological factors: Emerging research is exploring how trauma might influence gene expression, potentially impacting stress responses in future generations.

Cultural and social transmission: Studies are examining how cultural practices, historical narratives, and social inequalities can perpetuate the effects of trauma across generations.

Examples of Intergenerational Trauma

Intergenerational problems including oppression can often be found in families that have been traumatized in severe forms (e.g., sexual abuse, rape, murder, etc.). The consequences of intergenerational trauma are rarely if ever discussed unless a therapist or other mental health professional mentions it. However it is very real, so let's talk about it.

As we have just established, a parent or grandparent who never truly healed from or explored their own trauma may find it very difficult to provide emotional support to a family member suffering from his or her own trauma. Sadly, many families "cope" with intergenerational trauma by employing two (2) unhealthy coping mechanisms:

Denial: Refusing to acknowledge that the trauma happened.

Minimization: Ignoring the impact of the trauma and making the traumatic experience appear smaller than it really is.

13. DeAngelis, T. The legacy of trauma. *Monitor on Psychology*, 50:2, 36 (2019, February 1). https://www.apa.org/monitor/2019/02/legacy-trauma. Retrieved from American Psychology Association: https://www.apa.org/monitor/2019/02/legacy-

14. Yehuda, R., and Lehrner, A. Intergenerational transmission of trauma effects: putative role of epigenetic mechanisms. *World Psychiatry*, 17:3, 243–257 (2018, September 7). doi: 10.1002/wps.20568

THE CARE METHOD

Take a moment of introspection and think about your family dynamics. What are some coping mechanisms or intergenerational traumas that are a part of your family?

How Does Intergenerational Trauma Impact Us?

Now that you may have identified some of the intergenerational trauma that is present in your family, take a moment and think about how this has affected your family as a whole. Write down a few of these experiences below.

Inherited trauma can make deep imprints on your overall well-being. These are a few ways that digging into your past might help your present and future self:

a. The trauma reactions you feel today might stem from past events you weren't directly involved in or didn't personally experience. Maybe you weren't abused growing up, but your parents or grandparents were. Maybe you didn't face discrimination or live through a war,

INTERGENERATIONAL TRAUMA

but your great-grandparents did. In fact, we all lived through a global pandemic (COVID-19). This could be a good reference point for you.

b. Each person has unique reactions to stress and trauma, often categorized into the common responses of fight, flight, or freeze. These reactions can manifest in various ways, such as hyper-independence or tendencies toward people-pleasing.

c. What happens during those stress responses may be related to intergenerational trauma and can affect both your mental and physical wellness.

Who Is Affected the Most?

Anyone can experience intergenerational trauma, and some may argue that everyone experiences this phenomenon to some degree. However, people from marginalized groups—such as people of color and those in lower socioeconomic classes over several generations—may have more pronounced experiences with intergenerational trauma. Those who are descendants of people who have experienced violence from living in war zones and other hardships—such as World War II, effects of the Cold War, the Vietnam War, or conflicts in the Middle East—may also be more likely to experience intergenerational trauma.

Now that you have a sense of how intergenerational trauma has affected your family as a whole, it's time to be a little more specific. This time, think about *who* has been affected the most, and write down how these family members have been dealing with these traumas.

THE CARE METHOD

Now that we've narrowed it down to specifically *who* has been affected, I want you to think about your life (as an individual) for a moment. How do you think your own intergenerational trauma, if any, might have impacted your involvement with domestic violence?

Historical Trauma and Marginalized Groups

We have covered the history of intergenerational trauma in which we discovered that it was first discussed in relation to survivors of the Holocaust and their descendants. However, this type of intergenerational trauma also affects many other groups of marginalized communities all over the world, including:

a. Japanese Americans with ties to Japanese internment during World War II
b. Black and African American people
c. Those of Vietnamese, Cambodian, Ukrainian, and Rwandan descent
d. Australian Aboriginal tribes
e. Those belonging to North and South American Indigenous tribes, especially descendants of the Indian Reservation Schools in Canada and the United States

INTERGENERATIONAL TRAUMA

How Do We Pass It on to Our Children?

With everything that we've discussed thus far, we know that trauma is passed down through generations. You could actually have certain trauma responses that can be traced back to something a parent, relative, or significant adult did. So, including yourself, how has trauma been transmitted in your family?

Trauma can be transmitted in many ways from our genetics to conversations at the dinner table. Some experts in the medical community attributed intergenerational trauma to the stress of living with a traumatized person who may still be reliving horrific events. Others attributed intergenerational trauma to children becoming "containers" for their parents' unwanted pain. Here are a few ways trauma can be transmitted, especially in the modern day:

a. **Unspoken family narratives**: Families often develop unspoken narratives around traumatic events. These narratives can shape how future generations perceive the world and their place in it.
b. **Parenting behaviors**: When a parent or caregiver has unresolved trauma, it can impact their ability to provide a secure and nurturing environment. This might manifest as emotional distance, inconsistent parenting styles, or even emotional outbursts.
c. **Social inequalities**: Historical trauma can lead to social disadvantages that are carried across generations. For example, descendants of enslaved people might face systemic barriers to education, employment, and healthcare, perpetuating the cycle of trauma.

THE CARE METHOD

- **d. Stress responses**: Emerging research suggests that trauma might leave an imprint on genes, potentially influencing how future generations respond to stress. This can make them more susceptible to anxiety, depression, or other mental health issues.
- **e. Epigenetics**: As mentioned above, emerging research suggests that trauma can leave a mark on our genes, influencing how future generations respond to stress.

Epigenetics is a complex area of study, but it offers a potential explanation for how the biological effects of trauma can be transmitted across generations. Let's unpack this point.

Epigenetics

In the 1990s, researchers began to look at the biological mechanisms of intergenerational trauma via epigenetics. According to the Centers for Disease Control and Prevention, epigenetics is the study of how your behaviors and environment can cause changes that affect the way your genes work. Unlike genetic changes, epigenetic changes are reversible and do not change your DNA sequence, but they can change how your body reads a DNA sequence.

According to epigenetics, some of the ways trauma can be passed down include these:

- a. DNA modifications
- b. In utero
- c. Memory
- d. Cultural messages and conditioning
- e. Cultural patterns
- f. Cumulative emotional wounding
- g. Dominant family narratives
- h. Normalization of hatred, cruelty, and dehumanization toward others
- i. Parents bypassing or not coping with their trauma
- j. Aggressions and micro-aggressions

INTERGENERATIONAL TRAUMA

The Impact of Intergenerational Trauma on Your Family

The unfortunate truth about intergenerational trauma is that it can bring some families closer emotionally, but on the other hand, it can also cause some families to drift apart.

There are many ways intergenerational trauma might affect families, including these:

a. Disconnection

b. Denial

c. Detachment

d. Distance

e. Impaired self-esteem stemming from minimization of the child's own life experiences in comparison to the parents' trauma

f. Trauma bonding, or an emotional connection between an abuser and their target

g. Estrangement

h. Neglect

i. Abuse

j. Violence

From this list, choose three (3) ways trauma has affected your family and give an example for each one. Write your answers below.

THE CARE METHOD

Additional Negative Effects

Trauma and stress can increase the chances of chronic pain, certain illnesses, and behaviors that can impact wellness, including these:

a. Anxiety
b. Depression and suicidal ideation
c. Poor sleep hygiene
d. Heart disease
e. Substance use disorders (SUD)
f. Diabetes

These health issues are not only interconnected but can also create a vicious cycle, where one exacerbates the other. When the body and mind are constantly under the shadow of stress and trauma, they're pushed into a state of high alert, affecting not just your emotional well-being but your physical health too. It's important to remember that these are just some of the potential consequences. The specific effects of trauma and stress can vary depending on the individual and their unique circumstances.

Healing From Intergenerational Trauma

This is the most important part of this lesson. You need to understand what intergenerational trauma is, as well as its effects. However, the ultimate goal is to reach a place of healing.

Even for those who understand the ongoing nature of healing inherited trauma, there are ways to nurture yourself throughout the process. This can involve practices that enhance your body awareness. Remember, there's no single path or fixed definition of "healing" when it comes to intergenerational trauma. It's a deeply personal journey. However, acknowledging the reality of the trauma and its origins is a crucial first step. By validating the experience, you create a safe space for yourself and others impacted by it to begin the healing process.

INTERGENERATIONAL TRAUMA

Homework

Instructions

Take a moment to reflect on the concepts we've discussed in this chapter on intergenerational trauma and consider how they relate to your own life experiences. Write a thoughtful response to the following questions, addressing your level of awareness, perceived impact, and intentions for reducing the transmission of trauma to future generations.

1: Awareness

Let's rewind a little. Reflect on your level of awareness regarding intergenerational trauma prior to this chapter. Had you previously recognized the impact of historical or familial trauma on your own life experiences and behaviors, or did it only become apparent as you learned this material?

____

____

____

____

____

2: Impact

Describe how this chapter on intergenerational trauma has impacted your understanding of your own family history and personal experiences.

____

____

____

____

____

THE CARE METHOD

3: Reflection

Reflect on the different ways in which intergenerational trauma may have influenced your own beliefs, behaviors, and coping mechanisms throughout your life. Think about any patterns or cycles of trauma that you have observed in your family and how they may have affected your own life.

___

___

___

4: Intentions for Change

Identify specific changes or actions you intend to make in order to reduce the transmission of trauma to future generations. List them all.

___

___

___

___

___

5: Commitment

Commit to at least one actionable step you will take in the coming weeks to address intergenerational trauma in your own life and promote healing within your family. Write this step down, as well as smaller steps you intend to take to achieve this.

___

___

___

___

___

70

4

Resiliency

"Life doesn't get easier or more forgiving, we get stronger and more resilient."

—Steve Maraboli

Resilience is the key to overcoming life's hardest challenges and healing from past trauma. In this chapter, clients explore the concept of resilience, a vital trait that helps individuals recover and grow from adversity. Resilience is not just about surviving hardship—it's about developing the ability to bounce back, much like a rubber ball returning to shape after being compressed. This chapter invites clients to reflect on how they can cultivate resilience, especially when confronting personal and relational struggles that have shaped their lives.

As a counselor, your role is to help clients identify both internal and external sources of strength. This includes their support systems, coping mechanisms, and personal values. Guide clients in examining past experiences of adversity, encouraging them to reflect on how they managed to overcome those challenges, even during times of difficulty. By recognizing their past resilience, clients can begin to map out a way forward through their current struggles.

This chapter also highlights the importance of **self-awareness** in building resilience. Clients will be encouraged to identify when they are caught in negative cycles and to explore actionable steps they can take to break free. You will assist them in evaluating their support networks and personal strengths, helping them tap into the tools they already possess. Empowering clients in this way fosters a sense of control over their own healing journey.

As clients move through this chapter, emphasize that resilience is not about avoiding difficulties but about responding to them with adaptability and strength. Remind them that by participating in this program and seeking change, they have already shown resilience. This chapter aims to solidify that understanding, helping clients to continue building resilience as a key element in their personal growth and recovery.

Goals of This Chapter

Resilience is the foundation for navigating life's challenges with strength and grace. This chapter highlights the importance of building emotional strength and self-regulation to help clients face challenges in their relationships and personal lives. By cultivating resilience, clients are better equipped to handle stress, conflict, and emotional turmoil in ways that are both healthy and constructive.

Clients explore their own capacity for resilience, reflecting on past experiences where they demonstrated strength and perseverance. The goal is to help clients identify areas where they can continue to build resilience, ultimately leading to healthier emotional responses and improved relationship dynamics. This chapter is pivotal in the CARE Method as it provides clients with practical tools for emotional regulation and self-management, both of which are critical for fostering long-term change.

Colorado DVOMB Standards Competencies

This chapter aligns closely with the Colorado Domestic Violence Offender Management Board (DVOMB) standard on **self-regulation**. The DVOMB emphasizes the importance of self-regulation in reducing the risk of reoffending and promoting healthier, nonviolent behavior patterns.

Self-regulation is a key skill for managing emotions, particularly in moments of stress or conflict. Clients are encouraged to take responsibility for their emotional responses, learning to recognize when they are becoming dysregulated and employing strategies to regain control. By developing self-regulation, clients can reduce the likelihood of impulsive or harmful behaviors, making it a critical component of the CARE Method.

The therapeutic goals of this chapter align with the DVOMB standards by ensuring that clients not only understand the importance of resilience and self-regulation but also take active steps to implement these skills in their daily lives. By mastering self-regulation, clients can work toward healthier relationships and long-term personal growth.

Important Things to Know

We explore the concept of **resilience**, helping clients recognize their capacity to bounce back from challenges and adversity. Understanding and building resilience is crucial, especially as clients confront the impact of intergenerational trauma and the core values that have influenced their behaviors. By identifying their strengths and support systems, clients can develop the tools they need to move forward with confidence and self-awareness.

Next week, we'll move into **behavioral change**, which is a key aspect of personal growth. Clients will learn how to identify and alter harmful behaviors, particularly those that arise in stressful or triggering situations. By understanding the connection between their thoughts, emotions, and actions, clients will gain better control over their behaviors and develop healthier responses in relationships. This chapter on behavioral change lays the foundation for clients to approach their habits with greater awareness and responsibility.

Key Concepts and Terminology

Resilience: The ability to bounce back from adversity, setbacks, or challenges with strength and flexibility. It is described as the ability to return to one's original state, like a rubber ball, after experiencing pressure or difficulty.

Self-awareness: Recognizing personal traits and understanding one's emotional responses to stress or pressure. Self-awareness is a crucial trait of resilient individuals.

Optimism: The practice of maintaining a hopeful outlook even in the face of difficulty. It is listed as one of the characteristics of resilient individuals.

Coping mechanisms: Methods or strategies that individuals use to deal with stress, both in sudden and long-term pressures. Healthy coping mechanisms are critical for building resilience.

Reframing: A method to change the way one views situations or challenges to adopt a more positive perspective. Reframing how one thinks is emphasized as a tool for building resilience.

Resilient relationships: Relationships characterized by their ability to withstand conflict and challenges, bouncing back rather than breaking under stress.

Empathy in relationships: Resilient relationships rely on empathy, where both partners can understand and share each other's feelings, creating a safe space for emotional expression.

Healthy disagreement: In resilient relationships, partners practice respectful conflict resolution, focusing on finding solutions rather than attacking each other.

Discussion Prompts

The following prompts are designed to facilitate discussions that help clients reflect on their emotional responses, control impulses, and practice mindfulness to foster healthier relationships. These conversations aim to build awareness, encourage self-regulation, and support long-term personal growth.

Identifying emotional triggers:

- Ask clients to think about situations that tend to provoke strong emotional reactions and how they typically respond.
- **Discussion prompt**: "What situations or triggers tend to provoke intense emotions for you? How do you usually respond to these triggers, and how does that affect your relationships?"

Reflecting on impulse control:

- Encourage clients to explore moments when they struggled with controlling their impulses and the consequences of those actions.
- **Discussion prompt**: "Can you think of a time when you acted impulsively in a relationship? What were the consequences of your actions, and how could better impulse control have led to a different outcome?"

Building resilience:

- Help clients identify their sources of resilience and how they have successfully navigated challenges in the past.
- **Discussion prompt**: "When faced with adversity, what strengths or resources have you drawn on to help you get through difficult times? How can you build on these sources of resilience moving forward?"

Exploring mindfulness practices:

- Discuss how mindfulness techniques, such as breathing exercises or meditation, can support self-regulation and emotional awareness.

- **Discussion prompt**: "How can practicing mindfulness help you manage difficult emotions or impulses? What specific techniques do you think might work for you?"

Recognizing emotional intelligence:

- Explore how emotional intelligence, including recognizing and managing one's own emotions, can contribute to healthier relationships.
- **Discussion prompt**: "How well do you recognize your emotions as they arise? How can increasing your emotional intelligence help you respond more thoughtfully in stressful situations?"

Shifting negative thought patterns:

- Encourage clients to reflect on how cognitive restructuring can help them shift from negative thought patterns to more constructive ones.
- **Discussion prompt**: "Are there any recurring negative thoughts that affect how you respond to stress or conflict? How can you challenge these thoughts to create healthier responses?"

Accountability in self-regulation:

- Discuss the importance of taking responsibility for one's emotional reactions and behaviors.
- **Discussion prompt**: "How can taking responsibility for your emotional responses improve your relationships? What steps can you take to practice better self-regulation?"

Promoting healthy coping mechanisms:

- Ask clients to consider how they can replace unhealthy coping mechanisms with more constructive behaviors.
- **Discussion prompt**: "What are some of your current coping mechanisms when you're stressed or upset? Are there any that you'd like to replace with healthier alternatives?"

Contents

Chapter 4: Resiliency
What Is Resiliency?
What Makes You a Resilient Person?
Building Resilience in Adults
Resiliency in Relationships
Building Resilience in Children
Homework

4

Resiliency

"It's your reaction to adversity, not adversity itself that determines how your life's story will develop."

—Dieter F. Uchtdorf

Dealing with personal trauma is difficult, even for those of us who are professionally trained and work with clients on a daily basis. I want to commend you for being so strong, getting through the previous chapter, and being willing to be vulnerable enough to flip the page to chapter 4. This alone is proof that you are resilient. You may not feel it and your circumstances may not reflect it, but it is a fact that cannot be taken from you. So, in this chapter, I want us to unpack resilience because it's important that you not only have an accurate perspective of yourself, but that you also realize that hope is not lost. There is more to your life than your present circumstance.

What Is Resiliency?

Imagine a rubber ball. You squeeze it tight, then let go. It snaps back to its original shape. That's resilience in action. In life, resilience is that same ability to bounce back from challenges, setbacks, and adversity. It's not about avoiding problems, but about navigating them with strength and flexibility. Resilience isn't about being superhuman or feeling happy all the time. It's about allowing yourself to feel the hurt, the frustration, or the anger that comes with difficulty. But it's also about having the tools and resources to move forward in a healthy way.

THE CARE METHOD

In his Ted Talk titled *What Trauma Taught Me About Resilience*, Charles Hunt said this:

> "Sometimes we need to tell ourselves what to think when our mind starts telling us things that we don't need to hear: that you can and will overcome and succeed, and not just in spite of, but *precisely* because of. That with the proper perspective and a positive attitude, we have *power*."[15]

Do you think you are resilient? Why or why not?

15. https://www.youtube.com/watch?v=3qELiw_1Ddg&ab_channel=TEDxTalks

RESILIENCY

What Makes You a Resilient Person?

You might feel sad and hopeless or even feel like your life is over and you have no purpose, but in truth, the fact that you are still alive today, pushing through life even though you may not feel like it, makes you a resilient person. That's the foundation of resilience.

These are the characteristics of a resilient person:

a. Self-awareness
b. Connects with other people
c. Continues to grow and develop with life
d. Self-confidence
e. Recognizes when pressure begins to create problems
f. Knows how to cope with long-term pressure
g. Knows how to cope with sudden pressure
h. Optimism

What are your personal traits that make you resilient?

THE CARE METHOD

Building Resilience in Adults

There are four (4) ways to increase resilience:

1. Reframe how you think.
2. Get adequate sleep.
3. Find a substitute for sleep.
4. Explore the power of positivity.

What are some of the ways you have built resilience in your journey? Name a few things that help you keep going every day.

Resiliency in Relationships

Resilient relationships are characterized by their ability to withstand conflict and challenges. Just like a stretchy rubber band, they have the flexibility to bounce back and repair after experiencing tension. Unlike fragile eggshells, resilient relationships do not easily break under pressure. Here are some practices that contribute to the resilience of relationships:

1. **Showing up**: Resilient relationships require both partners to consistently show up for each other. This means being emotionally present, actively listening, and providing support when needed. By demonstrating reliability and dependability, partners strengthen their connection and build a foundation of trust.
2. **Seeing and being seen**: Empathy plays a crucial role in resilient relationships. It involves the ability to see and understand each other's perspectives, emotions, and experiences.

RESILIENCY

When both partners are able to empathize with one another, they create a safe space for vulnerability and build a deeper understanding of each other's needs.

3. **Sharing power**: Resilient relationships thrive on equal decision-making and power dynamics. Partners consult and collaborate with each other, making decisions together rather than exerting control or dominance. By sharing power, partners build mutual respect, trust, and a sense of equality within the relationship.

4. **Disagreeing well**: Conflict is inevitable in any relationship. However, in resilient relationships, partners practice healthy disagreement. This involves communicating with respect, actively listening to the other person's perspective, and finding constructive ways to address differences. Rather than attacking or blaming, resilient partners focus on finding solutions and understanding each other's needs.

5. **Taking breaks**: Resilient relationships recognize the importance of taking breaks during times of conflict or emotional overwhelm. Taking breaks allows both partners to pause, reflect, and cool down, preventing escalating arguments or hurtful behaviors. Using breaks as an opportunity for self-care and self-reflection helps partners return to discussions with a calmer mindset and a greater ability to find resolution.

It's important to note that healthy disagreement, rather than avoiding conflict altogether, is necessary for the strength and resilience of relationships. When partners are able to express their differing opinions and work through conflicts with respect and understanding, they build deeper connections and foster personal growth.

In conclusion, resilient relationships are characterized by partners who show up for each other, practice empathy, share power, engage in healthy disagreement, and use breaks constructively. By cultivating these practices, relationships become more resilient, allowing partners to navigate conflicts and challenges while maintaining a strong and fulfilling connection.

What are some of the ways your current or previous relationship has struggled?

THE CARE METHOD

Building Resilience in Children

The world can be a tough place, even for children. Sadly, trauma does not discriminate. Children can remember and experience the effects of trauma from as young as 18 months old.[16] Besides past trauma, children are constantly facing bullying, lack of resources, and low self-esteem. In addition, having a parent who is incarcerated or violent can severely undermine their sense of self-worth and belief in their future potential.

Here is how you can help your child build resilience:

1. **Be a role model**: Children are keen observers, mimicking the behaviors they see around them. Demonstrate resilience yourself. Talk openly about your own challenges and how you cope. Show them that setbacks are temporary and that perseverance leads to growth.
2. **Cultivate positive connections**: Strong social connections are a safety net for children. Help your child build positive relationships with family, friends, and caregivers. Encourage empathy and teamwork, fostering a sense of belonging and support.
3. **The power of "yet"**: Instead of focusing on limitations, use the power of "yet." When your child says, "I can't do this," reply with, "You can't do it yet, but I know you can learn with practice!" This growth mindset teaches children that challenges are opportunities to develop new skills.
4. **Celebrate effort, not just achievements**: Trophies are great, but the journey is even more important. Recognize your child's effort, determination, and problem-solving skills, not just the final outcome. This reinforces the idea that hard work and perseverance are valuable, regardless of the result.
5. **Let them experience healthy risks**: Bubble wrap might seem comforting, but it limits growth. Allow your child to experience age-appropriate risks, like climbing a jungle gym or trying a new sport. This helps them develop confidence, problem-solving skills, and the ability to cope with frustration.
6. **Teach healthy coping mechanisms**: Life throws curveballs, and children need tools to manage their emotions. Teach them relaxation techniques like deep breathing or mindfulness exercises. Encourage them to express their feelings in healthy ways through talking, drawing, or writing.

---

16. Dawson, K.S., and Bryant, R.A. Children's vantage Point of Recalling Traumatic Events. *PLoS One*, 11:19, e0162030 (2016). https://www.ncbi.nlm.nih.gov/pmc/articles/PMC5029877/; doi: 10.1371/journal.pone.0162030

RESILIENCY

7. **Let them fail (safely)**: Failure isn't the enemy; it's a stepping stone to success. Let your child experience setbacks in a safe environment. Help them learn from mistakes and develop strategies to try again in a different way.
8. **Be a supportive coach, not a rescuer**: There's a difference between helping and hovering. Instead of jumping in to fix every problem, guide your child through challenges. Ask questions, encourage them to brainstorm solutions, and celebrate their independence when they overcome obstacles.

THE CARE METHOD

Homework

Let's do this homework a little differently this time. Start by taking the resiliency quiz below. Remember to be as honest as possible. Don't give the answers you think will make you look good. Be honest and authentic. Then change will come.

Resiliency Quiz

Instructions: Answer the following questions and rate yourself on a scale of 1-5:
(Score: 1 = very little, 5 = very strong)

1. In a crisis or chaotic situation, I calm myself and focus on taking useful action.

1 2 3 4 5

2. I'm usually optimistic. I see difficulties as temporary and expect to overcome them.

1 2 3 4 5

3. I can tolerate high levels of ambiguity and uncertainty about situations.

1 2 3 4 5

4. I adapt quickly to new developments. I'm good at bouncing back from difficulties.

1 2 3 4 5

5. I'm playful. I find the humor in rough situations and can laugh at myself.

1 2 3 4 5

6. I'm able to recover emotionally from losses and setbacks. I have friends I can talk to. I can express my feelings to others and ask for help. Feelings of anger, loss, and discouragement don't last long.

1 2 3 4 5

RESILIENCY

7. I feel self-confident, appreciate myself, and have a healthy concept of who I am.

1 2 3 4 5

8. I'm curious. I ask questions. I want to know how things work. I like to try new ways of doing things.

1 2 3 4 5

9. I learn valuable lessons from my experiences and from the experiences of others.

1 2 3 4 5

10. I'm good at solving problems. I can use analytical logic, be creative, or use practical common sense.

1 2 3 4 5

11. I'm good at making things work well. I'm often asked to lead groups and projects.

1 2 3 4 5

12. I'm very flexible. I feel comfortable with my paradoxical complexity. I'm optimistic and pessimistic, trusting and cautious, unselfish and selfish, and so forth.

1 2 3 4 5

13. I'm always myself, but I've noticed that I'm different in different situations.

1 2 3 4 5

14. I prefer to work without a written job description. I'm more effective when I'm free to do what I think is best in each situation.

1 2 3 4 5

15. I "read" people well and trust my intuition.

1 2 3 4 5

79

THE CARE METHOD

16. I'm a good listener. I have good empathy skills.

1 2 3 4 5

17. I'm non-judgmental about others and adapt to people's different personality styles.

1 2 3 4 5

18. I'm very durable. I hold up well during tough times. I have an independent spirit underneath my cooperative way of working with others.

1 2 3 4 5

19. I've been made stronger and better by difficult experiences.

1 2 3 4 5

20. I've converted misfortune into good luck and found benefits in bad experiences.

1 2 3 4 5

Total Score: _______________

Interpretation:

80 or higher = very resilient

65-80 = better than most

50-65 = slow, but adequate

40-50 = you're struggling

40 or under = seek help!

80

RESILIENCY

Additional Questions

1. What does resilience mean to you? Provide personal examples of a time when you demonstrated resilience in overcoming a challenge or a setback. How did you cope with the situation, and what strategies did you employ to bounce back?

2. Think of a difficult situation you've faced in the past. How did you maintain a positive attitude or find the strength to persevere during that time? Reflect on the lessons you learned from overcoming that challenge and how it has influenced your resilience today.

5

Behavioral Change

"Your beliefs become your thoughts, your thoughts become your words, your words become your actions, your actions become your habits, your habits become your values, your values become your destiny."

—Mahatma Gandhi

Building on the resilience and introspection developed in previous sessions, chapter 5 invites clients to dive into the process of behavioral change. This chapter encourages clients to pinpoint specific behaviors they wish to change, while highlighting the importance of persistence and self-awareness in achieving meaningful transformation. Clients will learn that true behavioral change is a journey that requires consistent effort and a deep understanding of their own triggers and responses.

As a counselor, your role is to guide clients through the process of recognizing the habits and behaviors that have negatively impacted their relationships and lives. By helping clients reflect on the barriers that prevent behavioral change—such as cognitive distortions, lack of accountability, and ingrained habits—you can assist them in setting achievable goals for self-improvement. Encourage them to see the connection between resilience, as discussed in chapter 4, and their capacity for transformation. Behavioral change, much like resilience, demands repeated effort, reflection, and adaptation.

The key here is helping clients grasp that change is an ongoing process and often requires adjusting their responses to familiar challenges. The exercises in this chapter are designed to help clients identify their harmful behaviors, understand why these behaviors persist, and develop strategies to alter them. By creating an empathetic and encouraging environment, you can support clients in confronting the discomfort that often accompanies change while maintaining a commitment to progress.

This chapter prepares clients for the deeper work that will follow, particularly in understanding how cognitive distortions and emotional regulation impact their ability to change behavior in the long term.

Goals of This Chapter

Transforming behavior starts with understanding the process behind it. This chapter emphasizes self-regulation as a key foundation for promoting positive changes in both intimate partner relationships and personal growth. Clients will explore the connection between their thoughts, emotions, and actions, gaining insight into how these elements shape behavior patterns, particularly in the context of abusive tendencies.

As clients progress through this chapter, they are encouraged to reflect on past behaviors, recognize triggers, and begin the process of changing their responses to conflict and stress. The goal is to help clients identify barriers to behavioral change while equipping them with the tools to overcome these challenges. This chapter focuses on building accountability and responsibility, essential components in the journey toward healthier relationships.

Colorado DVOMB Standards Competencies

Chapter 5 aligns closely with the Colorado Domestic Violence Offender Management Board (DVOMB) standards, particularly emphasizing **self-regulation**, **dynamic DV risk factors**, **pro-social activities**, and **accountability/responsibility for one's behavior**. This chapter focuses on the process of behavioral change, highlighting self-regulation as a crucial component in managing impulses and emotional responses, especially in high-stress situations. Clients are encouraged to identify and address dynamic risk factors in their lives, taking proactive steps to reduce the likelihood of harmful reactions.

The integration of pro-social activities plays a vital role in this chapter, offering clients opportunities to engage in positive, community-based activities that provide a sense of purpose and belonging. By building healthy support networks, clients can replace negative behaviors with more constructive and fulfilling alternatives. Additionally, taking accountability for one's actions is a central theme, where clients are encouraged to understand the impact of their behaviors on others and commit to making amends.

These standards are integral to the CARE Method's therapeutic goals, ensuring that clients not only understand the need for behavioral change but also take actionable steps toward implementing these changes. By focusing on self-regulation, managing risk factors, engaging in pro-social activities, and assuming responsibility for their actions, clients are empowered to create lasting, positive change in their relationships and lives.

Important Things to Know

In this chapter, we delve into the concept of **behavioral change**, focusing on how clients can begin to alter negative behaviors and habits. This chapter builds on the previous discussions of resilience and emotional regulation, both of which are essential for sustaining long-term behavioral change. Understanding that change takes time and requires perseverance is key for clients as they work toward transforming their actions and thought patterns.

Next week, we will explore the concept of **amygdala hijack** and its effects on emotional responses. Clients will learn how their brain reacts in high-stress or triggering situations, helping them recognize when their emotions have taken control and how to regain composure. The foundation laid in this chapter on behavioral change is crucial as clients move forward, equipping them with the tools to manage emotional responses more effectively in future chapters.

Key Concepts and Terminology

Behavioral change: The process of altering one's actions, habits, or patterns of behavior over time. In the context of the CARE Method, behavioral change refers to the transformation of harmful behaviors into positive, healthy habits that improve relationships and personal well-being.

Stages of change (transtheoretical model): A framework for understanding how individuals progress through different stages when trying to change behaviors. The stages include precontemplation, contemplation, preparation, action, maintenance, and relapse. Recognizing these stages helps clients identify where they are in the process of change.

Relapse: A return to old, harmful behaviors after a period of improvement. Relapse is considered a normal part of the change process and is not viewed as failure. Clients learn how to navigate setbacks and continue moving forward.

Self-regulation: The ability to control one's emotions, thoughts, and behaviors in the face of challenges. Self-regulation is key to maintaining positive changes and avoiding impulsive reactions that could lead to relapse.

Accountability: Taking responsibility for one's actions and the consequences they have on others. In this chapter, clients are encouraged to reflect on how their behaviors have impacted their relationships and commit to making amends and improving.

Triggers: Situations, emotions, or environments that provoke harmful behaviors. Understanding personal triggers allows clients to anticipate and avoid situations that might lead to negative actions.

Cognitive restructuring: A method used to change unhelpful thought patterns that contribute to negative behaviors. Clients are encouraged to reframe their thoughts to support their behavioral change journey.

Discussion Prompts

These prompts are designed to facilitate reflection on current behaviors, encourage self-awareness, and help clients explore the barriers and opportunities for creating lasting change in their lives.

Recognizing the need for change:

- Encourage clients to reflect on specific behaviors they would like to change in their lives.
- **Discussion prompt**: "What are some behaviors or habits you currently have that you'd like to change? How have these behaviors impacted your relationships or personal growth?"

Understanding the stages of change:

- Discuss the different stages of change from the transtheoretical model, such as precontemplation, contemplation, and action.
- **Discussion prompt**: "Where do you see yourself in the process of change? Are you just starting to consider making a change, or have you already taken action to change a behavior?"

Exploring the barriers to change:

- Ask clients to think about why it's been hard for them to change certain behaviors in the past.
- **Discussion prompt**: "What challenges or obstacles have you faced when trying to change a habit or behavior? How have these barriers influenced your ability to create lasting change?"

Reflecting on relapse and resilience:

- Encourage clients to view relapse as part of the change process and reflect on times they experienced setbacks.
- **Discussion prompt**: "Can you think of a time when you tried to change a behavior but relapsed? What did you learn from that experience, and how can you apply those lessons as you continue to work on changing your behavior?"

Identifying positive reinforcements:

- Help clients recognize the rewards or positive reinforcements that motivate their behavioral changes.
- **Discussion prompt**: "What are some of the positive outcomes you've noticed when you've successfully made a change? How do these rewards help motivate you to continue working toward your goals?"

Breaking negative patterns:

- Discuss how negative patterns and habits can become ingrained and automatic over time.
- **Discussion prompt**: "What are some negative patterns or habits you've noticed in your behavior? How can you begin to disrupt these automatic responses and replace them with healthier behaviors?"

Accountability in behavioral change:

- Emphasize the importance of taking responsibility for one's actions during the process of behavioral change.
- **Discussion prompt**: "How can taking accountability for your actions help you stay on track with your behavioral change goals? What steps can you take to hold yourself accountable moving forward?"

Contents

Chapter 5: Behavioral Change
What Is Behavioral Change and What Does It Look Like?
Why Is It So Hard to Change a Behavior?
Transtheoretical Model and Stages of Change
The Six Stages of Change
Let's Talk About Behaviors You Have Struggled to Change.
Homework

5

Behavioral Change

"Behavior is the end result of a prevailing story in one's mind: change the story and the behavior will change."

—Dr. Jacinta Mpalyenkana

In this chapter, we're dealing with behavioral change. But remember what we learned in chapter 4 and how resilience is a key component of behavioral change. We learned what it means to be resilient and how important it is for us to have resilience in life. When we talk about behavioral change, it's important for you to know that change does not come easily and neither does it happen overnight. You need to have resilience to keep bouncing back and trying again, no matter how many times you fall away.

What Is Behavioral Change and What Does It Look Like?

When we talk about behavioral change, we're talking about transforming your current behaviors and habits, over time, into new (and positive) ones.[17] It involves altering how you behave in day-to-day situations, which can range from minor tweaks in your routine to major shifts in how you interact with others or manage your emotions and tasks.

What does this look like in the real world? Certain actions, reactions, or habits led you to where you are at this very moment. When we apply behavioral change, the goal is to alter those habits

17. American Psychological Association. (2018, April 19). APA Dictionary of Psychology—behavior change. Retrieved from American Psychological Association: https://dictionary.apa.org/behavior-change

THE CARE METHOD

from negative to positive so that the outcome changes. For example, maybe you struggle with aggression. In this case, behavioral change would involve identifying the root cause of your aggression and learning healthier ways to communicate your feelings, like talking things out calmly or using assertive language.

Name the behaviors in your life that you'd like to change.

Why Is It So Hard to Change a Behavior?

Our brains are wired to seek comfort and avoid discomfort. Change, by its very nature, disrupts our routines while simultaneously trying to establish new ones, and this can feel extremely uncomfortable.[18] So, it's no surprise our brains might try to steer us back to those familiar, even if not ideal, behaviors because they feel comfortable to us. Think about how you brush your teeth in the morning. It's probably second nature, right? That's because repeated behaviors become ingrained in our brains as automatic responses. This is why every time you try to change, you find yourself reverting back to those negative behaviors after some time.

18. Call, M. (2022, January 31). *Why is Behavior Change So Hard?* Retrieved from Accelerate Learning Community: https://accelerate.uofuhealth.utah.edu/resilience/why-is-behavior-change-so-hard

BEHAVIORAL CHANGE

Now, go back to the list of behaviors you said you'd like to change. For each one, write down why it's been hard for you to change this behavior.

Transtheoretical Model and Stages of Change

The transtheoretical model (TTM), also known as the stages of change model, offers a valuable framework for understanding the process of behavioral change. Developed by James Prochaska and Carlo DiClemente in the late 1970s, the TTM proposes that people move through distinct stages as they consider and implement behavioral changes.[19] Simply put, this model is a tool that helps us understand the stages we go through when we're trying to change a behavior.

The Six Stages of Change

Let's take a closer look at each stage:

1. Precontemplation
This stage is characterized by a lack of awareness or denial of a problem. If you are in this stage, you may not be ready to change and don't see a need for change. For example, a smoker in this stage may not see smoking as a problem and may not be interested in quitting.

2. Contemplation
In this stage, you begin to recognize that there is a problem and start to consider making a change. You may weigh the pros and cons of changing and are often ambivalent about making a change. You may even have thoughts such as "I should quit smoking, but I really enjoy it," or "I need to lose weight, but I don't have the time to exercise."

19. Cherry, K. (2022, December 19). The 6 Stages of Change: The Transtheoretical, or Stages of Change, Model. Retrieved from *Very Well Mind*: https://www.verywellmind.com/the-stages-of-change-2794868

THE CARE METHOD

3. Preparation

During this stage, you are actively preparing for the change. You may start looking for solutions and resources to help you make the change. For example, someone in this stage, while trying to quit smoking, may try using nicotine patches or gum.

4. Action

This stage involves taking specific action toward making the desired change. You would be making active changes in your behavior, such as starting a new diet or exercise routine. It is important to note that this stage can be challenging and often requires a great deal of effort. Yes, it is difficult, but it is not impossible.

5. Maintenance

This stage is focused on maintaining the changes that have been made. If you are in this stage, you are working to prevent relapse and maintain your new behaviors. This stage can last for a lifetime as you aim to maintain the changes you have made in the long term.

6. Relapse

Relapse is quite common when you are attempting to change a behavior. Remember when we spoke of how the brain is wired to resist change? This makes relapse all the more probable. You need to know that even if you do relapse, you shouldn't dwell on your frustration, disappointment, or feel like you are a failure. You can start again, but this time, you will be better prepared to deal with the challenge of trying to change because you will be aware of the triggers and possible setbacks that may occur.

Do you think you are capable of change? If you've tried to change in the past, what caused you to relapse or experience a setback?

BEHAVIORAL CHANGE

Let's Talk About Behaviors You Have Struggled to Change

It is important to note that relapse can occur at any stage of the process, and it is normal for individuals to cycle back and forth between stages. For example, someone in the maintenance stage may relapse and find themselves back in the contemplation stage. This is typical and should not be viewed as a failure.

Thinking of the behaviors you have struggled to change, have any of them caused issues in your interpersonal relationships?

THE CARE METHOD

Homework

As you reflect on any incidents you've been involved in related to domestic violence, it's essential to consider the underlying thought patterns or behaviors that might have been unhealthy and contributed to those situations. Understanding these dynamics is crucial for personal growth and development.

1. Consider the stage of change you found yourself in at the time of the DV incidents. Were you already recognizing the need for change, or were you still in the early stages of acknowledging the issue?

____

____

____

____

2. Moving forward to the present, assess your current stage of change. Have you gained a deeper understanding of the issues surrounding your behavior? Are you actively working toward positive changes in your thinking and interpersonal relationships?

____

____

____

____

3. What is an example of the ways you have begun to change?

____

____

____

____

BEHAVIORAL CHANGE

4. Identify any barriers that have hindered your journey toward change in the past.

5. These obstacles could be internal or external factors such as emotional struggles, lack of support, or societal influences (peer influence, wrong crowd, etc.). What are they and how are you challenging them today?

6

Mind-Altering Substances and Their Impact on Relationships

"Substance abuse doesn't just steal from the person who is using; it steals from everyone who loves them."

—Beverly Engel

In the previous chapter, we focused on behavioral change and the steps necessary to help clients transform negative habits into healthier ones. As we move forward, it is crucial to address the role that mind-altering substances play in both behavior and relationships. These substances, including alcohol, illicit drugs, and certain prescription medications, can profoundly impact an individual's decision-making and emotional regulation, often acting as barriers to positive change.

Mind-altering substances affect the way people think, feel, and behave, leading to impaired judgment and reduced inhibitions. While some clients may turn to these substances as a form of coping or temporary escape, the long-term consequences can be deeply harmful. Substance use can trigger or intensify existing negative behaviors, particularly in the context of interpersonal relationships. This chapter explores how substances can exacerbate aggression, emotional volatility, and impulsivity, contributing to unhealthy dynamics and the escalation of conflicts.

It is important to understand that while substances do not directly cause intimate partner violence (IPV), they can be a significant factor in intensifying abusive behaviors. Research shows a strong correlation between substance use and incidents of domestic violence, indicating that while substances are not the root cause, they can create an environment where abusive behaviors are more likely to emerge. Additionally, substance use can have a far-reaching impact on the entire family unit, particularly children, leading to emotional and psychological harm that can extend into adulthood.

As counselors, we must be equipped to recognize how substance use impacts the clients we work with. This chapter will provide insights into how substance use can act as a trigger for abusive behavior, worsen relational dynamics, and create patterns of instability within the family. By understanding these factors, we can better support our clients in their journey toward healthier behavior and relationships.

Throughout this chapter, lead your client to reflect on the ways substances may have played a role in their lives and relationships. Consider the challenges they face in addressing substance use and the impact it has had on their path toward change. This knowledge is essential in guiding them through the complexities of recovery, helping them rebuild trust and communication with their loved ones.

Goals of This Chapter

Mind-altering substances, whether licit or illicit, have the power to impair judgment, reduce inhibitions, and heighten emotional reactions. We will explore how substance use can exacerbate existing relational tensions and contribute to a cycle of unhealthy interactions, even though it is not the root cause of abusive behavior.

Through this exploration, clients will gain insight into how their use of substances may be influencing their ability to maintain healthy relationships and make constructive choices. The goal is to provide clients with a clearer understanding of the link between substance use and the escalation of conflict, encouraging them to reflect on the changes necessary for fostering healthier dynamics. We will also delve into the broader family impact, examining how substance use affects children and contributes to an environment of instability.

By the end of this chapter, clients should be able to recognize the significant role that mind-altering substances play in their behavioral patterns and relationship dynamics. Counselors will be better equipped to guide clients through the process of identifying these influences and working toward recovery and rebuilding trust. This chapter is a critical part of the CARE Method, as it offers strategies for clients to address substance use and its impact on their journey to lasting change.

Colorado DVOMB Standards Competencies

Chapter 6 aligns with the Colorado Domestic Violence Offender Management Board (DVOMB) standards, focusing on the competency related to **mood-altering substances**. The DVOMB emphasizes the need to understand the complex relationship between substance use and domestic violence, as substances can intensify aggressive behaviors and emotional volatility.

This chapter provides insight into how substance use can act as a catalyst for abusive behavior or exacerbate existing unhealthy dynamics. By addressing the influence of mind-altering substances, clients can better understand the ways in which substance use contributes to their decision-making and behavioral patterns. This knowledge is crucial in helping clients develop a more comprehensive approach to managing their behavior and preventing further incidents of abuse.

The integration of this competency within the CARE Method ensures that clients not only recognize the impact of substance use on their actions but also take active steps toward mitigating its influence on their relationships. By focusing on the connection between substance use and abusive behavior, this chapter supports the broader therapeutic goals of promoting self-awareness, accountability, and healthier interpersonal interactions.

Important Things to Know

In this chapter, we explore the **impact of mind-altering substances** on behavior, decision-making, and relationships. These substances, whether legal or illegal, can significantly impair judgment, reduce inhibitions, and heighten emotional responses, often leading to impulsive actions that strain interpersonal dynamics. It's important for clients to understand how substance use can serve as a trigger for negative behaviors or intensify existing unhealthy patterns, even though it may not be the root cause of such behaviors.

As we transition from the previous chapter on **behavioral change**, clients should be encouraged to reflect on how substance use might interfere with their efforts to adopt healthier habits. While the focus on changing behavior is crucial, the presence of substances in one's life can complicate this process, creating additional barriers to achieving lasting change. This chapter aims to help clients recognize the extent to which mind-altering substances influence their actions and relationships, providing a deeper understanding of the challenges they face in their journey toward transformation.

In the next chapter, we will delve into the concept of the amygdala hijack, which further examines how emotional responses can override rational thinking, especially in stressful or triggering situations. Understanding the amygdala hijack is essential, as it provides insight into the emotional triggers that can be exacerbated by substance use. By grasping how these substances can lower inhibitions and intensify emotional reactions, clients will gain a clearer picture of how they may contribute to the escalation of conflicts in their relationships.

Key Concepts and Terminology

Mind-altering substances: These include any substances that affect how a person thinks, feels, or behaves. This category encompasses alcohol, illicit drugs (such as marijuana, methamphetamine, cocaine, and heroin), and prescription medications when they are abused. While some individuals may use these substances for temporary relief from stress or pain, their impact on both the individual and their relationships can be deeply destructive.

Correlation between substance use and domestic violence: Research shows a strong correlation between substance use and incidents of domestic violence. Substance use does not cause intimate partner violence (IPV), but it can impair judgment and exacerbate aggressive behaviors, making violent episodes more likely to occur. Understanding this connection is essential for identifying how substance use can contribute to abusive incidents.

Impaired judgment: The use of mind-altering substances can impair an individual's ability to make sound decisions. This impairment can lead to impulsive behaviors, poor communication, and an escalation of conflicts within relationships. Impaired judgment is a key factor in how substances can act as a trigger for abusive or unhealthy behavior patterns.

Family impact: The effects of substance use extend beyond the individual to the entire family unit. Children living in households where substance use is prevalent are at a higher risk of experiencing emotional and psychological harm. This exposure can lead to developmental delays, emotional regulation issues, and the possibility of repeating these behaviors in adulthood. Understanding the broader impact on the family is crucial for addressing the intergenerational consequences of substance use.

Cycle of substance abuse and relationship breakdown: Substance use can create a cycle of dysfunction within relationships. It can lead to a breakdown in trust, communication, and emotional connection. Addiction can place a heavy burden on relationships, contributing to isolation and the erosion of healthy relational dynamics. Recognizing this cycle is an important step in breaking free from destructive patterns.

Triggers: In the context of substance use, triggers are specific situations, emotions, or environments that increase the likelihood of substance use or relapse. Identifying these triggers is a key component in helping clients manage their behavior and make healthier choices. Triggers can also include interpersonal conflicts or stressors that lead to substance use as a coping mechanism.

Recovery and healthy relationships: Recovery involves not only addressing substance use but also rebuilding trust and communication within relationships. It is a multi-step process that requires acknowledging the problem, seeking help, and committing to change. Understanding the role of substance use in one's behavior is a critical part of the recovery journey and the creation of healthier relationship patterns.

Discussion Prompts

The following discussion prompts are designed to guide clients in exploring the role of substance use in their lives, recognizing the impact on their decision-making and relationships, and developing strategies for moving toward recovery and healthier interactions.

Exploring the role of substances in your relationships:

- Encourage clients to reflect on how substance use has influenced their relationships, both positively and negatively.
- **Discussion prompt**: "How have mind-altering substances played a role in your relationships? Do you find that they intensify existing behaviors or trigger new ones?"

Recognizing the impact on decision-making and behavior:

- Help clients identify instances where substance use has impaired their judgment and contributed to negative behaviors.
- **Discussion prompt**: "Can you think of a situation where substance use led to an impulsive or regrettable decision? How did this impact your behavior and your relationships?"

Understanding the family impact:

- Discuss the broader effects of substance use on family dynamics, especially on children and other family members.

- **Discussion prompt**: "How do you think your substance use, if applicable, has affected those around you, particularly children or other family members? What changes have you noticed in family dynamics as a result?"

Breaking the cycle of substance abuse and relationship breakdown:

- Encourage clients to reflect on the cyclical nature of substance use and its impact on relationships, identifying patterns that may have emerged.
- **Discussion prompt**: "How have you noticed a cycle of substance use affecting your relationships? How might breaking this cycle contribute to healthier dynamics?"

Addressing substance use as a trigger for conflict:

- Discuss how substance use can act as a trigger for conflict or exacerbate existing tensions within relationships.
- **Discussion prompt**: "In what ways have substances acted as a trigger for conflict in your relationships? How have these substances influenced your ability to resolve conflicts effectively?"

Considering recovery and its impact on relationships:

- Help clients consider the potential positive changes that recovery from substance use could bring to their relationships.
- **Discussion prompt**: "How might your relationships improve if substances were no longer a factor in your life? What strengths do you have that could help you move away from substances and rebuild healthier relationships?"

Developing a plan for addressing substance use:

- Guide clients in creating a plan to address their substance use, focusing on how to make changes and rebuild trust in their relationships.
- **Discussion prompt**: "What steps are you ready to take, or have you taken, to address substance use and rebuild trust in your relationships? How can you start making these changes today?"

Contents

Chapter 6: Mind-Altering Substances and Their Impact on Relationships
Mind-Altering Substances
How Substances Impact Behavior and Relationships
Substance Use and Domestic Violence: Clarifying the Cause
Impact on the Family Unit and Children
The Cycle of Substance Abuse and Relationship Breakdown
Recovery and Healthy Relationships
Homework

6

Mind-Altering Substances and Their Impact on Relationships

"Addiction is a family disease. One person may use, but the whole family suffers."

—Unknown

In the previous chapter, we discussed behavioral change, and you learned about altering negative behaviors to create healthier patterns. In this chapter, we will explore how mind-altering substances such as alcohol, drugs, and certain medications can dramatically impact your behavior, decision-making, and relationships. It's essential to understand how substances can act as triggers for abusive behavior or worsen unhealthy dynamics within your interpersonal relationships.

Mind-Altering Substances

Mind-altering substances affect the way you think, feel, and behave. These can include licit and illicit drugs (like, alcohol, marijuana, methamphetamine, cocaine, and heroin), prescription medications (when abused), and other substances that impair your judgment and self-control. While some individuals may believe these substances offer temporary relief from stress or pain, their long-term impact on both the individual and their relationships can be destructive.

How Substances Impact Behavior and Relationships

Substance use can impair judgment, lower inhibitions, and exacerbate emotional reactions. This often leads to impulsive behaviors, aggression, and poor communication—factors that can contribute to conflict escalation in relationships. However, it's important to note that **substances**

do not cause intimate partner violence (IPV). While they may intensify aggression or emotional volatility, IPV is a pattern of controlling behavior that exists independently of substance use. Substance use may heighten existing tensions or contribute to abusive incidents, but it is not the root cause of abusive behavior.

How do you feel about the role substances may play in your own relationships? Do you feel they intensify existing behaviors or trigger new ones?

Substance Use and Domestic Violence: Clarifying the Cause

While substances do not directly cause IPV, research shows a strong correlation between substance use and domestic violence incidents. Studies have found that alcohol and drug use are present in approximately 40-60% of domestic violence cases.[20] Substance use can lower inhibitions and make violent behaviors more likely to emerge, but it is essential to remember that the presence of substances in a relationship does not excuse or justify abusive behavior.

Statistics also show that in many domestic violence arrests, the offender or the victim—or both—were under the influence of substances at the time of the incident. This connection is critical in understanding how substance use can create an environment that escalates abusive behavior but does not solely drive it.

20. Smith, J., et al. Substance Use and Domestic Violence: Correlation, Not Causation. *Journal of Interpersonal Violence*, 32(2), 253-270 (2017).

Impact on the Family Unit and Children

The effects of substance use are not limited to the couple in the relationship but extend to the entire family unit. Children who witness or are exposed to substance use in the household often experience emotional and psychological harm. Studies suggest that children living in households with substance abuse are at a higher risk for developmental delays, emotional regulation issues, and, in some cases, may repeat the same behaviors in adulthood.[21]

Substance abuse can disrupt family dynamics, creating instability and mistrust. Children may feel unsafe, neglected, or burdened with responsibilities beyond their years. The trauma associated with living in a home where both substance use and domestic violence occur can have long-lasting impacts on their sense of security and emotional well-being.

How do you think your substance use, if applicable, has affected those around you, especially children or other family members?

The Cycle of Substance Abuse and Relationship Breakdown

When mind-altering substances enter the equation, the cycle of abuse and dysfunction in relationships can intensify. Trust erodes, communication falters, and unhealthy behaviors escalate. Addiction, in particular, places an overwhelming burden on relationships, causing isolation and breakdowns in emotional connection.

21. National Institute on Drug Abuse. (2020). Effects of Substance Use on Children and Families.

How might your relationships improve if substances were no longer a factor in your life?

Recovery and Healthy Relationships

Healing from the effects of mind-altering substances requires not only addressing substance use but also learning how to rebuild trust and communication with your loved ones. Recovery is a multi-step process that includes acknowledging the problem, seeking help, and committing to change. As you begin to regain control over your behavior, it's essential to also work on creating healthier relationship patterns.

What strengths do you have that could help you move away from substances and rebuild healthier relationships?

MIND-ALTERING SUBSTANCES AND THEIR IMPACT ON RELATIONSHIPS

Homework

Reflect on how, if applicable, mind-altering substances may have played a role in escalating conflicts in your relationships. Answer the following questions:

1. How have mind-altering substances impacted your communication and behavior in your relationships?

____

____

____

____

2. What are some of the challenges you've faced in trying to reduce or eliminate substance use (if applicable), and how have they affected your relationships?

____

____

____

____

3. In what ways do you think your relationships would improve if you made changes related to substance use (if applicable)?

____

____

____

____

____

95

4. How have your loved ones expressed concern, if at all, about your substance use and its impact on their relationship with you?

5. What steps are you ready to take, or have you taken, to address substance use and rebuild trust in your relationships (if applicable)?

7

The Amygdala Hijack

"Feelings are something you have; not something you are."

—Shannon L. Alder

Emotional responses can sometimes overpower our ability to think clearly. In this chapter, clients will explore the concept of the **amygdala hijack**, a phenomenon where emotional reactions override rational thinking. This term describes moments when the emotional brain takes control, leading to impulsive reactions, particularly in stressful or triggering situations. The focus of this chapter is to help clients understand why this happens and provide them with strategies to regain control when they feel overwhelmed by their emotions.

As a counselor, your role is to guide clients in recognizing the early signs of an amygdala hijack—physical and emotional cues that indicate their emotions are escalating out of control. Encourage clients to reflect on past instances when they experienced this kind of emotional hijacking. Help them identify the triggers that set off these reactions and the consequences that followed. By examining these patterns, clients will gain insight into how their emotional responses have impacted their relationships and decision-making.

This chapter emphasizes the importance of self-regulation techniques, such as deep breathing, mindfulness, and taking a break from heated situations. As a counselor, assist clients in practicing these skills during the sessions for this chapter, helping them build the ability to pause before reacting impulsively. Encourage clients to use these techniques to reduce the intensity of emotional reactions and maintain control over their actions.

As clients move through this chapter, remind them that an amygdala hijack is a normal response to stress, but with practice and awareness, they can learn to manage their reactions more effectively. By the end of this chapter, clients should have a clearer understanding of their emotional triggers and feel empowered to implement strategies that prevent future emotional hijacking.

Goals of This Chapter

Understanding how the amygdala works encourages clients to identify their personal emotional triggers and explore how these have influenced past behaviors, particularly in moments of conflict or heightened stress. Through this exploration, clients will gain insight into how automatic emotional reactions can escalate situations and lead to impulsive or harmful decisions. The goal is to provide clients with practical tools, such as grounding techniques and mindfulness, to stabilize themselves during emotional crises and prevent negative outcomes.

By the end of this chapter, clients should feel more empowered to manage their emotions and avoid being overwhelmed by them. The techniques introduced here are crucial for fostering long-term emotional stability and healthier relationship dynamics. This chapter is a foundational part of the CARE Method, as it equips clients with the skills needed for effective emotional regulation and crisis management.

Colorado DVOMB Standards Competencies

Chapter 7 aligns with the Colorado Domestic Violence Offender Management Board (DVOMB) standards, particularly emphasizing **crisis management and stabilization, past experience/trauma, intergenerational patterns,** and **cognitive distortions**. This chapter explores the concept of the amygdala hijack, where emotional responses can override rational thinking, leading to impulsive reactions in stressful situations. Understanding this phenomenon helps clients recognize when they are losing control and teaches them to employ strategies like grounding exercises and mindfulness to manage emotions effectively.

The chapter also examines how past experiences and trauma influence emotional regulation. Clients are encouraged to reflect on how trauma and intergenerational patterns may have shaped their triggers and responses, enabling them to break the cycle of trauma and develop healthier coping mechanisms. Additionally, it addresses cognitive distortions, helping clients understand how inaccurate ways of thinking contribute to the amygdala hijack, and guides them in challenging and reframing these thought patterns for more balanced perspectives.

These competencies are integral to the CARE Method's therapeutic goals, ensuring clients understand the mechanics of the amygdala hijack and take active steps to manage their emotional responses. By focusing on crisis management, acknowledging past trauma, addressing intergenerational patterns, and challenging cognitive distortions, clients can move toward healthier emotional regulation and nonviolent interactions in their relationships.

Important Things to Know

In this chapter, we focus on the concept of the **amygdala hijack**, helping clients understand how the brain reacts to stress and emotional triggers. The amygdala, which plays a key role in processing emotions, can sometimes bypass rational thinking, leading to impulsive, emotionally driven reactions. This understanding is critical as clients begin to recognize their own triggers and how these biological responses can escalate conflict in their relationships.

Next week, we will build on this by exploring **emotional intelligence**. Clients will learn how to manage and harness their emotions in healthier ways, particularly by increasing their self-awareness and emotional control. The insights gained from understanding the amygdala hijack will serve as the foundation for developing emotional intelligence, enabling clients to approach their relationships with more empathy, self-regulation, and thoughtful responses rather than impulsive reactions.

Key Concepts and Terminology

Amygdala hijack: A term used to describe the process by which the amygdala, the brain's emotional center, overrides rational thought in moments of high emotional stress, leading to impulsive and often irrational reactions. Understanding this concept helps clients recognize when they are being controlled by their emotions and how to regain control.

Triggers: External or internal stimuli that provoke an emotional reaction, often linked to past experiences. In the context of the amygdala hijack, triggers are the catalysts that cause clients to lose control of their emotions.

Emotional regulation: The ability to manage and control one's emotional responses, particularly in stressful or triggering situations. Emotional regulation is a critical skill for avoiding the negative consequences of an amygdala hijack.

Self-awareness: Recognizing the signs of emotional escalation in oneself, such as physical sensations or mental shifts, that signal an impending amygdala hijack. Self-awareness is key to preventing emotional outbursts and maintaining control.

Crisis management: A set of strategies and tools designed to help clients stabilize their emotions during moments of heightened stress. Techniques such as deep breathing, grounding exercises, and mindfulness are introduced to help clients manage emotional crises more effectively.

Discussion Prompts

These discussion prompts aim to guide clients in identifying their emotional triggers, understanding the impact of the amygdala hijack on their behavior, and developing strategies for managing their emotions more effectively.

Identifying emotional triggers:

- Ask clients to reflect on situations where their emotions escalated quickly and consider what triggers might have caused that response.
- **Discussion prompt**: "Can you think of a situation where you felt your emotions spiral out of control? What was the trigger, and how did you react?"

Recognizing the signs of an amygdala hijack:

- Help clients explore the physical and emotional signs that occur when they are experiencing an amygdala hijack.
- **Discussion prompt**: "What physical signs do you notice in your body when you're feeling overwhelmed? How do these signals alert you to an emotional hijack?"

Understanding the consequences of impulsive reactions:

- Encourage clients to reflect on moments when an amygdala hijack led to impulsive decisions or harmful actions.

- **Discussion prompt**: "Can you recall a time when you reacted impulsively in the heat of the moment? What were the consequences, and how did that affect your relationships?"

Building emotional regulation skills:

- Discuss techniques for managing emotions and preventing an amygdala hijack, such as deep breathing, mindfulness, and grounding exercises.
- **Discussion prompt**: "What techniques have you tried to calm yourself during emotionally charged situations? How can you practice these techniques to better manage your emotions next time?"

Reflecting on past experiences:

- Ask clients to think about how their past experiences have shaped their emotional triggers and responses.
- **Discussion prompt**: "Looking back on your past, what experiences might have contributed to the emotional triggers you face today? How do these experiences still impact your reactions?"

Developing a plan for future emotional regulation:

- Help clients create a plan for recognizing and managing triggers before they escalate into an amygdala hijack.
- **Discussion prompt**: "What steps can you take to recognize when you're starting to feel triggered? How can you prevent your emotions from taking over and leading to a hijack?"

Contents

Chapter 7: The Amygdala Hijack
What Is the Amygdala Hijack?
Why Do We React to Other People's Emotional Dysregulation?
Signs and Symptoms of an Amygdala Hijack
Consequences
How Do We Stop an Amygdala Hijack?
How Can We Prevent an Amygdala Hijack?
Considerations
Homework

7

The Amygdala Hijack

"I don't want to be at the mercy of my emotions. I want to use them, to enjoy them, and to dominate them."

—Oscar Wilde

You're doing amazing so far. Behavioral change is certainly not easy, but it is very possible, and the fact that you are here means you're putting in the work for that change. In chapter 5, we focused on the different stages of change (TTM model). The sixth stage of the model, called "relapse," explains that one of its effects is frustration. When you're frustrated, you often feel like your emotions are all over the place and you feel like your body and your emotions have been hijacked. In this chapter, we're going to talk about what this is and why it happens.

What Is the Amygdala Hijack?

Imagine you're walking through a forest and suddenly, a large snake slithers across your path. In that split second, you don't stop to think; you immediately feel a surge of fear and your body jumps into action. Perhaps you freeze or scream, or maybe you run away as fast as you can. This reaction is so immediate and overpowering that there's no time for logical thinking. This, in essence, is an amygdala hijack.

The amygdala is a small, almond-shaped part of your brain that's crucial for processing emotions.[22] It's like the smoke detector of your brain. Simply put, its main job is to keep you safe by detecting

22. Guy-Evans, O. (2023, September 18). Amygdala Hijack: How It Works, Signs, & How To Cope. Retrieved from *Simply Psychology*: https://www.simplypsychology.org/amygdala-hijack.html

any threat, whether it's a physical danger like a snake or a psychological threat like a fear of speaking in public.

Dr. Daniel Goleman, a psychologist and science journalist, brought widespread attention to the concept of emotional intelligence and included the idea of the amygdala hijack in his theories. He first introduced this term in his 1995 book, *Emotional Intelligence*, to describe sudden, overwhelming emotional reactions that are disproportionate to the actual stimulus because of the emotional brain overwhelming the rational brain.[23]

During an amygdala hijack, this part of your brain takes over or hijacks the rest of your brain. This is a survival mechanism, deeply embedded in our brains, that helps us react without wasting precious time thinking about our next move when faced with immediate danger.[24] The amygdala sends out a distress signal that activates the sympathetic nervous system, making your body ready to fight, flee, or freeze. When this happens, your body releases stress hormones like adrenaline and cortisol, which prepare you for quick action.[25] Your heart beats faster, your breathing quickens, and your muscles tense up, all ready to respond to the danger.

Now, this sounds like a good thing, right? However, there is a flaw. The amygdala doesn't always know the difference between a real threat, like a snake, and what you perceive as a threat, like a tough conversation with a romantic partner. Sometimes, your amygdala can perceive something as a threat even if it isn't truly dangerous.[26] This misperception can lead to an amygdala hijack in situations where having an intense emotional response isn't really appropriate. In other words, your body is prepared to deal with a threat because your amygdala has hijacked your rational thought processes, thinking you're in danger even though you're not.

Unfortunately, this can make you react in ways that might not be the most helpful or appropriate for the situation. You might shout in anger, begin to throw objects, or emotionally withdraw completely. Later, when the hijack subsides, you might wonder why you reacted that way. Does this sound familiar?

---

23. Goleman D. (1995). *Emotional intelligence: Why It Can Matter More Than IQ.* New York, NY: Bantam Books.

24. Pedersen, T. (2021, October 14). All About Amygdala Hijack. Retrieved from *Psych Central*: https://psychcentral.com/health/amygdala-hijack

25. Guy-Evans, O. (2023, September 18). Amygdala Hijack: How It Works, Signs, & How To Cope. Retrieved from *Simply Psychology*: https://www.simplypsychology.org/amygdala-hijack.html

26. Pedersen, T. (2021, October 14). All About Amygdala Hijack. Retrieved from *Psych Central*: https://psychcentral.com/health/amygdala-hijack

Why Do We React to Other People's Emotional Dysregulation?

When someone says that your prefrontal cortex has been hijacked by the amygdala in response to other people's emotional dysregulation, it means that your immediate emotional response is overriding your ability to think rationally or calmly about the situation. What this means in everyday terms is that when you see someone else losing control of their emotions, your brain might react as if you are in danger or need to defend yourself.

Think of the worst overreaction you've ever had to a situation. What was the situation? What was your reaction? What was the truth you learned after the fact?

Signs and Symptoms of an Amygdala Hijack

During an amygdala hijack, the body undergoes a series of physical reactions as part of the fight-or-flight response. These symptoms are designed to prepare the body to quickly deal with whatever perceived threat you are facing. Here are the common physical symptoms associated with an amygdala hijack:[27]

a. Increased heart rate
b. Increased blood sugar for immediate energy
c. Expanded airways for more oxygen
d. Rapid breathing (hyperventilation)
e. Sweating
f. Trembling or shaking
g. Feeling flush or chills
h. Tightening of muscles
i. Dry mouth
j. Dilated pupils

What are some symptoms you experienced when you had an amygdala hijack in the situation you mentioned above?

27. Guy-Evans, O. (2023, September 18). Amygdala Hijack: How It Works, Signs, & How To Cope. Retrieved from *Simply Psychology*: https://www.simplypsychology.org/amygdala-hijack.html

Consequences

An amygdala hijack might feel like a dramatic emotional rollercoaster in the moment, but the consequences can extend far beyond the initial surge. Unfortunately, this can result in strained relationships, shame, regret, chronic stress, people calling you a volatile person, anxiety, or even PTSD.[28]

Can you think of some of the consequences you've faced as a result of that emotional outburst (amygdala hijack)?

How Do We Stop an Amygdala Hijack?

The amygdala hijack throws us into an automatic response, like a car hitting the gas without your foot on the pedal. Our bodies take action before we even have a chance to think. This doesn't mean you're stuck on a runaway emotional train! While the initial reaction might be automatic, you can learn to shift gears and regain control. It takes a conscious effort to deactivate the amygdala's alarm and fire up your frontal lobes, but you can do it. The key lies in recognizing the hijack in action.

So, what does this look like in real time? When you're faced with a perceived threat or intense stress, pay attention to your body. Is your heart racing? Do your palms get sweaty? What about your emotions? Do you feel anger rising in your heart, or extreme frustration, or even extreme fear? Catching these feelings in the moment won't be easy at first, but you just need a little practice. The next time you feel that familiar response rising, acknowledge it. Remind yourself that it's an automatic reaction, not necessarily the most logical one. This simple act of awareness can be a powerful tool to interrupt the hijack and regain control.

28. Smore Science Staff. (2024, February 15). The Incredible Impact of Amygdala Hijack On The Brain's Emergency Response. Retrieved from Smore Science: https://www.smorescience.com/the-incredible-impact-of-amygdala-hijack-on-the-brains-emergency-response/

From Dr. Goleman's studies on emotional intelligence, there are six (6) strategies for coping with amygdala hijack, namely:

1. Name the emotion
2. Six-second rule
3. Breathing
4. Change the setting
5. Share the emotional load
6. Draw on mindfulness

How Can We Prevent an Amygdala Hijack?

We all have emotional triggers. Identifying the situations, people, or topics that tend to set you off is crucial. Once you know these triggers, you can anticipate potential hijacks and prepare coping mechanisms through practicing mindfulness. By becoming more aware of your thoughts and emotions in the moment, you can detach from their intensity and respond more thoughtfully. Techniques like meditation or mindful breathing train you to observe your emotions without judgment, allowing you to have a more measured response.

Sometimes, negative thoughts fuel the emotional fire of an amygdala hijack. Learn to identify and challenge these automatic negative thoughts. Ask yourself, "Is this situation really that bad?" In other words, reframe the situation. I always encourage my clients not to be afraid to remove themselves from overwhelming situations or conversations to protect their emotional well-being. Sometimes, that's all you need to do to view the situation from a calmer state of mind.

Once again, think back to that situation you've been referring to throughout this chapter. Can you identify some of your emotional triggers in that situation?

In general, what are some of your emotional triggers?

Considerations

Let's face it, amygdala hijacks can happen to anyone, even if we have the best intentions. I want you to understand that setbacks are a natural part of the learning process. When you do get hijacked, don't beat yourself up. Instead, take some time to reflect on what happened. Think about the situation and your reaction. This mindful reflection can help you see things from a different perspective and identify ways to avoid similar triggers in the future. Remember, it's about learning from experience, not dwelling on it.

Homework

1. Identify and describe 3-5 triggers which have led to an amygdala hijack for you. Share some of the more recent events.

____

____

____

____

2. Identify and describe physical cues that you have experienced while triggered in the past.

____

____

____

____

3. Share some of the consequences that resulted from your amygdala hijack(s) in the past.

____

____

____

____

4. Share about the thoughts and emotions you experienced once you were calm and able to reason and reflect on your actions.

____

____

____

____

5. What impact did it have on others?

____

____

____

____

6. Were you able to make amends? If so, how? If not, why not?

____

____

____

7. How would you rate your current ability to detect triggers and control impulsive reactions to triggering situations? Mild, moderate, high? How can you improve?

____

____

____

8. Did you experience an amygdala hijack during any incidents related to domestic violence? Yes or no? If you could go back, what would you have done differently?

____

____

____

9. What is your plan for prevention of the amygdala hijack?

____

____

____

8

Emotional Intelligence

"Emotional intelligence is not about being emotional.
It's about being smart with your emotions."

—Josh Freedman

Understanding emotions is key to building healthier relationships. In this chapter, clients will explore the concept of emotional intelligence (EQ) and its impact on their interactions. Emotional intelligence refers to the ability to understand and manage emotions, both in oneself and others, and it plays a critical role in healthy communication, conflict resolution, and fostering empathy. This chapter is designed to help clients become more aware of their emotional responses and how they affect their relationships.

As a counselor, your role is to guide clients through the process of identifying and understanding their emotional triggers. Encourage clients to reflect on past situations where they reacted impulsively or emotionally. Help them pinpoint the emotions they experienced and explore how these responses affected their relationships, particularly during conflicts or stressful situations.

This chapter highlights the importance of building emotional awareness and regulation. By helping clients recognize their emotional states and manage them effectively, you will empower them to respond to relationship challenges with more control and intentionality. Practicing mindfulness, deep breathing, and pausing before reacting are all techniques clients can use to improve their emotional intelligence.

As clients move through this chapter, emphasize that emotional intelligence is a skill that can be developed over time. Remind them that becoming emotionally intelligent will not only enhance their relationships but also improve their ability to handle difficult situations with empathy and understanding. This chapter sets the foundation for healthier, more fulfilling relationships, giving clients the tools they need to navigate complex emotional landscapes.

Goals of This Chapter

In this chapter, the CARE Method focuses on helping clients develop emotional intelligence, also called emotional quotient (EQ), and its crucial role in understanding and managing emotions. Clients will explore how EQ enhances their ability to navigate complex emotions, both in themselves and in others. This chapter highlights the significance of building self-awareness, self-regulation, and empathy as essential tools for fostering healthier relationships and promoting personal growth. By cultivating emotional intelligence, clients become better equipped to handle conflict, stress, and interpersonal challenges in constructive and compassionate ways.

Clients are encouraged to explore their emotional triggers and reflect on how they have responded to conflict in the past. By increasing awareness of their emotional states, clients can begin to make more intentional choices that promote healthier relationship dynamics. This chapter provides practical tools for improving emotional regulation, conflict resolution, and the development of empathy, all of which are key components of emotional intelligence and essential for fostering positive, nonviolent interactions.

Colorado DVOMB Standards Competencies

This chapter aligns with the **Colorado Domestic Violence Offender Management Board (DVOMB) standards on insight and empathy, and self-regulation**. The DVOMB emphasizes the importance of developing **insight** into one's emotional responses and behaviors, fostering **empathy** to understand the impact of those behaviors on others, and cultivating **self-regulation** to manage emotions effectively and reduce impulsive or harmful reactions.

Insight, empathy, and self-regulation are critical components of emotional intelligence. By learning to understand their own emotional triggers, developing empathy for others, and practicing self-regulation, clients can better navigate difficult emotions and improve their interpersonal relationships. This chapter encourages clients to take responsibility for their actions by recognizing the emotional impact their behaviors have on others, and by applying emotional regulation strategies to prevent negative outcomes.

The therapeutic goals of this chapter align with the DVOMB standards by encouraging clients to develop insight, empathy, and self-regulation—key skills for reducing the risk of reoffending and cultivating healthier, nonviolent relationships.

Important Things to Know

In this chapter, we focus on the concept of **emotional intelligence**, guiding clients to understand and manage their emotions more effectively. Developing emotional intelligence is crucial in fostering self-awareness, empathy, and healthy communication, particularly in the context of relationships where emotional reactions can often escalate conflicts. By enhancing their emotional intelligence, clients will be better equipped to navigate difficult conversations, recognize emotional cues in themselves and others, and respond in ways that promote understanding rather than confrontation.

Next week, we will move into the topic of **triggers**. Clients will learn to identify and understand the specific situations or stimuli that provoke emotional responses and may lead to reactive behavior. The foundation of emotional intelligence built in this chapter will be essential as clients work on recognizing their triggers and developing strategies to manage them in a way that supports healthier relationships and personal growth.

Key Concepts and Terminology

Emotional intelligence/emotional quotient (EQ): The ability to recognize, understand, and manage one's emotions as well as the emotions of others. EQ plays a critical role in communication, empathy, and relationship building. It helps clients develop healthier, more emotionally intelligent responses to conflict and stress.

Self-awareness: Understanding one's emotions, triggers, and emotional responses in various situations. Developing self-awareness is the first step in emotional regulation and improving relational dynamics.

Empathy: The ability to understand and share the feelings of another person. Empathy helps clients foster deeper connections and more compassionate communication, which is essential in building trust and respect in relationships.

Self-regulation: The practice of controlling one's emotional impulses, particularly during stressful or triggering situations. Self-regulation is key to preventing impulsive behaviors that could lead to conflict or harm in relationships.

Insight: The ability to reflect on one's behaviors and emotional patterns, particularly in understanding how past experiences shape current actions and responses. Insight helps clients identify the root causes of their behaviors and work toward meaningful change.

Discussion Prompts

These discussion prompts are designed to facilitate reflection on how clients perceive and manage their emotions, and how their emotional intelligence impacts their interpersonal interactions. By discussing these topics, clients can enhance their self-awareness, improve conflict resolution skills, and strengthen relationships through emotional understanding.

Recognizing emotional triggers:

- Encourage clients to reflect on situations where their emotions have overpowered their rational thinking.
- **Discussion prompt**: "Can you recall a situation where your emotional response took over your logical thinking? How did your emotional reaction impact the outcome of the situation?"

Developing self-awareness:

- Ask clients to identify their emotional patterns and how they influence their relationships.
- **Discussion prompt**: "What are the common emotional patterns you've noticed in yourself? How do these patterns affect your relationships with others?"

Exploring empathy in relationships:

- Discuss how empathy contributes to emotional intelligence and improves relationship dynamics.
- **Discussion prompt**: "How do you show empathy in your relationships? In what ways does understanding your partner's emotions improve your connection?"

Managing emotional responses:

- Encourage clients to think about techniques they've used to regulate their emotions during stressful situations.
- **Discussion prompt**: "What strategies have you used in the past to manage your emotions during conflict? How can you improve your emotional regulation moving forward?"

Building emotional intelligence:

- Help clients reflect on how they can continue developing their emotional intelligence to foster healthier relationships.
- **Discussion prompt**: "How can you further develop your emotional intelligence to respond more thoughtfully in your relationships? What specific skills would you like to improve?"

Accountability in emotional regulation:

- Discuss the importance of taking responsibility for one's emotional reactions and how it impacts personal growth.
- **Discussion prompt**: "How can taking responsibility for your emotional responses lead to healthier communication in your relationships? What steps can you take to practice better emotional regulation?"

Enhancing empathy for conflict resolution:

- Explore how increasing empathy can lead to more effective conflict resolution and relationship repair.
- **Discussion prompt**: "In past conflicts, how could greater empathy have helped resolve issues? How can you use empathy to prevent conflicts in the future?"

Contents

Chapter 8: Emotional Intelligence
What Is Emotional Intelligence?
Where Does EQ Come From?
Developmental Stages of Emotional Intelligence
How Rich Is Your Emotions Vocabulary?
What Does Management of Emotions Mean?
How Can Emotional Intelligence Help Me in My Relationships?
Homework

8

Emotional Intelligence

"Emotional intelligence allows us to respond instead of react."

—Unknown

Amygdala hijack and emotional intelligence, also known as emotional quotient (EQ), are closely related. In this chapter, we'll focus more on emotional intelligence, but also the fascinating interplay between the amygdala hijack and emotional intelligence. These two topics shape our reactions to stress and help us navigate the complexities of human emotions. By understanding the science behind emotional hijacking and the power of EQ, we can learn to manage our emotions more effectively, and begin to create healthy relationships with the people we love.

What Is Emotional Intelligence?

Emotional intelligence (EQ) is a multifaceted construct encompassing a range of abilities related to understanding, managing, and utilizing emotions effectively.[29] It goes beyond simply experiencing emotions. It involves a conscious awareness of one's own emotional state and the ability to regulate them in response to internal and external stimuli. In simple terms, emotional intelligence is all about how well you understand and manage your own emotions, and how adept you are at picking up on the feelings of other people. If you have emotional intelligence, you can spot amygdala hijack not just in yourself but in others too and manage it before things get out of hand.

29. Williams, F. (2022, May 30). What to know about emotional intelligence. Retrieved from *Medical News Today*: https://www.medicalnewstoday.com/articles/components-of-emotional-intelligence

THE CARE METHOD

With this short definition, where do you think emotional intelligence (EQ) comes from?

Do you think EQ can be developed?

How do you think biology affects EQ?

Where Does EQ Come From?

The exact origins of emotional intelligence (EQ) are still being debated, but research suggests it likely stems from a combination of nature (genetics) and nurture (environment). There's evidence suggesting that certain brain regions associated with emotional processing and regulation might be partially influenced by genetics.[30]

30. Tait, B. (2020, April 22). Understanding The Neuroscience Behind Emotional Intelligence. Retrieved from *Forbes*: https://www.forbes.com/sites/forbescoachescouncil/2020/04/22/understanding-the-neuroscience-behind-emotional-intelligence/?sh=214913c97623

EMOTIONAL INTELLIGENCE

The quality of early parent-child interactions significantly impacts emotional development. Responsive and nurturing caregivers can help children learn to identify and manage their emotions effectively. On the contrary, neglectful or abusive environments can hinder emotional growth. Children observe and learn from the adults around them. Growing up in a household where emotions are openly expressed and managed constructively can contribute to the development of EQ.

Developing high emotional intelligence (EQ) isn't just about knowing what the right thing to do is; it's about consistently practicing those right actions until they become second nature. This process involves daily activities and interactions where you train your brain to respond in emotionally intelligent ways.

The exciting truth is that EQ is a skill you can develop, much like any other. Several brain regions play a crucial role in emotional intelligence, including the ventromedial prefrontal cortex (involved in decision-making), the frontal cortex (responsible for planning and control), the amygdala (which processes emotions), and the nucleus accumbens (linked to motivation and reward).[30] Each of these areas contributes to different aspects of EQ, making it a truly multifaceted skill that everybody needs to have.

Developmental Stages of Emotional Intelligence

There are different, nuanced models of developing emotional intelligence, but we're going to focus more on recognizing and dealing with your emotions by using a three-stage model.[30]

1. Emotional Awareness (Introduction and Recognition)

This is the initial stage where you are introduced to emotional stimulus. This could be through facial expressions, body language, or even the tone of voice. The focus here is on recognizing and labeling emotions, both in yourself and in others, by using different forms of media.

2. Emotional Understanding and Empathy (Decoding and Interpretation)

This stage goes beyond just recognizing emotions. It involves understanding the reasons behind them and the potential consequences. Empathy plays a crucial role here because it allows you to see things from another person's perspective and understand how they might be feeling.

3. Emotional Management and Regulation (Application and Control)

This final stage involves using the knowledge and understanding you gained in the previous stages to manage your own emotions and effectively respond to the emotions of other people around

THE CARE METHOD

you. In this stage, you will learn to regulate your emotions in healthy ways and build strong coping mechanisms. You can also use your understanding of emotions to build positive relationships and navigate social situations effectively.

While these stages offer a framework, it's important to remember that emotional intelligence development is a continuous process. You can't just go through the three stages and assume you've got enough EQ to last you a lifetime. You have to continually refine your EQ as you learn and grow.

How Rich Is Your Emotions Vocabulary?

A rich emotional vocabulary helps you accurately label your feelings and the feelings of others, which is a key component of emotional intelligence. In other words, it allows you to communicate your feelings more precisely. For example, instead of just saying you're feeling "good," you might specify that you're feeling content, optimistic, or enthusiastic. Similarly, instead of saying you're "upset," you might clarify whether you're feeling frustrated, disappointed, or overwhelmed.

If you're curious about expanding your own emotional vocabulary, you might start by identifying basic emotions such as happiness, sadness, anger, and fear. From there, you can explore more nuanced or complex emotions such as elation, grief, resentment, and apprehension. The more specific you can be about your emotions, the better you can understand and express your emotional experiences.

Mad	**Sad**	**Bad**	**Peaceful**	**Surprised**	**Happy**
Furious	Melancholy	Guilty	Calm	Shocked	Joyful
Irate	Depressed	Ashamed	Serene	Astonished	Elated
Fuming	Grief-stricken	Regretful	Tranquil	Amazed	Content
Annoyed	Despairing	Disappointed	Content	Startled	Ecstatic
Enraged	Heartbroken	Disheartened	Relaxed	Stunned	Grateful
Exasperated	Gloomy	Miserable	Harmonious	Awed	Cheerful
Outraged	Mournful	Worthless	Untroubled	Bewildered	Delighted
Aggravated	Downcast	Inferior	Still	Confounded	Jubilant
Livid	Dejected	Defeated	At ease	Dumbfounded	Blissful

EMOTIONAL INTELLIGENCE

Can you name three (3) emotions you experience on a daily, weekly, or continuous basis?

Think of the last argument you had with someone close to you. What vocabulary did you use in the moment? What vocabulary did you actually mean?

THE CARE METHOD

What Does Management of Emotions Mean?

Emotion management refers to the ability to understand, accept, and effectively regulate your own emotions, and at times, influence the emotions of others. Essentially, mastering your emotions involves recognizing what you feel, accepting these feelings, and managing them in a constructive way.

How do you often manage your emotions?

How Can Emotional Intelligence Help Me in My Relationships?

A core component of EQ is self-awareness, the ability to recognize and understand one's own emotions. This introspection allows you to identify your emotional triggers and the impact those emotions have on you and others. Healthy relationships rely heavily on clear and respectful communication. EQ equips you with the skills necessary to express your needs and wants assertively, while simultaneously practicing active listening. In other words, paying attention to your partner's verbal and nonverbal cues.

There are other ways EQ can help your relationships, such as these:

a. Resolving conflict
b. Building intimacy
c. Being able to support your partner emotionally
d. Controlling impulses
e. Creating empathy

EMOTIONAL INTELLIGENCE

Why do you think emotional intelligence is important in your relationships?

What are the signs that your relationships have not been emotionally intelligent?

Signs that show a lack of emotional intelligence in relationships can look like some of these:

a. You or your partner struggling with emotional regulation
b. A lack of empathy
c. Poor communication skills
d. Shifting the blame (lack of accountability)
e. Ignoring feedback

THE CARE METHOD

These are just a few signs of a lack of EQ in a relationship, but from everything you've learned today, can you list three (3) more signs of a relationship that lacks EQ?

What are the EQ areas you think you can improve on in your personal life?

EMOTIONAL INTELLIGENCE

Homework

Regardless of your starting point, there's always room to improve your emotional intelligence.

Take the following quiz and then answer the additional questions at the end of this homework. Be ready to share your answers with your group next week.

Emotional Intelligence Quiz

Instructions: For each statement, indicate how often it applies to you on a scale from 1 to 5.

1 – Rarely applies to me
2 – Occasionally applies to me
3 – Sometimes applies to me
4 – Often applies to me
5 – Always applies to me

Self-Awareness

1. I am aware of my strengths and weaknesses.

1 2 3 4 5

2. I can accurately recognize my emotions as they arise.

1 2 3 4 5

3. I understand how my emotions impact my thoughts and behavior.

1 2 3 4 5

4. I am comfortable expressing my feelings to others.

1 2 3 4 5

5. I regularly take time to reflect on my thoughts and emotions.

1 2 3 4 5

THE CARE METHOD

Self-Management

6. I can control impulsive behaviors, even when I'm experiencing strong emotions.

1 2 3 4 5

7. I am adept at setting and achieving personal goals.

1 2 3 4 5

8. I handle stressful situations with composure and resilience.

1 2 3 4 5

9. I am able to adapt to change and remain flexible.

1 2 3 4 5

10. I practice healthy habits to manage my emotional well-being.

1 2 3 4 5

Social Awareness

11. I am attentive to the emotions and needs of others.

1 2 3 4 5

12. I can accurately read non-verbal cues in social interactions.

1 2 3 4 5

13. I show empathy and compassion toward others.

1 2 3 4 5

14. I am skilled at resolving conflicts peacefully.

1 2 3 4 5

15. I appreciate diversity and value different perspectives.

1 2 3 4 5

116

EMOTIONAL INTELLIGENCE

Relationship Management

16. I communicate effectively and openly with others.

1 2 3 4 5

17. I build and maintain strong, positive relationships.

1 2 3 4 5

18. I am able to influence and inspire others toward a common goal.

1 2 3 4 5

19. I collaborate well with others in group settings.

1 2 3 4 5

20. I handle criticism and feedback constructively.

1 2 3 4 5

Scoring: After answering all the questions, separate your responses into the four categories below and add up your scores for each one:

______ Self-Awareness (Questions 1-5)

______ Self-Management (Questions 6-10)

______ Social Awareness (Questions 11-15)

______ Relationship Management (Questions 16-20)

Interpretation: Compare your total score for each category to the ranges below to interpret your results:

5-9: Low
10-14: Below average
15-19: Average
20-24: Above average
25: High

117

THE CARE METHOD

Additional Questions

1. Share the results of your EQ quiz. What are the areas you excelled in and what are the areas for improvement?

2. Based on what you learned in chapter 8 about emotional intelligence (EQ) and the signs a relationship is not emotionally intelligent, what areas do you think you can improve upon?

3. Discuss the importance of emotional intelligence in fostering healthy communication and conflict resolution within intimate partner relationships.

4. Explore the role of empathy in intimate partner relationships and its connection to emotional intelligence. How does the ability to understand and share your partner's feelings contribute to relationship satisfaction and longevity?

9

Triggers

"Your triggers are your teachers. They show you where you're not free."

—Nicolette Sowder

Triggers can unexpectedly bring powerful emotions to the surface, often linked to past trauma. In this chapter, clients will learn about triggers—emotional reactions to certain stimuli or situations that can evoke intense memories or feelings. These triggers can range from a smell, a sound, or even a phrase, instantly transporting clients back to the emotional state of a past distressing event. The goal of this chapter is to help clients recognize and manage these triggers effectively to prevent negative emotional responses from escalating.

As a counselor, your role is to guide clients in identifying their personal triggers. Encourage clients to reflect on past situations when they were emotionally triggered and the events that led up to it. Help them explore how those triggers manifested physically and emotionally. By understanding the triggers and the ways they react to them, clients can become more conscious of the early warning signs.

This chapter also focuses on equipping clients with tools to manage their reactions to triggers, such as mindfulness, deep breathing, and grounding techniques. As clients practice these strategies, they will gradually improve their ability to pause and respond intentionally, rather than react impulsively. Your role is to support clients as they practice these techniques, helping them to navigate the discomfort that may arise during emotionally charged situations.

As clients move through this chapter, remind them that being triggered is not a sign of weakness but an opportunity to heal old wounds. By gaining control over their triggers, clients will be better equipped to handle challenging emotions and stressful situations in a healthier, more mindful way.

Goals of This Chapter

Understanding what sets us off can be the first step toward emotional freedom. Clients will explore both internal and external triggers and how these can lead to emotional responses that may feel disproportionate to the current situation. This chapter emphasizes the importance of developing self-awareness to identify triggers and implementing healthy coping strategies to manage reactions in a more constructive way.

Clients are encouraged to reflect on their personal experiences with triggers, considering how past trauma has shaped their emotional responses in the present. The goal is to help clients become more conscious of the early warning signs of being triggered, enabling them to employ emotional regulation techniques before the situation escalates. Through this process, clients will develop greater control over their emotions and behaviors, reducing the likelihood of impulsive or harmful reactions.

Colorado DVOMB Standards Competencies

Chapter 9 aligns with the Colorado Domestic Violence Offender Management Board (DVOMB) standards, focusing on **past experience/trauma**, **intergenerational patterns**, **self-regulation**, and **cognitive distortions**. This chapter explores the concept of triggers, helping clients understand how certain stimuli can provoke intense emotional reactions and lead to maladaptive behaviors. By examining their history, clients identify events that have contributed to these triggers, gaining insight into their emotional responses.

Intergenerational patterns also influence the formation of triggers. Clients are encouraged to explore how family behaviors and responses have shaped their emotional reactions. Recognizing these patterns allows them to break the cycle and develop healthier coping mechanisms. Self-regulation is key in managing triggers, and this chapter provides tools such as mindfulness and grounding exercises to help clients maintain control and respond thoughtfully rather than impulsively.

This chapter also addresses cognitive distortions, guiding clients in identifying and challenging faulty thinking patterns that can intensify reactions to triggers. By reframing these thoughts, clients can reduce the intensity of their emotional responses. These competencies are integral to the CARE Method, ensuring that clients not only understand their triggers but also develop practical skills to manage them, promoting more balanced interactions in relationships.

Important Things to Know

In this chapter, we'll explore what **triggers** are, how they are formed, and how they impact behavior. Last week, we focused on **emotional intelligence**, where clients learned about managing their emotions and understanding how these emotions influence their reactions in relationships. Now, with triggers, we build on this knowledge by discussing how external and internal stimuli can suddenly cause a powerful emotional response, often tied to past trauma.

Next week, we'll shift our focus to **habits**, examining how repeated behaviors shape our daily lives and how those habits are linked to emotional triggers. Understanding triggers is essential in helping clients manage their emotional responses and prevent destructive behaviors, setting the stage for exploring how long-standing habits can either reinforce or help overcome those patterns.

Key Concepts and Terminology

Triggers: External or internal stimuli that evoke strong emotional responses, often linked to past trauma or stressful experiences. Triggers can cause clients to react impulsively or feel overwhelmed, and recognizing these is crucial for emotional regulation.

Past trauma: Previous adverse events that influence current emotional reactions and behavior. Understanding how past trauma affects current responses helps clients manage their triggers and begin the healing process.

Emotional regulation: The ability to control and manage emotional responses, particularly in the face of triggers. Emotional regulation is essential for preventing impulsive or harmful behaviors.

Self-awareness: The process of recognizing one's emotional states and triggers. This self-awareness allows clients to anticipate and manage reactions more effectively.

Coping mechanisms: Strategies clients use to manage emotional reactions when triggered. Developing healthy coping mechanisms is key to breaking cycles of reactive behavior and fostering emotional stability.

Discussion Prompts

The following prompts are designed to help clients understand their triggers, explore how they've affected their lives, and develop strategies to manage their emotional responses more effectively.

Identifying triggers:

- Encourage clients to identify the specific situations, people, or environments that trigger strong emotional responses.
- **Discussion prompt**: "What are some common triggers in your life that provoke intense emotions? How do these triggers typically affect your thoughts and behavior?"

Exploring past trauma:

- Ask clients to reflect on how past experiences have shaped their emotional triggers.
- **Discussion prompt**: "Can you identify any connections between your current emotional triggers and past traumatic events? How have these experiences influenced your responses to certain situations?"

Managing triggered responses:

- Help clients explore ways to manage their emotional reactions when they are triggered.
- **Discussion prompt**: "What techniques have you found helpful for managing your emotions when you're triggered? How can you use these techniques to prevent overreacting in the future?"

Reflecting on the impact of triggers on relationships:

- Discuss how emotional triggers can affect relationships, particularly in moments of conflict.
- **Discussion prompt**: "How have your emotional triggers impacted your relationships? What steps can you take to reduce the negative effects of being triggered in future interactions?"

Developing a plan for managing triggers:

- Encourage clients to create a plan for addressing their triggers in a healthy way.
- **Discussion prompt**: "How can you anticipate and prepare for situations that might trigger strong emotional responses? What steps can you take to manage your reactions and maintain control?"

Contents

Chapter 8: Triggers
What Are Triggers?
What Types of Triggers Are There?
Common Triggers for Stress
What Does "Triggered" Mean?
How Do Triggers Form?
Different Coping Strategies
Homework

9

Triggers

"There's nothing negative about being triggered. It's a calling to heal our wounds. It's a calling to self-reflect and to get curious about the reaction we are having."

—Dr Nicole LePera

We dealt with emotional intelligence in the previous chapter, which is very important to keep in mind as you work your way through this chapter, which is about triggers. Emotional intelligence deals with how to manage your emotions, but what do you do when your body has an emotional reaction to a sudden encounter or stimuli, a.k.a. a "trigger"? This is what we will be discussing in this chapter.

What Are Triggers?

Have you ever smelled a certain type of perfume and suddenly found yourself whisked back in time to a specific moment in your childhood? Or heard a song that instantly made you feel the same sadness you did years ago? If so, you've experienced what psychologists call triggers.

Triggers are sensory experiences—like sights, sounds, or smells—that can unexpectedly set off intense emotional reactions or memories, especially from traumatic events.[31] These reactions can feel as though you're reliving the past, and they can happen without any warning.

31. Pedersen, T. (2022, April 28). What Are Triggers, and How Do They Form? Retrieved from *Psych Central*: https://psychcentral.com/lib/what-is-a-trigger#what-is-a-trigger

The Science Behind Triggers

Do you remember the chapter on amygdala hijack? Believe it or not, the amygdala is involved in the process of being triggered. Remember, the amygdala plays a central role in processing emotional stimuli and triggering the fight-or-flight response. It is constantly evaluating sensory input and searching for potential threats.[32] When we encounter a trigger, the amygdala interprets it as a potential danger and initiates the fight-or-flight response. This results in the release of stress hormones like cortisol and adrenaline, leading to increased heart rate, sweating, and muscle tension.

The hippocampus, located in the medial temporal lobe, is responsible for memory consolidation and retrieval. When your body perceives a sensory stimulus, the amygdala then sends signals to the hippocampus, prompting the retrieval of a specific memory associated with that stimulus.[32] In the case of triggers, this retrieved memory is often linked to a traumatic or distressing event.

Traumatic experiences can significantly impact the way the amygdala and hippocampus interact. During a traumatic event, the amygdala becomes hyperactive, forming a strong association between the sensory details of the experience (sights, sounds, smells) and the intense emotions you felt when that stressful event originally occurred. This heightened sensitivity is the reason why stimuli—no matter how insignificant they may seem, even if they faintly resemble the things that were present during the trauma—can trigger a flood of emotions and different physiological responses.[32]

What Types of Triggers Are There?

Triggers can be all sorts of things, depending on the memory they're connected to, but they can be split into different categories such as:[33]

a. **Sensory triggers**: These are the classic ones we often hear about. They can be sights you saw (like a burning building if you had a fire scare), sounds you heard (like screeching tires from a car accident), smells you encountered (like smoke if you were in a fire), tastes you experienced (maybe a certain medicine you had to take during a bad illness), or even sensations (like the feel of rough water if you almost drowned).

32. Edwards, S. (2024, February 6). Understanding how traumatic memory is stored in the brain. Retrieved from *Counseling Directory*: https://www.counselling-directory.org.uk/memberarticles/understanding-how-traumatic-memory-is-stored-in-the-brain

33. Johnson, C. (2023). 7 Types of Triggers and 7 Coping Strategies. Retrieved from *Care Counseling*: https://care-clinics.com/7-types-of-triggers-and-7-coping-strategies/

b. **Emotional triggers**: Sometimes, a strong emotion you're feeling in the present can trigger a memory that evokes a similar feeling. Feeling angry might remind you of a past fight, or feeling sad could bring back a time of loss.

c. **Situational triggers**: Certain places or situations can be triggers too. Maybe a dark hallway reminds you of getting lost as a child, or a crowded room triggers anxiety if you're prone to feeling overwhelmed.

d. **Relational triggers**: Interactions with certain people or types of people can be triggers. Maybe someone who reminds you of a bully, or even a situation like being criticized can bring back bad memories.

From these four (4) categories, what types of triggers do you struggle with the most and why?

Common Triggers for Stress

Triggers can either be a result of external or internal stimuli.[34] Here are a few examples:

External

- Financial issues
- Life changes
- Loud sounds
- Work-related pressure
- Relationship issues
- Being too busy
- Being ignored

Internal

- Pessimism
- Unrealistic expectations
- Rejection
- Fear
- Physical discomfort
- Lack of self-control
- Memories

Split this block into two (2) columns. In one column, write your external triggers, and in the other column, write your internal triggers.

What Does "Triggered" Mean?

In recent years, "triggered" has become a popular term in casual conversation. It's often used to describe someone who is upset, offended, or simply disagrees with something.[35] This informal

34. Cuncic, A. (2023, August 23). What Does It Mean to Be "Triggered": Types of Triggers and Coping Strategies. Retrieved from *Very Well Mind*: https://www.verywellmind.com/what-does-it-mean-to-be-triggered-4175432

35. Pedersen, T. (2022, April 28). What Are Triggers, and How Do They Form? Retrieved from *Psych Central*: https://psychcentral.com/lib/what-is-a-trigger#what-is-a-trigger

usage has caused some confusion and can downplay the true experience of being triggered in a clinical sense.

Going back to the definition above, being triggered refers to experiencing a strong emotional or physical reaction to a particular stimulus, often related to a past trauma or deeply impactful memory. When you're triggered, something in the present environment reminds you of the past experience, causing your brain to react as if you are reliving that moment again. This reaction can happen suddenly and intensely, and it often feels involuntary, catching you off-guard.

Being triggered can feel overwhelming. You might suddenly feel scared, anxious, or upset without fully understanding why. Physically, you might experience a racing heart, sweating, or shaking. Emotionally, it can lead to sadness, anger, or a feeling of detachment from reality.

How Do Triggers Form?

Triggers are closely tied to our memories. When something traumatic happens, our brains link certain sensory details, like the sound of a car backfiring or the smell of burning wood, with that moment. Later on, encountering the same sensory details can bring that memory back to life, along with all the associated emotions.

When we experience a traumatic event, our brains don't just register the core event itself. Our senses—sight, smell, sound, taste, and even touch—capture the surrounding details and encode them alongside the emotional response.[36] This creates a vivid sensory memory of the experience.

Years later, encountering elements from that sensory memory can trigger a powerful emotional response. A familiar scent, a specific sound, or even a visual cue can activate the amygdala, the brain's fear center. This can lead to a cascade of physiological and emotional responses, essentially causing us to relive the trauma in the present moment.

In some cases, the trigger may be so subtle that we're not even consciously aware of the sensory connection. For example, a person who experienced having to hide in a closet from a home intruder might experience unexplained anxiety when in a small, stuffy room without realizing the muted sounds coming through the walls are what is triggering the feeling.

36. Pedersen, T. (2022, April 28). What Are Triggers, and How Do They Form? Retrieved from *Psych Central*: https://psychcentral.com/lib/what-is-a-trigger#what-is-a-trigger

Triggers form through a process closely tied to how our brains handle memory and learning, particularly in response to intense or traumatic experiences. Here's a closer look at how this happens:[37]

1. **Association during intense events**: When you experience something very intense or traumatic, your brain notes all the sensory details surrounding the event (what you see, hear, smell, etc.) along with the emotional response you have to that event. This can include everything from the exact location, specific sounds, the weather, or even particular smells associated with that moment. For instance, if someone was in a car accident during a rainstorm, the sound of rain might later become a trigger.
2. **Memory encoding**: These details are encoded in your memory along with the emotional and physical sensations experienced during the event. The brain's limbic system, which includes structures like the amygdala and hippocampus, plays a crucial role in processing emotions and memory. The amygdala, responsible for detecting fear and preparing for emergency events, tags these memories as significant and stores them.
3. **Conditioned responses**: Through a process known as classical conditioning (a learning process that occurs through associations between an environmental stimulus and a naturally occurring stimulus), these sensory details become conditioned stimuli. That means that even without the traumatic event happening again, encountering the sensory details alone can trigger the same emotional and physical response as the original event. This is why, for example, hearing a car backfire might trigger someone who has experienced gunfire.
4. **Reactivation of memories**: When you later encounter a similar sensory detail (a trigger), your brain reacts by activating the memory of the trauma, including the emotional and physical reactions initially experienced. This can feel as though the traumatic event is happening all over again because the original memory was encoded along with the high levels of stress or fear.
5. **Reinforcement**: If the person repeatedly responds to triggers in a certain way, the response can become reinforced. This means the connection between the sensory detail (trigger) and the traumatic memory grows stronger, making it more likely that the trigger will provoke a strong reaction in the future.

---

37. Cohen, R.T., and Kahana, M.J. A memory-based theory of emotional disorders. *Psychol. Rev., 129*(4), 742-776 (2022, April 7). doi: 10.1037/rev0000334. Retrieved from National Library of Medicine: https://www.ncbi.nlm.nih.gov/pmc/articles/PMC9256582/

TRIGGERS

It's not just traumatic memories that can be triggered. People living with substance use disorder might find that seeing a bottle of alcohol or visiting a place where they used to drink can trigger a strong urge to use the substance again.

Triggers are not always negative, even though the term is often associated with negative stimuli. What are some positive or happy triggers from your childhood? These are things that trigger happiness, love, or other positive emotions and reactions.

Different Coping Strategies

Triggers can be disruptive and emotionally charged experiences. However, there are various strategies you can employ to manage your response and regain control. Here are some effective coping mechanisms to consider:[38]

Awareness and Recognition

- **Awareness**: The first step in coping with triggers is to become aware of them. Recognizing the situations, thoughts, emotions, or sensory cues that trigger distressing reactions is essential. Keeping a journal to track triggers and reactions can be helpful in identifying patterns and understanding specific triggers better.
- **Check the facts**: Find out what is true and if this truth aligns with your interpretation of the events.
- **Reframe**: Work to transform your negative perception and thoughts about the stimuli into positive ones.

38 Faster Capital. (2024, March 16). Triggered response: Exploring the Science Behind Triggered Responses. Retrieved from *Faster Capital*: https://fastercapital.com/content/Triggered-response—Exploring-the-Science-Behind-Triggered-Responses.html

Grounding Techniques

- **5-4-3-2-1 grounding**: Focus on your five (5) senses. Name five (5) things you can see, four (4) things you can touch, three (3) things you can hear, two (2) things you can smell, and one (1) thing you can taste. This simple exercise can help bring your attention back to the present moment.
- **Deep breathing**: Take slow, deep breaths in through your nose and out through your mouth. Focus on the sensation of your breath filling your lungs and abdomen. This can help regulate your heart rate and calm your nervous system.

Cognitive Restructuring

- **Challenge negative thoughts**: When triggered, negative thoughts can spiral out of control. Challenge these thoughts by asking yourself if they are realistic and helpful. Try to reframe the situation in a more positive light.
- **Positive affirmations**: Repeat positive affirmations to yourself, like "I am strong," "I can handle this," or "This feeling is temporary." Affirmations can help counteract negative self-talk and boost your sense of control.

Relaxation Techniques

- **Progressive muscle relaxation**: Tense and relax different muscle groups in your body, starting with your toes and working your way up. This can help release physical tension associated with anxiety.
- **Visualization**: Imagine yourself in a calming and peaceful place. Focus on the sights, sounds, and smells of this environment. Visualization can help distract you from your trigger and promote relaxation.

Lifestyle Modifications

- **Self-care**: Prioritize activities that promote your overall well-being. This could include getting enough sleep, eating a healthy diet, exercising regularly, and practicing mindfulness meditation. A healthy lifestyle can enhance your resilience in dealing with triggers.
- **Social support**: Talk to a trusted friend, family member, or therapist about your triggers. Having a support system can provide you with validation, encouragement, and coping strategies.

Professional Help

- **Therapy:** If you're struggling to manage your triggers on your own, consider seeking professional help. A therapist can teach you effective coping mechanisms and help you process past trauma.

Homework

1. Think carefully about what triggers you (it could be an emotion, a smell, a word, a person, an activity, a place, an object, a thought, etc.). Write down the triggers that you experience regularly.

____

____

____

2. What feelings do you experience when you recognize you are being triggered?

Do you feel anger, shame, fear, frustration, or something else? How intense are these feelings?

____

____

____

3. Think about the moments when you felt threatened or insecure in a relationship. What were the triggers for these feelings and how did you cope with them?

____

____

____

4. Have you ever lashed out verbally or physically at a partner? Reflect on what triggered that response and how you could have handled it differently.

____

____

____

____

5. Still thinking about your past relationships and now bringing in your answers to the questions above, are there recurring patterns of behavior or triggers that led to conflicts or violence? Describe them, looking for the patterns in your previous answers.

6. Describe a situation where you felt the need to control a conversation or interaction with your partner. What was the underlying trigger for this need and how did it manifest in real time? (Did it manifest as anger? Throwing objects? Strong verbal language?)

7. How do your reactions impact your relationships? Describe both the short-term and long-term effects on your relationships as a result of your reactions to triggers.

10

Habits and the Mind

"We are what we repeatedly do. Excellence, then, is not an act, but a habit."

—Aristotle

Habits play a powerful role in shaping our actions and relationships. In this chapter, clients will explore the concept of habits and how they influence behaviors and daily life. Habits are automatic patterns that guide routines, impact relationships, and even affect mental states. By understanding how habits are formed, clients can begin identifying the patterns that drive their actions and take control of behaviors that no longer serve them.

As a counselor, your role is to help clients recognize the distinction between positive and negative habits, guiding them to reflect on how these habits have impacted their lives, especially within their relationships. Encourage clients to identify any destructive patterns, such as habits of avoidance, emotional shutdowns, or even aggression, and reflect on how they were formed. Use this as an opportunity to discuss how these automatic behaviors have reinforced negative cycles in their interpersonal relationships.

This chapter highlights the importance of awareness and intentionality in breaking negative habits. As you guide clients through this process, focus on helping them develop a plan to replace harmful habits with healthier ones. Support them in identifying cues that trigger their habitual responses and brainstorm new ways to respond. Tools such as mindfulness, journaling, or practicing alternative behaviors can be powerful in fostering new, positive habits.

As clients work through this chapter, remind them that changing habits takes time and consistency, but with focus and determination, it is possible to reshape their behaviors. At the completion of this chapter, clients should have a clearer understanding of how habits influence their decision-making and possess practical strategies to begin transforming harmful habits into ones that promote growth and healthier relationships.

Goals of This Chapter

Our habits shape more than just our routines; they define how we interact with others. Clients will learn that habits, much like automatic responses, are often formed by past experiences and, if left unchecked, can lead to negative outcomes in relationships. This chapter emphasizes the importance of recognizing and reshaping these habits to create more positive patterns of behavior, ultimately contributing to healthier relationships and better decision-making.

Clients are encouraged to reflect on both the positive and negative habits they have developed over time and how these habits have impacted their personal lives, particularly in their interpersonal relationships. By understanding the formation of these behaviors, clients can begin to actively work on replacing harmful habits with pro-social activities—behaviors that contribute to the well-being of others and society. This chapter also highlights the importance of consistency and intention when breaking old habits and forming new, more constructive ones.

Colorado DVOMB Standards Competencies

Chapter 10 aligns with the Colorado Domestic Violence Offender Management Board (DVOMB) standards, particularly emphasizing **pro-social activities** and **intergenerational patterns**. This chapter highlights the importance of engaging in pro-social activities as a way to break negative behavior cycles and foster positive, community-oriented habits. By participating in activities that encourage social connection, responsibility, and positive reinforcement, clients can develop a sense of belonging and purpose, which is essential for creating lasting change.

Intergenerational patterns are also a key focus of this chapter. Clients reflect on how family behaviors and attitudes have influenced their current actions. Understanding these patterns enables clients to see how engaging in pro-social activities can help break the cycle of intergenerational trauma and create a positive legacy for future generations. By modeling healthy behavior and community involvement, clients can shift family dynamics and set a better example for their children and loved ones.

These standards are integral to the therapeutic goals of the CARE Method. By addressing intergenerational patterns and encouraging active participation in positive community activities, clients can build a foundation for healthier relationships and a more supportive social network. This chapter serves as a crucial step in guiding clients toward a life that is not only free of violence but also rich in connection and personal growth.

Important Things to Know

Last week, we dove into the topic of **triggers** and how certain experiences, sounds, or situations can bring up intense emotional reactions rooted in past traumas. As clients begin to recognize their personal triggers, they can start learning to manage their responses and reduce harmful behaviors.

In this chapter, we shift the focus to **habits and the mind**. Clients will explore how deeply ingrained habits, much like triggers, can shape their behaviors—both positively and negatively. Understanding how habits form and identifying unhelpful patterns will be key to helping clients take control of their actions.

Next week, we will transition into **attachment theory**, where clients will learn how early relational experiences with caregivers have shaped their attachment styles and, ultimately, their behaviors in intimate relationships. This exploration of habits prepares clients to better understand how deeply rooted behaviors influence their attachment patterns and emotional responses.

Key Concepts and Terminology

Habit: A regular behavior that becomes automatic over time, often based on past experiences and repetitive actions. Habits can either be positive or negative, impacting personal relationships and decision-making processes. In this chapter, clients learn how to identify and change harmful habits.

Cognitive restructuring: A technique used to shift unhelpful thought patterns. By mentally rehearsing positive actions and changing negative thought processes, clients can develop healthier behaviors and break free from destructive habits.

Meditation: A mindfulness practice that helps clients focus on the present moment and reduce automatic negative responses. Meditation is used as a tool to retrain the mind and create new, more positive habits.

Visualization: A technique that allows clients to emotionally and mentally envision their desired future. Through visualization, clients can teach their body and mind how to respond differently in challenging situations, fostering behavioral change.

Self-awareness: The recognition of one's own emotional and behavioral patterns. By developing self-awareness, clients can identify habits that no longer serve them and make conscious decisions to change.

Discussion Prompts

These prompts are designed to help clients reflect on their habits, identify areas for improvement, and develop strategies to create positive, lasting changes. By exploring the mind's role in shaping habits, clients can take the first steps toward breaking unhealthy cycles and building more constructive routines.

Understanding habit formation:

- Encourage clients to explore how their habits are formed and reinforced over time.
- **Discussion prompt**: "What are some habits you have developed that have impacted your behavior in relationships? How were these habits formed, and what cues or rewards keep them in place?"

Identifying unhealthy habits:

- Help clients recognize habits that may negatively affect their interpersonal relationships.
- **Discussion prompt**: "Can you identify one unhealthy habit that has caused tension in your relationships? How does this habit typically play out, and what impact does it have on those around you?"

Breaking the habit loop:

- Discuss the components of the habit loop (cue, routine, reward) and how clients can begin to change it.
- **Discussion prompt**: "What are the triggers or cues that lead to unhealthy habits in your daily life? What steps can you take to interrupt the routine and replace it with a healthier behavior?"

Creating positive habits:

- Guide clients in thinking about habits they would like to develop to improve their relationships and emotional well-being.
- **Discussion prompt**: "What is one new habit you would like to build that could contribute to healthier relationships? What reward could you create to reinforce this habit?"

Exploring the role of the mind:

- Encourage clients to reflect on the mental processes involved in habit formation and change.
- **Discussion prompt**: "How do your thoughts and mental patterns influence your habits? How can practicing mindfulness or cognitive restructuring help you shift away from negative habits?"

Overcoming setbacks:

- Help clients anticipate and manage challenges they may face when trying to change their habits.
- **Discussion prompt**: "What obstacles have you encountered when trying to break a bad habit in the past? How can you prepare to handle setbacks as you work to develop new, healthier habits?"

Building self-awareness:

- Encourage clients to reflect on how their awareness of their habits has evolved.
- **Discussion prompt**: "How aware are you of the habits that affect your emotions and behaviors? How can increasing your self-awareness help you take control of your habits?"

Using accountability to support change:

- Discuss how accountability can play a role in habit change.
- **Discussion prompt**: "Who in your life can help you stay accountable as you work to change a habit? How can you use this support system to stay committed to your goals?"

Contents

Chapter 10: Habits and the Mind
What Are Habits and How Do We Develop Them?
Let's Look at Albert Bandura's Social Cognitive Theory
What Does the Mind Have to Do With Habits and Behavioral Changes?
Learning How to Control Your Mind
Homework

10

Habits and the Mind

"We need to break free from the habits of mind and behavior, to discover the possibilities of who we can become."

—Larry Brooks

In the previous chapter, we talked about triggers—what they are, how they are formed, and how they impact our lives. Habits are similar to triggers in that they also impact our lives for a very long time. I like to think of it like this: a trigger causes us to react to our environment, but a habit causes us to shape our environment. Let's talk about it.

What Are Habits and How Do We Develop Them?

Habits are the small decisions and actions we perform every day, without much thought, that eventually become automatic.[39] From brushing your teeth in the morning or putting on your socks before your pants, habits shape our lives in significant ways. While some habits can be beneficial, others might be less helpful.

Habits form through a process known as the **habit loop**. This loop consists of three (3) main components: the cue, the routine, and the reward.[39] Understanding these three elements can help us grasp how habits form and how we can change them.

39. Psychology Today Staff. (2024). Habit Formation. Retrieved from *Psychology Today*: https://www.psychologytoday.com/za/basics/habit-formation

THE CARE METHOD

1. **Cue**: A cue triggers your brain to initiate a behavior. It can be anything that acts as a signal, such as an alarm clock ringing, which signals you to wake up and start your morning routine.
2. **Routine**: This is the behavior that follows the cue. It can be physical, mental, or emotional. For example, if your cue is feeling tired in the afternoon, your routine might be to drink a cup of coffee.
3. **Reward**: This is what your brain gets out of the habit. Rewards help your brain decide if this particular loop is worth remembering for the future. In our coffee example, the reward might be the burst of energy you feel after drinking caffeine.

Over time, this loop becomes more and more automatic as it is reinforced in your daily life. Essentially, the more you repeat a behavior in response to a specific cue, the less you think about it because it becomes a part of your subconscious. You know that you have to brush your teeth, take a shower, and get dressed every morning. Maybe your routine involves a workout or eating breakfast at a specific time. These are all things you probably don't really think about because you do them every morning like clockwork.

Name one (1) healthy habit you have developed and one (1) unhealthy habit.

HABITS AND THE MIND

How and where did you develop these habits?

Let's Look at Albert Bandura's Social Cognitive Theory

Have you ever learned a new skill by watching someone else do it? This process of learning through observation is a core principle of social cognitive theory, developed by psychologist Albert Bandura.

Social cognitive theory expands on the idea of social learning theory, which proposes that our behaviors are acquired through observing other people's actions.[40] Bandura goes a step further, emphasizing that we are not simply passive observers, but **active agents** in our own learning and development.[40] This means we are capable of influencing our own behavior and shaping our goals.

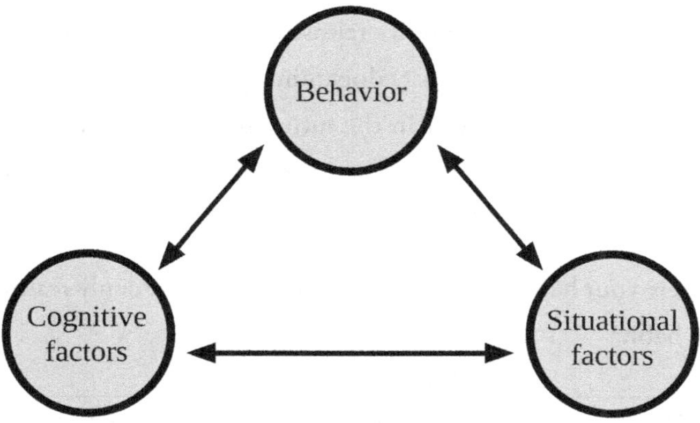

40. Bandura, A. Social cognitive theory: An agentic perspective. *Asian Journal of Social Psychology*, 2(1), 21–41, (1999).

THE CARE METHOD

Bandura believed that behavior isn't shaped only by the environment but also by how we interact with that environment based on our actions and thoughts. Here's how it breaks down:

- **Personal factors**: Your own ideas, feelings, and expectations influence how you see and react to things.
- **Behavioral factors**: These are the actions you decide to take and how you manage and regulate yourself.
- **Environmental factors**: Everything around you, like your friends, family, where you live, and your community, impacts your behavior too.

These factors constantly interact with each other. For instance, doing well on a task (a behavioral factor) might boost your confidence (a personal factor), which might encourage you to seek more challenging tasks (an environmental factor).

What Does the Mind Have to Do With Habits and Behavioral Changes?

When we repeatedly perform an action, the brain creates neural pathways that strengthen with each repetition. These pathways make the behavior more automatic over time.[41] The prefrontal cortex is the area of the brain responsible for decision-making, self-control, and regulating behavior. It's especially active when you're making conscious decisions about whether to follow or resist a habit.[42] Then there's dopamine, which you've heard of in previous chapters. This neurotransmitter plays a key role in the brain's reward system. It's released when you perform activities that are pleasurable or satisfying. When a behavior releases dopamine, you feel good, and your brain takes note of the action, encouraging you to repeat it in the future to experience the reward again.[41] This is why breaking habits or changing ingrained behaviors requires effort—because our brains are wired for efficiency and favor established pathways.

Can you pinpoint where your habit developed from, or did you suddenly realize down the line that you had developed a habit?

---

41. MacLachlan, S. (2021, December 22). The Science of Habit. Retrieved from *Healthline*: https://www.healthline.com/health/the-science-of-habit#1

42. Trafton, A. (2012, October 29). How the brain controls our habits. Retrieved from *MIT News*: https://news.mit.edu/2012/understanding-how-brains-control-our-habits-1029

HABITS AND THE MIND

Learning How to Control Your Mind

Dr. Joe Dispenza has a philosophy that understanding the mechanics of the mind is the first step toward controlling it. In a powerful YouTube video,[43] he explains that a habit is formed when the mind functions on autopilot better than the body. This means a habit is formed when the mind operates in redundant patterns and habits that are based on past experiences and deep-seated beliefs that affect your present. In other words, your brain becomes wired to live in your past experiences and emotions, which means when you wake up every day, those past feelings become your present reality.

To change these brain waves that are wired to live in the past, you need to do certain things:

- **Meditation**: Make meditation a habit.
- **Cognitive restructuring**: Mentally rehearse the action that you want.
- **Visualization**: Teach your body (emotionally) what the future will feel like.

Dr. Dispenza talks about the concept of a "familiar past," which refers to our tendency to live in the past and to predict the future based on past experiences. But he also says, "You can be the creator of your own reality." Even though our habits and emotions are shaped by our past experiences, we can change what defines us by letting go of the past and envisioning the future we want.

Reflect on habits and their impact on interpersonal relationships.

43. Dr. Joe Dispenza on YouTube. You Are the Creator of Your World: https://www.youtube.com/watch?v=v7KQsS2kLM4

THE CARE METHOD

Homework

1. Identifying unhealthy habits:

Describe at least two (2) unhealthy habits you have that have caused issues in your interpersonal relationships. Be specific about how these habits have affected your interactions and the consequences they have had.

2. Understanding the impact:

Reflect on how these unhealthy habits have influenced your communication, trust, and overall relationship dynamics with others. Provide examples to illustrate these impacts.

HABITS AND THE MIND

3. Planning for change:

What specific changes do you believe are necessary to improve your interpersonal relationships? Identify at least two (2) potential barriers you might face in making these changes. Additionally, explain how you will use the power of your mind, such as positive thinking, mindfulness, or self-discipline, to stay focused and overcome these.

11

Attachment Theory and Attachment Styles

"Attachment is the base from which all development occurs. It's not the absence of conflict that signifies security, but the ability to navigate conflict together."

—Dr. Dan Siegel

Early relationships can leave a lasting imprint on how we connect with others. In this chapter, clients will explore attachment theory, which examines how early interactions, particularly with caregivers, shape behaviors in later relationships. Attachment theory identifies different styles of relating to others, each of which affects how individuals navigate intimacy, trust, and emotional expression. Understanding these attachment styles is key to uncovering the relational patterns that clients may have struggled with, especially in close, intimate relationships.

As a counselor, your role is to guide clients in reflecting on how their early experiences with caregivers influenced their attachment style and how that style plays out in their current relationships. Encourage them to examine how they approach emotional closeness, their fears of abandonment or intimacy, and their communication patterns with partners. By understanding their attachment style, clients can start to identify both strengths and areas of growth in how they connect with others.

This chapter also emphasizes helping clients explore the four primary attachment styles: secure, anxious, avoidant, and anxious-avoidant. As you guide them through each style, help clients recognize where they might fall on the spectrum and what behaviors they might exhibit in response to emotional closeness or stress within relationships.

Throughout this material, stress the importance of becoming more self-aware in order to build healthier, more secure connections. By the end, clients should have a greater understanding of how their attachment style affects their relationships and leave the final session equipped with insights into how they can work toward more secure, fulfilling partnerships.

Encourage clients to carry these reflections into future sessions and chapters, particularly as they work on cultivating healthier dynamics in relationships.

Goals of This Chapter

As clients explore their attachment styles, they are encouraged to reflect on how past relationships, especially with caregivers, have contributed to their current behaviors in intimate and interpersonal connections. The goal is for clients to recognize the attachment patterns they may have adopted and begin working toward building more secure and healthier relationships.

By gaining insight into their attachment styles, clients can identify the areas they need to improve, especially in how they approach emotional intimacy and manage fears of abandonment or rejection. This chapter is pivotal in helping clients foster emotional growth and healthier relational dynamics.

Colorado DVOMB Standards Competencies

Chapter 11 aligns with the Colorado Domestic Violence Offender Management Board (DVOMB) standards, focusing on **attachment issues** and **intergenerational patterns**. It explores how early childhood attachment styles can influence behavior in intimate relationships and how these patterns are often passed down through generations. Understanding attachment issues is crucial in addressing the roots of abusive behaviors, as clients reflect on how early relationships with caregivers have shaped their ability to form secure connections.

Intergenerational patterns are also emphasized, guiding clients to examine how their caregivers' attachment styles may have influenced their own relational patterns. By understanding this transmission, clients can identify and break the cycle of insecure attachments, fostering healthier behaviors in their current and future relationships. This chapter provides strategies for addressing attachment issues, emphasizing the development of secure and healthy connections.

These standards are integral to the CARE Method's therapeutic goals, ensuring clients understand how attachment issues and intergenerational patterns impact their behaviors. By recognizing and altering maladaptive attachment behaviors, clients can work toward establishing more positive, stable, and nurturing relationships, breaking free from cycles of attachment-related distress.

Important Things to Know

In this chapter, we explore **attachment theory** and its profound impact on how we form relationships, focusing on the four main **attachment styles**. Clients will learn how early interactions with caregivers shape their behaviors in relationships, particularly around trust, emotional expression, and intimacy. Recognizing these patterns is crucial for understanding the dynamics that may be contributing to unhealthy relationship behaviors or emotional disconnect.

By understanding their attachment style, clients can reflect on how past experiences influence their current relationships, allowing them to make more conscious choices that promote growth and healing. This awareness provides an opportunity to identify challenges in their relational patterns and take steps toward more secure and fulfilling connections.

Next week, we will build on this foundation by focusing on **what makes a healthy relationship**. Clients will explore the key components of healthy relationships, such as mutual respect, effective communication, and emotional support, using the insights gained from this chapter and previous chapters. These elements will empower clients to cultivate stronger, more positive relationships as they move forward.

Key Concepts and Terminology

Attachment styles: Patterns of behavior in relationships, shaped by early interactions with caregivers. There are four main types of attachment styles—secure, anxious, avoidant, and anxious-avoidant—that influence how individuals experience intimacy, trust, and emotional expression in their relationships.

Secure attachment: A healthy attachment style where individuals are comfortable with emotional closeness, trust, and reliance on others, fostering stable and fulfilling relationships.

Anxious attachment: A style characterized by fear of abandonment and a need for constant reassurance in relationships. Individuals with anxious attachment often feel insecure about their partner's love and commitment.

Avoidant attachment: A style in which individuals value independence over emotional intimacy, often avoiding closeness and vulnerability in relationships.

Anxious-avoidant attachment: A combination of both anxious and avoidant traits, where individuals may fear abandonment but simultaneously resist emotional closeness, leading to conflicted and unstable relationships.

Trust: The belief in the reliability and honesty of a partner. Trust is essential for fostering secure attachment and healthy emotional connections in relationships.

Emotional intimacy: The ability to share and express deep emotions with another person, creating a bond based on mutual vulnerability and understanding.

Discussion Prompts

These prompts will help clients reflect on their attachment styles and explore how their past experiences influence their current relationships.

Identifying your attachment style:

- Encourage clients to explore which attachment style they identify with and how it manifests in their relationships.
- **Discussion prompt**: "Which of the four attachment styles—secure, anxious, avoidant, or anxious-avoidant—do you believe fits you best? How do you see this attachment style influencing your current relationships?"

Exploring early caregiver relationships:

- Help clients reflect on their early experiences with caregivers and how these relationships may have shaped their attachment style.

- **Discussion prompt**: "How did your relationship with your primary caregivers as a child influence your ability to trust and form close bonds with others? Can you draw any connections between your childhood experiences and your adult relationships?"

Recognizing the impact on intimacy:

- Discuss how different attachment styles affect emotional intimacy and vulnerability in relationships.
- **Discussion prompt**: "How comfortable are you with emotional intimacy and vulnerability? How do you think your attachment style affects your willingness to trust and depend on others?"

Changing attachment patterns:

- Encourage clients to consider ways they can work toward developing a more secure attachment style.
- **Discussion prompt**: "What steps can you take to change any unhealthy patterns in your attachment style? How might therapy, self-awareness, or other strategies help you move toward a more secure attachment?"

Managing attachment conflicts:

- Help clients reflect on how attachment styles influence conflict and communication in relationships.
- **Discussion prompt**: "How do you typically handle conflict in your relationships? Do you notice any patterns that might be tied to your attachment style, such as withdrawing or seeking constant reassurance?"

Exploring codependency and attachment:

- Discuss the overlap between attachment issues and codependency in relationships.
- **Discussion prompt**: "Do you ever find yourself becoming overly dependent on your partner for emotional validation or security? How might this be connected to your attachment style, and what can you do to foster a healthier dynamic?"

Building secure relationships:

- Guide clients toward understanding how they can develop more secure and fulfilling relationships.

- **Discussion prompt**: "What are some actions you can take to build more secure and trusting relationships? How can improving communication, setting boundaries, and increasing emotional awareness help you achieve this?"

Reflecting on emotional awareness:

- Discuss the role of emotional awareness in identifying and managing attachment-related behaviors.
- **Discussion prompt**: "How aware are you of your emotions when you're feeling insecure or anxious in a relationship? How can emotional awareness help you respond more thoughtfully to situations that trigger attachment-related stress?"

Contents

Chapter 11: Attachment Theory and Attachment Styles

What Are Attachment Styles?

Secure Attachment

Anxious Attachment

Avoidant Attachment

Anxious-Avoidant Attachment

Attachment Styles in Relationships

Can I Change My Attachment Style?

Additional Information

Homework

11

Attachment Theory and Attachment Styles

"Attachment security doesn't mean there are no conflicts;
it means conflicts can be managed with trust and respect."

—Amir Levine

Relationships will always have some level of difficulty because we're dealing with other unique human beings. This is why it is important to gain deep insight into who you are and why you behave the way you do. We talked about habits in chapter 9 and how we can change learned behaviors by learning how to control our minds. In this chapter, we are going to focus on attachment styles, which are also learned behaviors in a way, but they tend to manifest differently from a habit. So, let's break this down.

What Are Attachment Styles?

Have you ever wondered why you behave the way you do in relationships? Whether it's with friends, family, or romantic partners, the way we connect with others has a lot to do with our attachment styles. These styles were formed early in our lives, based on how we bonded with our primary caregivers. In other words, attachment styles are basically different ways we behave in relationships. They are the foundation of our relational behaviors. They influence how comfortable we are with intimacy, trust, and expressing emotions.

The concept comes from a psychological theory primarily developed by John Bowlby (Bowlby's Theory) and further developed by Mary Ainsworth.[44] They observed how children responded to

44. Cassidy, J., Jones, J.D., and Shaver, P.R. What Is Attachment Theory. *Development and Psychopathology*, 1415–1434 (2013). doi: 10.1017/S0954579413000692. Retrieved from *The Attachment Project.*

THE CARE METHOD

being separated from their parents and identified distinct ways children would use their relationships with their parents to cope with stress and anxiety. Because these patterns extend into adulthood and play a big role in how we form and maintain relationships, it's important to understand each style and find which one we fall under.

There are four (4) main types of attachment styles,[45] namely these:

1. Secure attachment
2. Anxious attachment
3. Avoidant attachment
4. Anxious-avoidant attachment

Understanding your attachment style will help you identify the areas you need to work on in your life in order to have healthy, positive relationships. Let's break each one down.

Secure Attachment

If you have a secure attachment style, you're likely comfortable with emotional intimacy.[45] You probably find it easy to get close to others and are comfortable depending on them and having them depend on you. You're also likely to have a positive view of relationships and handle conflicts with maturity and compassion.

Common traits:

- Comfortable with intimacy
- Reliable and consistent
- Straightforward and honest
- Constructive approach to conflict
- Committed but independent
- Emotionally supportive

45. The Attachment Project. (2023, July 29). Attachment Styles & Their Role in Relationships. Retrieved from *The Attachment Project*: https://www.attachmentproject.com/blog/four-attachment-styles/

ATTACHMENT THEORY AND ATTACHMENT STYLES

Anxious Attachment

People who have an anxious attachment style often fear that their partner does not love them or might leave them.[46] This often leads to them behaving acting in a clingy or overly dependent way with their partner. If this is your attachment style, you might find that you need a lot of validation and reassurance in relationships, which can sometimes overwhelm your partners or even your family and friends.

Common traits:

- Fear of abandonment or rejection
- Overly emotional and easily agitated
- Need constant reassurance
- Distrustful of the relationship and/or their partner

Avoidant Attachment

If you identify with the avoidant attachment style, you might be a person who values their independence above all else. You often feel that getting too close to someone is risky so it's safer to maintain your distance. Even in close relationships, you might keep parts of yourself private, resisting complete vulnerability.[46]

Common traits:

- Avoids intimacy or vulnerability
- Rigid and guarded
- Suppresses their feelings
- Uncomfortable with emotions
- Self-reliant

46. The Attachment Project. (2023, July 29). Attachment Styles & Their Role in Relationships. Retrieved from *The Attachment Project*: https://www.attachmentproject.com/blog/four-attachment-styles/

THE CARE METHOD

Anxious-Avoidant Attachment

Finally, we have the anxious-avoidant style, which is a mix of anxious and avoidant, as you may have already guessed. The anxious-avoidant attachment style involves a desire for close relationships, but a fear of trusting and depending on others.[47] This often leads to inner conflict, uncertainty, and erratic behaviors within relationships.

Common traits:

- Can be confusing and ambiguous
- Avoids emotional attachment due to fear
- Struggles to maintain healthy boundaries
- Emotionally extreme
- Difficulty trusting people

Attachment Styles in Relationships

Intimate relationships have a way of activating our attachment styles. A healthy dependence on each other is a natural part of a secure relationship. When our needs for intimacy, trust, and emotional support are met, we feel secure and loved. This sense of security is what allows us to be vulnerable and open with a partner.

You can often discern your partner's attachment style through their behavior and the way they respond when you directly express your desire for closeness. A secure partner will always be open to communicating and reaching a compromise, while an anxious or avoidant partner could create a co-dependent dynamic with their partner.

Some attachment styles will naturally have stable and healthier relationships than others. However, all attachment styles can have good relationships, as long as they are paired with the right type of style. For example, a secure and a secure will obviously be very healthy together. On the other hand, an anxious and an avoidant style would be an unlikely pair due to how opposite they are in nature. However, these two styles can still have a healthy relationship.[48]

47. The Attachment Project. (2023, July 29). Attachment Styles & Their Role in Relationships. Retrieved from *The Attachment Project*: https://www.attachmentproject.com/blog/four-attachment-styles/

48. Huang, S. (2024, January 23). Attachment Styles and How They Affect Adult Relationships. Retrieved from *Simply Psychology*: https://www.simplypsychology.org/attachment-styles.html

ATTACHMENT THEORY AND ATTACHMENT STYLES

Can I Change My Attachment Style?

Yes, attachment styles can change. However, this often requires self-reflection and the help of a professional therapist. Therapy is very important because you will need a professional to work with you on developing healthier relationship patterns. The goal will always be to try to develop a secure attachment style, but as I said, you can still have healthy and long-lasting relationships if you learn to manage your style, regardless of what it is. Remember, having a particular attachment style is not a life sentence. With awareness and effort, you can reshape the way you relate to others.

What do you think your current attachment style is and what are the areas you think you can improve in to possibly change your attachment style?

Additional Information

While the four (4) main styles (secure, anxious, avoidant, and anxious-avoidant) provide a general framework, it's important to remember that attachment can exist on a spectrum. Some people may exhibit characteristics of multiple styles or fall somewhere in between the categories. Attachment styles can also be linked to various mental health conditions. For instance, anxious attachment has been associated with anxiety disorders, while avoidant attachment can be linked to depression and self-esteem issues. Then there's also early childhood trauma, such as neglect or abuse, which can significantly impact your attachment style and possibly lead to the development of insecure patterns and behaviors.

THE CARE METHOD

Homework

Attachment Style Questionnaire

Instructions: Please read each statement and rate how much you agree or disagree with it on a scale from 1 to 5, where 1 means "strongly disagree" and 5 means "strongly agree."

1. Secure Attachment

I find it easy to get close to others.

1 2 3 4 5

I am comfortable depending on others and having others depend on me.

1 2 3 4 5

I don't worry about being abandoned or someone getting too close to me.

1 2 3 4 5

2. Anxious Attachment

I often worry that my partner doesn't really love me.

1 2 3 4 5

I find that others are often reluctant to get as close as I would like.

1 2 3 4 5

I often worry that my partner will leave me.

1 2 3 4 5

142

ATTACHMENT THEORY AND ATTACHMENT STYLES

3. Avoidant Attachment

I am uncomfortable being close to others.

1 2 3 4 5

I find it difficult to trust others completely.

1 2 3 4 5

I find it difficult to allow myself to depend on others.

1 2 3 4 5

4. Anxious-Avoidant Attachment

I am afraid that I will get hurt if I get too close to others.

1 2 3 4 5

I want to be close to others, but I feel uncomfortable with too much closeness.

1 2 3 4 5

I have mixed feelings about close relationships; I desire them, but also fear them.

1 2 3 4 5

Scoring:

To determine your attachment style, calculate the total score for each category:

Secure Attachment: Add your scores for statements 1, 2, and 3: ______
Anxious Attachment: Add your scores for statements 4, 5, and 6: ______
Avoidant Attachment: Add your scores for statements 7, 8, and 9: ______
Anxious-Avoidant Attachment: Add your scores for statements 10, 11, and 12: ______

The highest score indicates your predominant attachment style. If you have high scores in multiple categories, you may have a mixed attachment style.

THE CARE METHOD

Additional Questions

1. Think back to your childhood experiences with caregivers (mother, father, or guardian). Did you feel consistently loved and supported, or were there periods of neglect or emotional unavailability? How do you think these experiences shaped your expectations in relationships?

____

____

____

____

____

2. Have you noticed any recurring patterns in your behavior in your past relationships such as jealousy, possessiveness, or difficulty expressing your emotions clearly?

____

____

____

____

____

3. What specific situations or behaviors would typically trigger your feelings of insecurity, anger, or possessiveness in your relationships? How do you typically react in those moments?

____

____

____

____

____

____

144

ATTACHMENT THEORY AND ATTACHMENT STYLES

4. Go back to the secure attachment style and pick one (1) trait that you would like to develop more in yourself. Explain why you chose this trait and how you think it can contribute to you becoming a healthy partner in the future.

____

____

____

____

____

5. What does the quiz result say about your attachment style? What is your most predominant style and how do you feel about it?

____

____

____

____

____

145

12

What Makes a Relationship Healthy?

"The meeting of two personalities is like the contact of two chemical substances: if there is any reaction, both are transformed."

—Carl Jung

At the heart of every strong relationship lies a foundation of mutual respect and trust. In this chapter, clients will embark on a journey to uncover the core qualities that make relationships both healthy and fulfilling. A truly healthy relationship thrives on open communication, emotional safety, and personal growth—qualities that empower both individuals. Unlike relationships driven by control or dominance, these connections allow each partner to feel deeply valued and supported, fostering an environment of mutual care and understanding.

As a counselor, your role is to guide clients in identifying the attributes of healthy relationships, as well as recognizing when those qualities are absent. Clients may have never experienced or witnessed a healthy relationship before, making it essential to provide clear examples and practical tools. You'll encourage them to reflect on their past relationships, pointing out patterns of behavior that contributed to unhealthy dynamics and helping them envision a different way forward.

Clients will also assess their current relationships, looking closely at how they communicate, manage conflict, and support one another. Help clients to see that a healthy relationship does not mean one free of conflict, but one in which conflicts are addressed constructively and respectfully. This section emphasizes that a key marker of a healthy relationship is a balance of power and responsibility, where both partners are equally invested in maintaining the well-being of the relationship.

As clients move through this chapter, they will begin to understand that healthy relationships require ongoing effort, honesty, and vulnerability. Your task is to empower them to seek out and build relationships that nourish rather than diminish them, helping them to break free from any toxic cycles of behavior they may have been part of in the past.

Goals of This Chapter

Understanding the qualities of a healthy relationship is essential for breaking free from harmful patterns. Many clients may have developed a skewed understanding of relationships due to past trauma, unhealthy role models, or abusive dynamics. A key goal of this chapter is to equip clients with the tools and insights necessary to differentiate between destructive relationship patterns and those founded on mutual respect, trust, and healthy communication.

As clients work through this material, they will be invited to reflect on their past relationships and begin identifying which elements were healthy and which were not. By gaining this awareness, they can start developing a clearer picture of what a healthy, functional relationship should look like and how they can contribute to it moving forward.

Your role as a counselor is to guide clients in understanding that a healthy relationship is more than just love or compatibility. It is founded on accountability, trust, communication, and mutual respect. Through this reflection process, clients will be encouraged to examine the behaviors and values they bring into their relationships and how these can be adapted to create a safe, nurturing environment for both partners.

Colorado DVOMB Standards Competencies

This chapter aligns closely with the Colorado Domestic Violence Offender Management Board (DVOMB) standards on **insight and empathy**, **accountability/responsibility for behaviors**, and **healthy sexual behavior**. The DVOMB underscores the importance of developing insight into one's actions and understanding their impact on intimate relationships. By fostering a deeper comprehension of the dynamics of healthy relationships, clients can identify patterns that may have contributed to destructive behaviors, including those related to unhealthy or coercive sexual behavior, and work toward healthier interactions.

The chapter encourages clients to take responsibility for their role in relationships by reflecting on past behaviors and identifying where accountability was missing. This includes an emphasis on recognizing and fostering healthy sexual behavior, which is a crucial component of respectful and consensual relationships. By developing empathy, clients can better appreciate their partner's needs and perspectives, moving away from controlling or harmful behaviors, whether emotional, physical, or sexual. This self-awareness, paired with an empathetic approach, is vital for building nonviolent, respectful relationships that honor the sexual autonomy and well-being of both partners.

The standards reinforce the therapeutic goals of this chapter by ensuring that clients not only gain insight into their past behaviors but also actively work toward establishing healthier patterns in all aspects of their relationships. Developing empathy, taking responsibility, and understanding healthy sexual behavior are key elements in fostering long-term, positive changes in how clients engage with others.

Important Things to Know

In the previous chapters, we've explored various aspects of relationships and behaviors, including **attachment styles** and the foundations of a healthy relationship. This chapter shifts the focus to helping clients understand the specific qualities that contribute to a truly **healthy relationship**. Often, clients may have a distorted or incomplete idea of what a healthy relationship looks like due to past experiences, trauma, or dysfunctional role models.

In this chapter, you'll work with clients to break down the characteristics of a healthy relationship—such as mutual respect, trust, and communication—and help them recognize whether these qualities have been present or absent in their own relationships. You will guide them through an exploration of their past relationships, encouraging them to assess whether those relationships were truly healthy and supportive, or if they exhibited unhealthy patterns that may have gone unnoticed at the time.

Next week, we will build on this by exploring the dynamics of **codependency and trauma bonding in relationships**. Clients will begin to understand how unhealthy emotional bonds form and how these patterns can trap individuals in destructive relationship cycles. This chapter on healthy relationships sets the foundation for clients to recognize the warning signs of codependency and trauma bonding, and to begin building the tools they need for lasting change.

Key Concepts and Terminology

Honesty and accountability: In a healthy relationship, honesty means being truthful with your partner and not making excuses for your actions. Accountability requires both partners to take responsibility for their behavior, admitting mistakes and making amends. This builds trust and strengthens the relationship.

Connections with others: Maintaining social connections outside the relationship is crucial. Healthy relationships allow both partners to maintain individuality, friendships, and family connections, creating a balanced and well-rounded support system. Trust is built when both partners respect each other's space without jealousy or control.

Trust and support: Trust is the foundation of emotional safety within a relationship, allowing both partners to be their authentic selves without fear of betrayal. Support means being there for each other during difficult times and encouraging personal growth, reinforcing mutual trust and partnership.

Non-threatening behavior: A healthy relationship is free of physical, emotional, and psychological threats. Non-threatening behavior involves respecting boundaries, and ensuring that no coercion, intimidation, or violence is used to control the partner.

Sexual safety: A key part of a healthy relationship is ensuring that both partners feel safe and respected in all aspects of their sexual relationship. Consent should be enthusiastic, clear, and ongoing, ensuring both parties are comfortable discussing boundaries and desires openly.

Financial independence: Healthy relationships involve transparency and shared decision-making around finances. Each partner should have financial autonomy while contributing fairly to shared expenses and financial goals. Open communication about finances helps avoid conflicts and promotes equality in the relationship.

Negotiation and fairness: Healthy relationships involve compromise, with both partners striving to meet each other halfway. The goal is to address both partners' needs equitably without manipulation or taking advantage of the other. Fair negotiation helps maintain balance and mutual respect.

Discussion Prompts

The following discussion prompts can help foster meaningful conversations and self-reflection, encouraging them to engage deeply with the material.

Defining healthy relationships:

- Ask clients to describe what a healthy relationship means to them and what qualities they believe are essential for a successful partnership.
- **Discussion prompt**: "When you think of a healthy relationship, what qualities come to mind? How do you define a relationship that is built on trust, respect, and understanding?"

Honesty and accountability:

- Encourage clients to reflect on how they approach honesty and accountability in their relationships.
- **Discussion prompt**: "Reflect on a time when you were completely honest and accountable with your partner. How did this strengthen or challenge the relationship? What impact did taking responsibility for your actions have?"

Trust and support:

- Help clients explore their experiences with trust and support in their past and current relationships.
- **Discussion prompt**: "Think about a relationship where you felt truly supported and trusted. How did that relationship differ from others? What actions helped build that trust?"

Connection with others:

- Engage clients in considering the balance needed to maintain individual connections outside of their romantic relationships.
- **Discussion prompt**: "How do you and your partner handle time spent apart or with other people? How do you ensure that maintaining friendships outside of the relationship does not lead to jealousy or mistrust?"

Negotiation and fairness:

- Encourage clients to think about the importance of compromise and fairness in maintaining relationship balance.
- **Discussion prompt**: "Consider a time when you had to compromise in your relationship. How did finding a fair solution impact the dynamic between you and your partner?"

Non-threatening behavior:

- Prompt clients to examine any instances of non-threatening or threatening behavior in their relationships and how it affects safety and emotional security.
- **Discussion prompt**: "Have there been moments in your relationships where you felt unsafe, either physically or emotionally? What would non-threatening behavior look like in those situations?"

Contents

Chapter 12: What Makes a Relationship Healthy?
What Makes a Relationship Healthy?
Honesty and Accountability
Connections With Others
Trust and Support
Non-Threatening Behavior
Sexual Safety
Financial/Economic Independence
Negotiation and Fairness
Responsible Parenting
Homework

12

What Makes a Relationship Healthy?

"Far too many people are looking for the right person,
instead of trying to be the right person.

—Gloria Steinem

The previous chapter was all about attachment styles and the underlying theme was about how to have a healthy relationship regardless of your attachment style. In this chapter, we will focus more on what makes a relationship healthy. If the goal is to be an individual with a healthy mindset and healthy relationships, you need to know how to achieve this.

What Makes a Relationship Healthy?

When we talk about healthy relationships, most people often think of love and some form of compatibility (religious, sexual, mutual interests). However, a truly healthy relationship is built on a foundation of mutual respect, trust, communication, and understanding.[49] These days you'll hear people using the word "safe" to describe what a healthy relationship means to them. The truth of the matter is that a relationship that is truly healthy comprises specific characteristics[50] such as these:

- Honesty and accountability
- Connections with others

49. Cleveland Clinic. (2023, June 5). 12 Signs You're in a Healthy Relationship. Retrieved from Cleveland Clinic: https://health.clevelandclinic.org/signs-of-a-healthy-relationship

50. Campbell University. (2016, December). Characteristics of a Healthy, Functional Romantic Relationship. Retrieved from Campbell University: https://assets.campbell.edu/wp-content/uploads/2016/12/22122441/characteristics-of-healthy-romantic-relationships.pdf

THE CARE METHOD

- Trust and support
- Non-threatening behavior
- Sexual safety
- Financial/economic independence
- Negotiation and fairness
- Responsible parenting

What is your idea of a healthy relationship? Do you have an example of a healthy relationship in your life? For example, your grandparents' marriage, your friends who have been in a committed relationship for years, or even people who have managed to create a great blended family.

Honesty and Accountability

Building a healthy relationship requires a foundation of honesty and accountability. Being truthful with your partner and not making excuses, even when it's difficult, builds trust and strengthens your bond as a couple. Accountability goes hand-in-hand with honesty, meaning both you and your partner have to take responsibility for your individual actions and decisions, and you must be willing to admit your mistakes.[51]

51. Campbell University. (2016, December). Characteristics of a Healthy, Functional Romantic Relationship. Retrieved from Campbell University: https://assets.campbell.edu/wp-content/uploads/2016/12/22122441/characteristics-of-healthy-romantic-relationships.pdf

WHAT MAKES A RELATIONSHIP HEALTHY?

Are you honest about your mistakes in relationships? Do you take accountability for your actions, or do you deflect and blame it on your partner?

Connections With Others

Both you and your partner must maintain your connections with others if you want to have a healthy relationship. Having thriving social circles and healthy family relationships creates a well-rounded support system for both of you and keeps you accountable. It's important to respect each other's individuality and allow space for personal interests and friendships without feeling jealous or threatened. In other words, you both have to maintain your individuality to some degree.

How do you feel about your partner spending time with other people or doing social activities without you present?

THE CARE METHOD

Trust and Support

Trust and support are very important because they create a safe space for both of you to be your authentic selves with each other.[52] You can only feel confident that your partner has your best interests at heart and won't intentionally betray or hurt you when there is trust. Supporting one another also reinforces trust. You need to encourage each other during emotionally challenging times but also when it comes to one or both of you trying to achieve something significant.

Did you trust and support your partners in your past or current relationships?

Non-Threatening Behavior

In a healthy relationship, both partners should feel safe. This safety transcends just the physical and includes emotional and psychological aspects. Non-threatening behavior means respecting each other's boundaries and never resorting to violence, coercion, guilt, or intimidation to exert control or dominance. This means you should both feel comfortable enough to express yourselves and make your own decisions without fear.[53]

52. Bonior, A. (2018, December 28). What Does a Healthy Relationship Look Like? Retrieved from *Psychology Today*: https://www.psychologytoday.com/za/blog/friendship-20/201812/what-does-healthy-relationship-look

53. Campbell University. (2016, December). Characteristics of a Healthy, Functional Romantic Relationship. Retrieved from Campbell University: https://assets.campbell.edu/wp-content/uploads/2016/12/22122441/characteristics-of-healthy-romantic-relationships.pdf

WHAT MAKES A RELATIONSHIP HEALTHY?

What (if any) kind of threatening behavior have you displayed in relationships in the past and why?

Sexual Safety

Sexual safety is a vital aspect of a healthy intimate relationship. You should only engage in sexual activity when there is clear, enthusiastic, and ongoing consent from your partner, and this goes both ways. Both of you should feel comfortable discussing your sexual desires, boundaries, and what you do and do not consent to.[54] Remember to practice safe sex regardless of the situation.

What are your thoughts on consent? Have you always honored your partner's boundaries and vice versa?

54. Campbell University. (2016, December). Characteristics of a Healthy, Functional Romantic Relationship. Retrieved from Campbell University: https://assets.campbell.edu/wp-content/uploads/2016/12/22122441/characteristics-of-healthy-romantic-relationships.pdf

THE CARE METHOD

Financial/Economic Independence

Financial independence and equality are also very important aspects of any healthy relationship. Both of you should have autonomy over your finances and contribute equitably to the shared expenses and financial decisions of your individual households or a shared home.[55] Financial transparency and open communication about money matters will always help avoid conflicts and power imbalances within the relationship.

Are you open and honest with your partner about your finances? What are your thoughts on how finances should be handled within a relationship?

Negotiation and Fairness

Being willing to meet halfway and find solutions that address both partners' needs is an important skill to have in a relationship.[56] The goal should always be to strive for equitable treatment and avoid manipulation or taking advantage of one another. In a healthy relationship, you have to be willing to compromise and reach an agreement that is fair to both of you.

55. Campbell University. (2016, December). Characteristics of a Healthy, Functional Romantic Relationship. Retrieved from Campbell University: https://assets.campbell.edu/wp-content/uploads/2016/12/22122441/characteristics-of-healthy-romantic-relationships.pdf

56. Bonior, A. (2018, December 28). What Does a Healthy Relationship Look Like? Retrieved from *Psychology Today*: https://www.psychologytoday.com/za/blog/friendship-20/201812/what-does-healthy-relationship-look

WHAT MAKES A RELATIONSHIP HEALTHY?

Do you find it easy to compromise in a relationship, or is it your way or the highway?

Responsible Parenting

If children are part of the relationship, responsible parenting should be non-negotiable.

Both parents have to work together to raise the children, sharing the duties fairly, and making decisions that prioritize their well-being.[57] You both have to create a safe and nurturing environment for your children and be good role models.

If you have kids or if you plan on having kids in the future, what do you think your role should be as a responsible parent?

57. Quinlan, C. (2023, May 23). How to Be Good Partners in Parenting. Retrieved from *Marriage.com*: https://www.marriage.com/advice/parenting/how-to-be-good-partners-in-parenting/

THE CARE METHOD

Homework

1. Has there ever been a time when you might not have been honest or accountable in your relationships? How did it impact the relationship?

2. Do you believe that your partner is your equal in a relationship?

3. In the past, have you felt comfortable with your partner maintaining friendships and other important relationships and interests outside of you?

4. How have you typically handled disagreements within your relationships? (intimidation, manipulation, threats, violence, emotional isolation or withdrawal, etc.)

154

WHAT MAKES A RELATIONSHIP HEALTHY?

5. What are some of the ways you can become a healthier partner in your intimate relationships? What are specific dynamics you'd like to see moving forward? (more trust and support, honesty, accountability, etc.)

____

____

____

____

____

____

155

13

Codependency and Trauma Bonding in Relationships

"Codependency is the dance of dysfunction. It's the belief that you can fix someone else, but the truth is, you can only fix yourself."

—Terry Kellogg

Some relationships trap individuals in toxic cycles that are difficult to break free from. This chapter will uncover the hidden forces behind codependency and trauma bonding. Codependency arises when one partner becomes deeply dependent on the other for emotional support and identity, often sacrificing their own well-being in the process. Trauma bonding, in contrast, develops through a cycle of abuse and reconciliation, where one partner forms a powerful emotional attachment to their abuser, drawn in by periods of calm or affection that follow the abuse.

As a counselor, it's crucial to help clients recognize the signs of both codependency and trauma bonding in their relationships. Many clients may not realize that these behaviors are harmful because they can feel deeply attached to their partner, mistaking the intensity of these bonds for love or commitment. You'll guide clients through the process of identifying how these patterns of behavior have kept them trapped in unhealthy cycles of dependency, control, and emotional volatility.

In this chapter, clients will explore how trauma bonding often roots itself in a relationship through inconsistent rewards—moments of affection after episodes of abuse. This creates a powerful emotional loop, making it difficult for the victim to leave, despite the harm being done. Similarly, codependent relationships foster a lack of personal boundaries and an unhealthy need for validation and approval from their partner.

As clients progress through this chapter, your role is to help them begin to untangle these harmful attachments. Encourage them to reflect on their own emotional needs, self-worth, and personal boundaries. It's essential to help clients see that breaking free from these toxic patterns requires them to reclaim their sense of self and recognize that love should not come at the expense of their own mental and emotional health.

Throughout this chapter, emphasize that while the journey to breaking trauma bonds and codependent patterns is challenging, it is also an essential step toward building healthier, more balanced relationships in the future.

Goals of This Chapter

In this chapter, clients will begin to explore the complex dynamics of codependency and trauma bonding in relationships. These patterns, often rooted in past trauma and unhealthy attachment, can create powerful emotional ties that keep individuals trapped in destructive relationships. A key goal of this chapter is to help clients understand the nature of these bonds, particularly how cycles of abuse and intermittent affection contribute to the formation of trauma bonds. Clients will also learn to identify the behaviors associated with codependency, which often involve an unhealthy reliance on a partner for emotional validation or identity.

As clients reflect on their past and current relationships, they will be encouraged to assess whether these dynamics are present. By recognizing how trauma bonding and codependency have shaped their behavior, clients can begin to break free from these harmful patterns. Your role as a counselor is to guide clients through this process of self-awareness, helping them to understand that while these bonds may feel strong, they are built on unhealthy foundations.

This chapter invites clients to take the first steps toward reclaiming their sense of self, encouraging them to set boundaries and seek relationships based on mutual respect rather than dependency or manipulation. It also emphasizes the importance of developing internal sources of validation and healing from past traumas to build healthier, more balanced connections moving forward.

Colorado DVOMB Standards Competencies

This chapter aligns closely with the Colorado Domestic Violence Offender Management Board (DVOMB) standards on **past experiences/trauma** and **mental health needs and supports**. The

DVOMB highlights the importance of understanding how past trauma, particularly in the context of abusive or dysfunctional relationships, contributes to the development of codependency and trauma bonding. By examining the impact of these past experiences, clients can better understand why they may be drawn to unhealthy relationships and how these patterns have influenced their behavior.

The chapter encourages clients to recognize the psychological and emotional effects of trauma bonding and codependency, and to take ownership of their recovery. It highlights the need to address underlying mental health needs and offers support in helping clients build healthier emotional foundations. The standard reinforces the therapeutic goals of this chapter by ensuring that clients not only recognize the effects of trauma and codependency but also actively work toward creating healthier, non-dependent relationship dynamics.

Important Things to Know

Last week, we focused on understanding what makes a **relationship healthy** and the key qualities that contribute to mutual respect, trust, and communication. In this chapter, we shift our attention to more complex relationship dynamics by examining **codependency** and **trauma bonding**—patterns that often develop in unhealthy or abusive relationships.

This chapter will help clients recognize how codependent behaviors may be rooted in an unhealthy emotional reliance on their partner. We'll explore how trauma bonding—a cycle of abuse followed by affection—can create powerful emotional ties that are difficult to break. As a counselor, your role is to help clients understand that while these bonds may feel strong, they are destructive and not reflective of healthy, supportive relationships.

Next week, we will build on this chapter by exploring **cognitive distortions** and their connection to behavioral responses. This will help clients understand how faulty thinking patterns shape emotional reactions and can reinforce codependent or abusive relationship dynamics.

Key Concepts and Terminology

Codependency: A dysfunctional pattern of behavior where individuals excessively rely on others for their sense of self-worth and identity, often at the expense of their own needs and well-being.

This dynamic often leads to unhealthy attachment, where one partner prioritizes the other's needs while neglecting their own.

Trauma bonding: A psychological phenomenon that occurs when a person forms an emotional attachment to an abusive partner. The bond is often strengthened by cycles of abuse followed by periods of kindness, making it difficult for the victim to leave the relationship. Trauma bonding reinforces codependency by creating an emotional dependence on the abuser.

Cognitive dissonance: A mental state where an individual holds contradictory beliefs or ideas. In trauma bonding, cognitive dissonance occurs when a person simultaneously views their abuser as both caring and harmful, leading to confusion and difficulty breaking free from the relationship.

Emotional dependence: A state where one partner relies on the other for validation, safety, and self-worth, often leading to a loss of autonomy. Emotional dependence is a key component of both codependency and trauma bonding, reinforcing harmful relational patterns.

Isolation and control: In abusive relationships, abusers often isolate their victims from support networks and exert control over their actions, reinforcing dependence and making it harder for the victim to leave.

Enabling: A behavior that unintentionally supports or perpetuates unhealthy or destructive behaviors in a loved one, often seen in codependent relationships. Enabling can prevent both individuals from developing healthier ways of relating to each other.

Discussion Prompts

The following discussion prompts can encourage self-reflection and help clients gain deeper insights into the unhealthy dynamics of codependency and trauma bonding.

Defining codependency:

- Ask clients to reflect on how they view their relationships and whether they recognize any codependent behaviors.
- **Discussion prompt**: "When you think about your past or current relationships, do you see any patterns where you relied on your partner for your self-worth or identity? How did this affect your own well-being?"

Recognizing trauma bonding:

- Encourage clients to think about their experiences in relationships where they may have felt attached despite mistreatment.
- **Discussion prompt**: "Have you ever been in a relationship where you felt emotionally tied to someone even though the relationship was harmful? What kept you in that relationship, and how did it impact your ability to leave?"

Identifying emotional dependence:

- Help clients explore how emotional dependence has played a role in their relationships.
- **Discussion prompt**: "In your relationships, have you ever felt that your happiness or sense of security depended solely on the other person? How did this influence the way you interacted with your partner?"

Examining enabling behaviors:

- Ask clients to reflect on instances where they may have enabled unhealthy behaviors in their relationships.
- **Discussion prompt**: "Have there been times when you took responsibility for someone else's problems or avoided conflict to 'keep the peace'? How did this dynamic affect the relationship and your personal well-being?"

Breaking the cycle of trauma bonding:

- Encourage clients to consider steps they can take to break free from unhealthy attachments.
- **Discussion prompt**: "What steps can you take to start breaking the cycle of trauma bonding? How can building a support network and setting boundaries help you regain your sense of self?"

Contents

Chapter 13: Codependency and Trauma Bonding in Relationships
What Does It Mean to Be Codependent?
What Are the Characteristics of a Codependent Person?
What Is Trauma Bonding?
Characteristics of Trauma Bonding
The Relationship Between Codependency and Trauma Bonding
Homework

13

Codependency and Trauma Bonding in Relationships

"Codependency is using a relationship to fill a bottomless void due to not feeling whole and loved as an individual. It's not the need to be loved that's the issue, it's the inability to love one's self that causes the dysfunction."

—Graham R. White

There are several hallmarks of a healthy relationship, as we discussed in the previous chapter. However, codependency and trauma bonding can often masquerade as healthy signs in a relationship due to psychological factors. It is vital to understand what these terms mean and how they show up in relationships, which is what we are discussing in this chapter.

What Does It Mean to Be Codependent?

Let's start by looking at the definition of this term. "Codependency refers to a dysfunctional pattern of behavior where individuals excessively rely on others for their sense of self-worth and identity, often at the expense of their own needs and well-being."[58] It often involves a one-sided, imbalanced relationship dynamic where one person prioritizes the needs of the other to the detriment of their own emotional well-being.

Codependency isn't just about needing others. While it might appear as selflessness or devotion, this can be emotionally draining and even enabling of destructive behaviors because the person's

58. Psychology. Codependency. Retrieved from Psychology.tips: https://psychology.tips/codependency/

THE CARE METHOD

sense of identity and well-being become intertwined with another person. Codependency can affect all types of relationships, not just romantic ones. It can be present in friendships, family dynamics, or even work relationships.

There are also instances, quite often, when codependency overlaps with enabling behavior. Codependents might unintentionally enable unhealthy behaviors in their loved ones, such as addiction or irresponsibility, by rescuing them from consequences or taking over their problems. While they believe they are helping, this actually hinders the other person's growth and reinforces the unhealthy dynamic.

What Are the Characteristics of a Codependent Person?

Codependency can be quite difficult to recognize in your own life because this behavior might have gone on for so long that it feels normal to you now. Understanding how codependency manifests will help you recognize the signs and begin to create healthier dynamics in your relationships. There are several characteristics of codependency,[59] however, we will only cover six (6) of the most common ones below.

1. **Low self-worth**: People with codependency often struggle with low self-esteem so they seek external validation to feel worthy or lovable.
2. **Poor boundaries**: They have difficulty saying no or asserting their needs out of fear of rejection or abandonment.
3. **Enabling behaviors**: They might enable unhealthy behaviors in their loved ones, like addiction, by taking care of problems or trying to "rescue" them.
4. **Caretaking tendency**: They may fall into a caretaker role, feeling excessively responsible for others' feelings, actions, or issues.
5. **Conflict avoidance**: Codependent people often avoid conflict or confrontation, sacrificing their own needs to keep the peace in relationships.
6. **Fear of abandonment**: They can have an intense fear of being alone or abandoned, which can lead them to go to great lengths to avoid this.

59. Fort Behavioral Health. Addiction, Health & Wellness, Recovery, Therapy. (May 25, 2021). 9 Warning Signs of a Codependent Relationship. Retrieved from *Fort Behavioral Health* blog: https://fortbehavioral.com/addiction-recovery-blog/9-warning-signs-of-a-codependent-relationship/

CODEPENDENCY AND TRAUMA BONDING IN RELATIONSHIPS

Imagine yourself on the receiving end of your past actions. How might your behaviors have impacted your partner's sense of self-worth, security, and emotional well-being?

What Is Trauma Bonding?

Trauma bonding, also known as Stockholm syndrome, refers to the psychological phenomenon where victims develop strong emotional bonds with their abusers.[60] It occurs as a result of intermittent reinforcement, where moments of kindness or affection from the abuser are interspersed with periods of abuse or mistreatment.

Trauma bonds are an insidious consequence of abuse. They create a powerful emotional attachment between the victim and the abuser, making it incredibly difficult to leave the abusive situation. But why do these bonds form in the first place? The answer lies in a complex interplay of human needs, manipulation tactics, and the unpredictable nature of abuse in general.

Humans are social creatures with a deep-seated need for connection and belonging. When an abuser becomes the primary source of affection and validation, the fear of losing them becomes overwhelming. This can be especially true for victims who have already experienced abandonment or trauma in their past. The abuser exploits this fear by threatening to leave the relationship if they don't get their way. This manipulation reinforces the cycle of abuse and strengthens the trauma bond.

60. Cleveland Clinic. (March 29, 2023).Here's What Trauma Bonding Really Is and How to Recognize the Signs. Retrieved from Cleveland Clinic: https://health.clevelandclinic.org/trauma-bonding

THE CARE METHOD

We discussed attachment styles in chapter 10. Reflect on your own attachment style, and ask yourself if it could be possible to create an unhealthy attachment (trauma bond) with your partner?

Characteristics of Trauma Bonding

These are some of the characteristics of trauma bonding:[61]

1. **Cognitive dissonance**: Victims of trauma bonding may experience cognitive dissonance, where they simultaneously hold contradictory beliefs about their abuser (e.g., seeing them as both caring and abusive).
2. **Emotional dependence**: They become emotionally dependent on their abuser for validation, safety, and a sense of belonging.
3. **Isolation and control**: Abusers often isolate their victims from support networks and exert control over their lives, intensifying the bond of dependency.
4. **Survival mechanism**: Trauma bonding may serve as a survival mechanism, helping victims cope with the psychological and emotional trauma of abuse by forming a perceived alliance with the abuser.
5. **Difficulty leaving**: Victims of trauma bonding may struggle to leave the abusive relationship despite knowing it is harmful, due to the strong emotional attachment and fear of the unknown.

61. Fonseca, N.Q.L., and Oliveira, B.Q. Trauma Bonding: concepts, causes, and mechanisms in intimate relationships. *Revista Científica Multidisciplinar Núcleo do Conhecimento* (November 16, 2021). https://www.nucleodoconhecimento.com.br/psychology/intimate-relationships; doi: 10.32749/nucleodoconhecimento.com.br/psychology/intimate-relationships

CODEPENDENCY AND TRAUMA BONDING IN RELATIONSHIPS

Breaking a trauma bond requires significant emotional work and often external support. It involves recognizing the patterns of abuse, understanding the nature of trauma bonding, seeking help from professionals or support groups, and gradually rebuilding one's sense of self-worth and autonomy.

The Relationship Between Codependency and Trauma Bonding

Codependency and trauma bonding often coexist in abusive or dysfunctional relationships. Codependent individuals may be more susceptible to trauma bonding due to their tendencies to prioritize the needs of others, have low self-esteem, and avoid conflict. Similarly, trauma bonding reinforces codependent behaviors by deepening emotional dependence and attachment to the abuser.

Both codependency and trauma bonding can perpetuate cycles of abuse and dysfunction in relationships, making it challenging for individuals to break free from unhealthy dynamics. Recovery from codependency and trauma bonding typically involves therapy, self-awareness, setting boundaries, and building a support network to regain autonomy, self-worth, and healthy relationship skills.

THE CARE METHOD

Homework

Codependency Questionnaire

Instructions: Answer the following questions to assess your tendencies toward codependent behavior. Be honest with yourself and choose the response that best applies to you. For each question, assign the following point values to your answers:

A) Yes, frequently = 3 points
B) Sometimes = 2 points
C) Rarely = 1 point
D) No, never = 0 points

1. Do you often find yourself prioritizing other people's needs over your own, even if it negatively impacts your well-being?

    A) Yes, frequently
    B) Sometimes
    C) Rarely
    D) No, never

2. Do you have difficulty setting boundaries or saying no to others, even when you know it's necessary for your own self-care?

    A) Yes, frequently
    B) Sometimes
    C) Rarely
    D) No, never

3. Do you feel responsible for the emotions, actions, or problems of others, often taking on a caretaker role in your relationships?

    A) Yes, frequently
    B) Sometimes
    C) Rarely
    D) No, never

CODEPENDENCY AND TRAUMA BONDING IN RELATIONSHIPS

4. Do you have difficulty expressing your own thoughts, feelings, or needs in relationships, fearing conflict or rejection?

   A) Yes, frequently

   B) Sometimes

   C) Rarely

   D) No, never

5. Do you often feel guilty or ashamed when you prioritize your own needs or assert boundaries in relationships?

   A) Yes, frequently

   B) Sometimes

   C) Rarely

   D) No, never

6. Do you find yourself seeking validation and approval from others to feel worthy or lovable?

   A) Yes, frequently

   B) Sometimes

   C) Rarely

   D) No, never

7. Do you tend to stay in relationships even when they are unhealthy or abusive, hoping that things will improve or change?

   A) Yes, frequently

   B) Sometimes

   C) Rarely

   D) No, never

8. Do you struggle with feelings of low self-esteem or self-worth, often seeking external validation to feel better about yourself?

   A) Yes, frequently

   B) Sometimes

   C) Rarely

   D) No, never

THE CARE METHOD

Scoring: After answering all the questions, add up your total score: ________

Interpretation:

18-24 points: High likelihood of codependency. You often prioritize others over yourself, struggle with boundaries, and may have low self-esteem or difficulty in maintaining healthy relationships. It's important to seek support and consider strategies for improving your self-care and relationship dynamics.

10-17 points: Moderate likelihood of codependency. You may experience some codependent tendencies but might be able to manage them with increased self-awareness and support.

4-9 points: Low likelihood of codependency. You exhibit some healthy relationship behaviors, but there may still be areas to work on.

0-3 points: Minimal likelihood of codependency. You likely have healthy boundaries and self-esteem, though continuous self-reflection is always beneficial.

CODEPENDENCY AND TRAUMA BONDING IN RELATIONSHIPS

Additional Assignment

Instructions: Reflect on your past or current relationships and answer the following questions honestly. Focus on your own behaviors and patterns rather than those of your partner.

1. Reflect on a past or current relationship where you exhibited codependent behaviors. Describe specific instances where you prioritized your partner's needs over your own well-being. How did this impact your self-esteem and overall happiness?

____

____

____

____

2. Identify a boundary that you struggled to set in a past or current relationship. Why was it challenging for you to assert this boundary? How did not asserting this boundary affect the dynamics of the relationship?

____

____

____

____

3. Think about a time when you stayed in a relationship despite knowing it was unhealthy or abusive. What factors influenced your decision to stay? Reflect on how this experience has shaped your understanding of relationships and your own self-worth.

____

____

____

____

____

14

Understanding Cognitive Distortions and Their Connection to Behavioral Responses

"Our thoughts, when distorted by negative emotions, create worlds that don't really exist."

—Steve Maraboli

The way we think shapes the way we live—this chapter uncovers how distorted thinking patterns, known as cognitive distortions, impact clients' behaviors and relationships. Cognitive distortions are deeply ingrained thought patterns that skew perceptions of reality, often leading to harmful behaviors, especially within close relationships. These faulty perceptions create an emotional filter that warps the truth, causing clients to react impulsively or irrationally.

As a counselor, your role is to help clients identify the cognitive distortions that may be fueling their destructive behaviors. Many clients may not even be aware of how these thought patterns are affecting their lives. This chapter is about gaining awareness of how negative thinking patterns—such as all-or-nothing thinking, overgeneralization, and catastrophizing—impact emotional regulation and relational dynamics.

Clients will begin to see that distorted thinking shapes their emotional responses and consequently, their behavior. Encourage them to explore specific situations where they may have fallen into patterns of cognitive distortions and the outcomes of those responses. Helping them recognize how these distortions have influenced past conflicts, decisions, or reactions in their relationships is key.

As they progress through this chapter, your task is to guide them in challenging and reframing these distortions. With practice, clients can learn to replace faulty thoughts with more balanced perspectives, ultimately leading to healthier behavioral responses. Through this process, they will learn to interrupt the cycle of distorted thinking, reducing impulsivity and making more conscious, thoughtful choices in their relationships.

Goals of This Chapter

Faulty thinking can lead to a spiral of negative emotions and reactions, especially in relationships. In this chapter, clients will explore how cognitive distortions—irrational thought patterns—shape their perceptions, emotions, and behaviors. These distortions often cause individuals to misinterpret situations, resulting in heightened emotional responses and impulsive or harmful actions. The goal is to help clients recognize these thinking errors and understand how they contribute to destructive behaviors, particularly within intimate relationships.

As clients work through the material, they will be encouraged to identify specific cognitive distortions they may be prone to, such as all-or-nothing thinking, overgeneralization, or catastrophizing. By becoming aware of these thought processes, clients can begin to challenge and reframe their distorted thinking, which is crucial for making healthier decisions and responses in relationships. Your role as a counselor is to guide clients in linking their thought patterns to their emotional and behavioral responses, helping them see how cognitive distortions have fueled harmful actions in the past.

Colorado DVOMB Standards Competencies

Chapter 14 aligns with the Colorado Domestic Violence Offender Management Board (DVOMB) standards on **cognitive distortions** and **dynamic DV risk factors**. The DVOMB emphasizes the importance of addressing cognitive distortions that contribute to dynamic risk factors for domestic violence. By identifying and correcting distorted thinking, clients can reduce the risk of engaging in behaviors that perpetuate violence or harm within relationships.

The chapter encourages clients to take ownership of their thought processes and how these influence their actions. By addressing cognitive distortions, clients can better manage the dynamic factors that increase their risk for violent or abusive behavior. The standard reinforces the therapeutic goals of this chapter by ensuring that clients not only recognize and challenge harmful thought patterns but also actively work toward creating more positive and responsible behaviors in their relationships.

Important Things to Know

Last week, we explored the dynamics of **codependency and trauma bonding**, focusing on how unhealthy emotional ties can form and trap individuals in destructive relationship patterns. This chapter will delve deeper into the psychological mechanisms behind these behaviors by examining **cognitive distortions**—irrational thought patterns that distort reality and often lead to harmful emotional and behavioral responses.

In this chapter's sessions, you will help clients identify specific cognitive distortions, such as catastrophizing or black-and-white thinking, and understand how these patterns contribute to the escalation of conflicts or negative emotional responses. Clients will learn to challenge these distorted thoughts and replace them with healthier, more balanced perspectives, which can improve their emotional regulation and relationships.

Next week, we'll build on this by addressing the **Four Horsemen of the Relationship Apocalypse and their antidotes,** focusing on how destructive communication patterns like criticism and defensiveness can be replaced with positive communication strategies to further support healthy relationship dynamics.

Key Concepts and Terminology

Cognitive distortions: Inaccurate and irrational thought patterns that lead individuals to misinterpret situations and influence their emotional and behavioral responses. These distortions are often linked to negative emotions such as anxiety, depression, or anger, and they can significantly impact how individuals perceive their relationships and the world around them.

All-or-nothing thinking: A type of cognitive distortion where situations are seen in extremes—either completely good or completely bad. This kind of thinking often leads to overreactions, such as believing that if one thing goes wrong, the entire relationship is doomed.

Overgeneralization: Drawing broad, negative conclusions based on a single event. In relationships, this could involve assuming that because one argument occurred, the entire relationship is a failure or that future conflicts are inevitable.

Catastrophizing: A distortion where individuals expect the worst possible outcome in a situation, regardless of the evidence to the contrary. This can lead to unnecessary fear and avoidance in relationships.

Mind reading: A common cognitive distortion where one assumes they know what the other person is thinking without any real evidence. This can lead to misunderstandings, miscommunication, and unnecessary conflicts.

Magnification and minimization: This involves exaggerating the importance of negative events or downplaying the significance of positive ones. In relationships, this could manifest as overemphasizing mistakes and disregarding positive efforts made by a partner.

Emotional reasoning: The belief that feelings are equivalent to facts. For example, if someone feels insecure or unlovable, they conclude that they are, in fact, unlovable, regardless of their partner's actual behavior.

Self-regulation: The ability to manage one's emotional reactions and behaviors, particularly in stressful or conflict-laden situations. Understanding and managing cognitive distortions is key to developing better self-regulation and healthier relationship dynamics.

Discussion Prompts

The following discussion prompts can help facilitate meaningful reflection and discussion on how cognitive distortions influence thoughts and actions.

Recognizing cognitive distortions:

- Encourage clients to identify cognitive distortions they might commonly engage in and how those distortions impact their behavior.
- **Discussion prompt**: "Think about a recent conflict or challenging situation. What thoughts were running through your mind at the time? Can you identify any cognitive distortions, such as all-or-nothing thinking or catastrophizing?"

Impact on relationships:

- Ask clients to reflect on how distorted thinking has affected their relationships.
- **Discussion prompt**: "How have your negative or distorted thoughts influenced your behavior in relationships? What effect did those behaviors have on your partner or other loved ones?"

Challenging negative thought patterns:

- Encourage clients to think about ways they can challenge and reframe cognitive distortions in the future.
- **Discussion prompt**: "What is one cognitive distortion you tend to experience frequently? How can you challenge this thought with evidence and develop a more balanced perspective?"

Exploring emotional responses:

- Help clients link their cognitive distortions to their emotional reactions and behavioral responses.
- **Discussion prompt**: "When you have negative thoughts, how do they affect your emotions? For example, if you assume someone is upset with you, how does that change the way you feel or behave?"

Developing healthier thought patterns:

- Guide clients toward strategies that can help them replace cognitive distortions with healthier, more rational thought processes.
- **Discussion prompt**: "What are some techniques you can use to reframe distorted thoughts? How could using these strategies improve your emotional well-being and relationships?"

Contents

Chapter 14: Understanding Cognitive Distortions and Their Connection to Behavioral Responses

What Are Cognitive Distortions and Where Do They Come From?

How Do Cognitive Distortions Affect Our Central Nervous System?

Creating Range for Behavioral Response

How to Challenge and Treat Cognitive Distortions

How Do Distortions Impact Our Communication With Others?

Homework

14

Understanding Cognitive Distortions and Their Connection to Behavioral Responses

"You don't have to control your thoughts;
you just have to let them stop controlling you."

—Dan Millman

In the previous chapter, we talked about codependency and trauma bonding, both of which are dysfunctional behaviors formed by a distortion of the facts or dynamics of a relationship. This brings us to the concept of **cognitive distortions**. The brain is a complex organ that is constantly creating neuro pathways according to our life experiences. However, sometimes these neuro pathways, or patterns, are birthed from distorted information. Simply put, the patterns are formed based on false information. Let's discuss this.

What Are Cognitive Distortions and Where Do They Come From?

Cognitive distortions are inaccurate or faulty thought patterns based on assumptions that distort our perspectives and lead us to misinterpret situations.[62] They act like mental filters, coloring our perception of reality with negativity and fueling unhelpful emotions like anxiety, depression, and anger. These distortions are not uncommon. Everyone experiences them from time to time. However, when they become persistent and pervasive, they can significantly impact our mental well-being and daily lives.

62. Guy-Evans, O. (2023, November 9). 13 Cognitive Distortions Identified In CBT. Retrieved from *Simply Psychology*: https://www.simplypsychology.org/cognitive-distortions-in-cbt.html

The concept of cognitive distortions was pioneered by Dr. Aaron Beck, a prominent psychiatrist, in the 1960s.[63] Through his work in cognitive behavioral therapy (CBT), Dr. Beck identified several common cognitive distortions that underlie negative thinking patterns.

There are several types of cognitive distortions that can sneak into our thought processes. Let's look at a few of the most common ones:[64]

1. **All-or-nothing thinking**: This distortion sees things in extremes—everything is either perfect or a complete failure. You might think, "If my partner doesn't text me back immediately then it means they don't love me anymore." It has to be one extreme or the other. There's no middle ground.
2. **Overgeneralization**: Here, you take one negative experience and assume all your future experiences will be the same. For instance, after a bad date, you might conclude, "I'm always going to be alone."
3. **Mental filter**: This involves picking out a single negative detail and dwelling on it exclusively, thus perceiving the whole situation as negative. For example, your partner might compliment your outfit and tell you how handsome you are, but then they say, "I think this tie would look better than the one you have on," and this one comment ruins your whole night. Every other positive your partner said flies out the window.
4. **Disqualifying the positive**: You dismiss positive experiences as insignificant or due to luck, not your own ability. You might downplay a compliment by thinking, "They were just being nice." By doing this, you maintain a negative belief despite evidence to the contrary.
5. **Jumping to conclusions**: This can occur in two (2) ways:
   a. **Mind reading**: You assume the thoughts and intentions of others. For example, you might conclude someone thinks negatively of you without sufficient evidence.
   b. **Fortune telling**: You catastrophize about the future, predicting negative outcomes without evidence.

63. Guy-Evans, O. (2023, November 9). 13 Cognitive Distortions Identified In CBT. Retrieved from *Simply Psychology*: https://www.simplypsychology.org/cognitive-distortions-in-cbt.html

64. UPMC HealthBeat. (2022, April 20). Cognitive Distortions Explained With 10 Examples. Retrieved from *UPMC HealthBeat*: https://share.upmc.com/2021/05/cognitive-distortions/

6. **Magnification (catastrophizing) or minimization**: In this distortion, you either exaggerate the importance of your mistakes and shortcomings or someone else's achievements (magnification), or you minimize the importance of your desirable qualities or someone else's faults (minimization). This is also known as the "binocular trick," e.g., "He's so much smarter than me; I'm just not good enough."
7. **Emotional reasoning**: You believe that what you feel must be true automatically. If you feel stupid and boring, then you must be stupid and boring. In other words, you equate your feelings with facts.
8. **"Should" statements**: You hold yourself and others to unrealistic standards, which leads to guilt and frustration. You have a set of ironclad rules about how you and others should act. People who break these rules anger you, and you feel guilty when you violate these rules. You try to motivate yourself with shoulds and shouldn'ts, as if you need to be whipped and punished before you can expect to do anything. For example, "I should always be friendly," or "I should be able to handle this."
9. **Labeling and mislabeling**: This is an extreme form of overgeneralization. Instead of describing an error in the context of a specific situation, you attach a negative label to yourself or others. For instance, you forget your partner's birthday and conclude, "I'm such an idiot," rather than recognizing the mistake as a normal human oversight.
10. **Personalization**: You take responsibility for events outside your control, even if you had nothing to do with it. For example, if your spouse slams a cabinet door, you might think, "I must have done something to make them mad."

Sources of Cognitive Distortions

Research has revealed a connection between cognitive distortions and mental health disorders. For instance, a 2023 study highlighted that these distorted patterns of thought are more commonly observed in individuals with depression than in those without it.[65] Moreover, a 2020 international study further solidified this relationship by describing negative thoughts as a hallmark feature of depression.[66] Why is this the case? When someone is depressed, their ability to process information

65. Rnic, K., Dozois, D.J., and Martin, R.A. Distorted thoughts as a mediator of depressive symptoms in patients with major depressive disorder: a longitudinal study. *Health and Quality of Life Outcomes*, 12:3, 88 (2023, August 14). doi: 10.1186/s12955-023-02178-y

66. Mahali, S.C., Beshai, S., Feeney, J.R., and Mishra, S. Associations of negative cognitions, emotional regulation, and depression symptoms across four continents: International support for the cognitive model of depression. *BMC Psychiatry*, 20:1, 18 (2020, January 13). doi: 10.1186/s12888-019-2423-x

and react to their environment changes significantly. The world may seem more threatening or hopeless, and this skewed perception feeds the cycle of depression, reinforcing negative thinking patterns. This is why cognitive distortions are not just common in those with depression but are also a defining feature of the condition. It is important to know that although there is a strong connection between distortions and mental health, it is not set in stone that these distortions actually cause mental health disorders

However, depression isn't the only mental health condition linked with cognitive distortions. Anxiety, for example, can exacerbate and be exacerbated by patterns like catastrophizing (expecting the worst) or mind-reading (assuming you know what others are thinking) among other things.[67] Other mental health issues, such as obsessive-compulsive disorder (OCD), PTSD, and eating disorders also involve distinct cognitive distortions.[68]

How do these distortions develop? Cognitive distortions generally aren't inborn but form over time, often in response to adverse events or situations. When people experience trauma, prolonged stress, or are repeatedly exposed to certain patterns of thinking through their environment and relationships, they may develop these unhelpful thought patterns.[68] Cognitive distortions often start as a shorthand to make sense of complex emotions or situations but can become habitual and automatic (Ackerman, 2017).[69] Over time, if these patterns remain unchecked, they can become deeply ingrained, making them more difficult to identify and challenge.

Name the cognitive distortions you relate to in your personal life.

---

67. Özdemir, I., and Kuru, E. Investigation of Cognitive Distortions in Panic Disorder, Generalized Anxiety Disorder and Social Anxiety Disorder. *Journal of Clinical Medicine*, 12:19, 6351 (2023, October 23). doi: 10.3390/jcm12196351

68. Huziej, M. (2023, November 27). All about Cognitive Distortions. Retrieved from *CPD Online College*: https://cpdonline.co.uk/knowledge-base/mental-health/cognitive-distortions/

69. Ackerman, C.E. (2017, September 29). Cognitive Distortions: 22 Examples & Worksheets (& PDF). Retrieved from *Positive Psychology*: https://positivepsychology.com/cognitive-distortions/

How Do Cognitive Distortions Affect Our Central Nervous System?

Take a look at the below diagram of how cognitive distortions affect our central nervous system (CNS). When we input information, this is the path it takes through our CNS, including the prefrontal cortex (PFC), and then it produces an output. I'm sure you recognize the amygdala hijack by now.

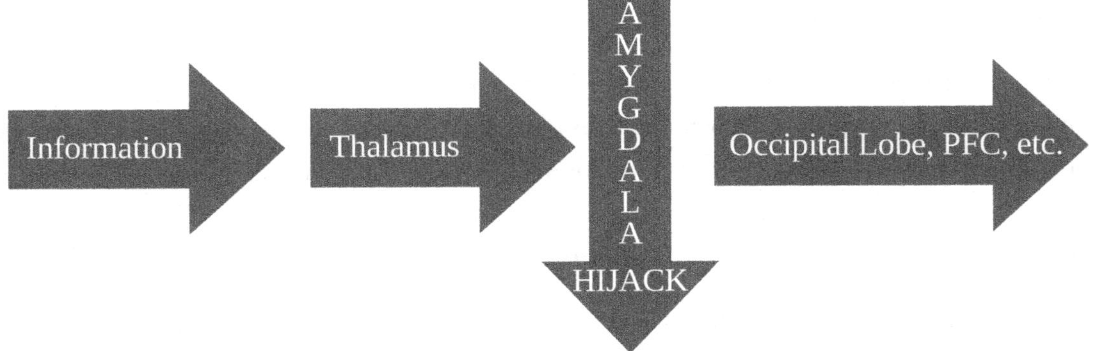

Creating Range for Behavioral Response

Creating a range for behavioral responses involves developing a spectrum of possible reactions and strategies to handle various situations, particularly when confronted with stress, conflict, or decision-making scenarios. This concept is central in psychology and behavioral therapy, where the goal is often to expand the repertoire of an individual's responses, rather than resorting to automatic or habitual reactions that may not be optimal. Here's how you can work on creating and broadening your range of behavioral responses:[70]

a. Step back from the situation.
b. Identify the thought.
c. Analyze the situation from different perspectives.
d. Avoid extremes and absolutes.
e. Remove any mental label you have assigned to the situation.
f. Focus on the positive.
g. Weigh the evidence and replace the initial thought with a neutral thought.

70. Herndon, J.R. (2024, February 6). 12 Examples of Cognitive Distortions and How to Cope with Them. Retrieved from *Very Well Health*: https://www.verywellhealth.com/cognitive-distortions-5226061#toc-when-to-see-a-healthcare-provider

What is the most common cognitive distortion (thought) in your life right now? Using the steps above, challenge this thought.

How To Challenge and Treat Cognitive Distortions

One effective approach to challenge and treat cognitive distortions is through cognitive behavioral therapy (CBT). This method involves identifying and reframing negative thoughts. You can ask yourself questions such as "Is this thought reasonable?" or "What evidence supports or contradicts my belief?" "Could there be another explanation for someone's behavior that isn't about me?" "Am I confusing a thought with a fact?"

Another approach is mindfulness, which helps in becoming more aware and observant of your thoughts and feelings. This awareness can lead to better management of emotional responses and a more balanced perspective on situations.

How Do Distortions Impact Communication With Others?

Throughout this chapter, we've explored the concept of cognitive distortions and their impact on our thoughts and behaviors. By recognizing these distorted thinking patterns and challenging them with rational thought processes, we can significantly improve our communication with others.

Effective communication is a lifelong journey. By recognizing and challenging cognitive distortions, we can cultivate a more rational and balanced way of thinking. This, in turn, empowers us to connect with others on a deeper level, build stronger relationships, and navigate the complexities of human interaction from a healthy mindset.

UNDERSTANDING COGNITIVE DISTORTIONS AND THEIR CONNECTION TO . . .

Homework

1. Reflect on a recent situation where you felt overwhelmed by negative emotions. What was the situation?

2. Identify any cognitive distortions that were present in your thoughts during this situation (e.g., all-or-nothing thinking, catastrophizing).

3. Now, challenge that distortion with evidence to the contrary. Are there other ways to interpret the situation?

THE CARE METHOD

4. How could you have reframed your thoughts to provide a more rational response/reaction?

____

____

____

____

____

5. If you happen to encounter a similar situation in the future, how can you develop a more balanced and realistic thought process to guide your response?

____

____

____

____

____

15

The Four Horsemen of the Relationship Apocalypse and Their Antidotes

"When you react, you let others control you.
When you respond, you are in control."

—Bohdi Sanders

Communication can either strengthen a relationship or lead to its demise—this chapter examines the destructive patterns known as the "Four Horsemen of the Relationship Apocalypse," a concept developed by Dr. John Gottman. These four detrimental behaviors—criticism, defensiveness, contempt, and stonewalling—are strong predictors of relationship breakdown if they go unaddressed. Recognizing and understanding these communication patterns is crucial, as they often serve as the foundation for conflicts that can escalate into relational and even physical abuse.

As a counselor, your role is to help clients identify when these communication patterns are present in their relationships and guide them toward healthier alternatives. It is important for clients to realize that these behaviors are not just harmful but solvable with the right approaches—known as the antidotes. Helping clients recognize the role of these destructive patterns allows them to take responsibility for their behavior and choose more constructive ways of interacting with their partners.

This chapter outlines each of the Four Horsemen in detail, along with the antidotes. Criticism, for example, is countered by using a gentle startup, allowing clients to express needs and concerns without attacking their partner's character. Defensiveness, a common response to criticism, can be resolved by taking responsibility for one's role in the conflict. Contempt, the most harmful of the four, is dissolved by fostering appreciation and respect in the relationship, while stonewalling, or shutting down during conflict, can be alleviated through physiological self-soothing techniques.

By helping clients recognize and replace these toxic behaviors, this chapter empowers them to break free from destructive cycles and begin the process of building healthier, more respectful communication patterns. This understanding also contributes to the broader goal of violence prevention by addressing the underlying communication issues that can lead to abusive behaviors.

Goals of This Chapter

Destructive communication patterns can undermine even the strongest relationships. These behaviors often lead to the breakdown of relationships and can be precursors to conflict and abuse. The goal of this chapter is to help clients recognize these toxic communication patterns and replace them with healthier alternatives, known as the antidotes: gentle startup, taking responsibility, expressing feelings and needs, and self-soothing.

Clients will be encouraged to reflect on past relationship conflicts where one or more of the Four Horsemen were present and to consider how the antidotes could have transformed the outcome. Through this reflection process, clients will gain the tools to foster more respectful and constructive communication in future interactions. As a counselor, your role is to help clients identify these patterns in their relationships and equip them with strategies to shift toward healthier behaviors, promoting mutual respect, understanding, and personal accountability.

By practicing the antidotes to these toxic behaviors, clients will learn how to set healthy boundaries and engage in pro-social activities that support the well-being of both partners, ultimately building more stable and fulfilling relationships.

Colorado DVOMB Standards Competencies

Chapter 15 aligns with the Colorado Domestic Violence Offender Management Board (DVOMB) standards, emphasizing **accountability/responsibility**, **boundaries**, **dynamic DV risk factors**, and **insight and empathy**. It stresses the importance of taking full responsibility for one's actions, guiding clients to confront their behaviors and recognize their impact on others. By being genuinely accountable, clients can move beyond denial, work toward making amends, and create healthier relationship patterns.

Understanding and respecting boundaries is also central to this chapter. Clients learn about healthy boundary-setting, distinguishing between assertiveness and aggression. By becoming aware of their own boundaries and respecting others' boundaries, they can foster more respectful interactions. The chapter also addresses dynamic DV risk factors, prompting clients to identify and manage these factors to reduce the likelihood of future harmful behaviors.

Insight and empathy are crucial components, encouraging clients to develop a deeper understanding of their emotions and the experiences of others. By fostering empathy, clients can recognize the emotional impact of their actions, promoting a more compassionate approach to their relationships. These standards are integral to the CARE Method, ensuring clients understand accountability and boundaries while gaining the insight necessary for meaningful change. This chapter serves as a vital step in fostering personal transformation and healthier relational patterns.

Important Things to Know

Last week, we explored **cognitive distortions** and their role in shaping emotional responses and behaviors. Clients gained an understanding of how these distorted thought patterns can lead to harmful behaviors within their relationships. In this chapter, we'll focus on communication patterns by introducing the **Four Horsemen of the Relationship Apocalypse**—criticism, defensiveness, contempt, and stonewalling—and how these toxic behaviors erode relationships over time.

You will help clients recognize when they are engaging in these destructive patterns and guide them toward healthier alternatives, known as antidotes. By learning to replace criticism with gentle startup, defensiveness with taking responsibility, contempt with building appreciation, and stonewalling with self-soothing, clients can begin to communicate in ways that foster respect and connection, rather than conflict.

Next week, we will build on this chapter by examining the **four styles of communication,** where clients will explore how adopting an assertive communication style can further strengthen their ability to interact with others in a healthy, balanced manner.

Key Concepts and Terminology

Emotional flooding: A state where overwhelming emotions make it impossible to think clearly or engage in constructive dialogue. Physiological symptoms include a rapid heartbeat and adrenaline rush, making rational communication difficult. Managing emotional flooding is essential for maintaining control during conflict

Criticism: A destructive communication pattern that attacks a person's character rather than addressing a specific behavior. Criticism often involves blame and accusatory language, damaging the relationship by making the other person feel personally attacked. It undermines the possibility of constructive dialogue.

Defensiveness: The act of protecting oneself from perceived attacks by making excuses, counterattacking, or refusing to take responsibility. Defensiveness shuts down productive conversation and escalates conflicts rather than resolving them.

Contempt: The most damaging of the Four Horsemen, contempt involves sarcasm, mockery, or insulting behavior that communicates a sense of superiority and disdain. It erodes respect and creates an environment of resentment and hostility, making resolution and connection nearly impossible.

Stonewalling: Shutting down emotionally or physically withdrawing from a conversation when feeling overwhelmed. Stonewalling leaves the other partner feeling unheard and rejected, further damaging the relationship by avoiding the issue rather than addressing it.

Antidotes: These are the solutions or counterstrategies to the Four Horsemen, listed next.

Gentle startup: Instead of criticism, use "I" statements to express feelings and needs calmly and without accusation.

Taking responsibility: Instead of being defensive, acknowledge your role in the issue and commit to working on a solution.

Describing feelings and needs: Rather than showing contempt, openly communicate your emotions and needs without attacking your partner's character.

Physiological self-soothing: Instead of stonewalling, take a break to calm down and re-engage in the conversation when both partners are ready.

Discussion Prompts

The following discussion prompts can help facilitate reflection and conversation about how these destructive communication patterns show up in their relationships and how to address them.

Identifying the Four Horsemen:

- Help clients recognize which of the Four Horsemen (criticism, defensiveness, contempt, or stonewalling) they most often engage in.
- **Discussion prompt**: "When thinking about past arguments or conflicts, which of the Four Horsemen do you recognize in your behavior? How do you think this has impacted your relationships?"

Recognizing criticism and its antidote:

- Encourage clients to reflect on how often they use criticism and how it affects their partner.
- **Discussion prompt**: "Think about a time when you criticized your partner rather than addressing a specific issue. How could using a gentle startup instead have changed the outcome of that situation?"

Exploring defensiveness and its antidote:

- Guide clients to recognize moments when they have been defensive and avoided responsibility.
- **Discussion prompt**: "When you've felt blamed or attacked, how have you responded defensively? How could taking responsibility, even for a small part of the issue, have led to a more productive conversation?"

Addressing contempt and its antidote:

- Ask clients to consider moments where contempt has shown up in their communication.
- **Discussion prompt**: "Have you ever used sarcasm, insults, or put-downs in an argument? How do you think this has affected your partner, and how could focusing on expressing your feelings and needs help improve communication?"

Dealing with stonewalling and its antidote:

- Help clients reflect on times they've shut down or withdrawn during conflicts.
- **Discussion prompt**: "When have you felt overwhelmed during a conflict and chosen to stonewall or shut down? How could practicing self-soothing and asking for a break improve how you handle tough conversations?"

Applying the antidotes:

- Encourage clients to reflect on how the antidotes for the Four Horsemen could improve their relationships.
- **Discussion prompt**: "Which of the antidotes do you feel would be the most helpful in your current or past relationships? How can you start incorporating these strategies to improve communication moving forward?"

Contents

Chapter 15: The Four Horsemen of the Relationship Apocalypse and Their Antidotes
The Four Horsemen of the Relationship Apocalypse
Two Types of Couples
Changing Your Communication Pattern From the Four Horsemen to Using the Antidotes
Homework

15

The Four Horsemen of the Relationship Apocalypse and Their Antidotes

"Most couples don't get any training in relationships, and often they don't learn how to communicate with each other until they go to therapy, and that's often too late."

—John Gottman

In this chapter, we are going to deal with the different types of communication styles that often lead to the breakdown of relationships. This is particularly important because it piggybacks the previous chapter about cognitive distortions. We learned in chapter 13 that these inaccurate or negative thought patterns and perspectives are a result of assumptions. Unfortunately, negative thought patterns often lead to negative speech patterns. We all tend to verbalize our thoughts, whether good or bad, and the latter, especially, is often the cause of relationships falling apart. Let's talk about how this manifests in relationships.

The Four Horsemen of the Relationship Apocalypse

History

In 1986, Dr. Gottman established the "Love Lab" at the University of Washington.[71] This innovative laboratory allowed them to observe couples in a controlled environment, recording their interactions and physiological responses. Over a period spanning more than 40 years, Dr. Gottman and his team studied thousands of couples. Through extensive observation and analysis, they identified specific communication patterns that predicted marital breakdown. Their research revealed

71. The Gottman Institute. (2024). Gottman Love lab. Retrieved from the Gottman Institute: https://www.gottman.com/love-lab/

THE CARE METHOD

four (4) key communication styles that consistently appeared in couples headed for divorce. These negative behaviors, often fueled by strong emotions, were labeled the "Four Horsemen of the Relationship Apocalypse."[72]

The Four Horsemen of the Relationship Apocalypse represent destructive forces that can lead to the end of a relationship.[73]

1. Criticism

Criticism focuses on attacking a person's character rather than a specific behavior. It often uses accusatory language and blame.[73] For example, instead of saying, "I feel hurt when you leave your dirty dishes in the sink," a critical statement might be, "You're so inconsiderate, always leaving messes everywhere!"

2. Defensiveness

Defensiveness is the urge to protect yourself from blame by making excuses, justifying your actions, or counter-attacking your partner.[73] It deflects responsibility and hinders productive communication. An example of defensiveness might be, "It's not my fault the dishes are dirty, you never clean up after yourself either!"

3. Contempt

Contempt is the most destructive horseman. It involves putting down your partner and using sarcasm, mockery, or hurtful insults.[73] Contempt breeds resentment and erodes respect. An example of contempt might be, "Honestly, how can you not even do the simplest chores? You're hopeless!"

4. Stonewalling

Stonewalling is the act of shutting down emotionally and withdrawing from communication.[73] This might involve silence, changing the subject, or walking away mid-conversation. Stonewalling leaves the other person feeling unheard and frustrated.

---

72. The Gottman Institute. (2024). Research. Retrieved from the Gottman Institute: https://www.gottman.com/about/research/

73. Moore, M. (2022, February 24). 4 Relationship Behaviors That Often Lead to Divorce. Retrieved from *Psych Central*: https://psychcentral.com/blog/predicting-divorce-the-four-horsemen-of-the-apocalpyse#the-four-horsemen-defined

THE FOUR HORSEMEN OF THE RELATIONSHIP APOCALYPSE AND THEIR ANTIDOTES

Two Types of Couples

Dr. Gottman's research went beyond simply identifying the Four Horsemen. He categorized couples based on their communication styles. Here's the key distinction:

1. **The masters of relationship**: These couples rarely used the Four Horsemen. Instead, they excelled at utilizing the antidotes: gentle start-ups, taking responsibility, expressing feelings and needs, and self-soothing. This fostered a more positive and respectful communication dynamic, leading to stronger and more resilient relationships.
2. **The disasters**: These couples frequently fell into the trap of the Four Horsemen. Their communication was riddled with criticism, defensiveness, contempt, and stonewalling. This created a toxic environment that eroded trust and satisfaction, ultimately jeopardizing the relationship's stability.

Changing Your Communication Pattern From the Four Horsemen to Using the Antidotes

Thankfully, each Horseman has an antidote, which is a counter behavior that helps solve the conflict.[74] These are the antidotes Gottman lists:

a. Using a gentle startup
b. Taking responsibility
c. Describing your own feelings and needs
d. Doing physiological self-soothing

74. The Gottman Institute. (2024). The Four Horsemen: The Antidotes. Retrieved from the Gottman Institute: https://www.gottman.com/blog/the-four-horsemen-the-antidotes/

THE CARE METHOD

Criticism

The antidote: Using a gentle startup. Express your feelings and needs by using "I" statements. This allows your partner to understand your perspective without feeling attacked.

Examples of the antidote:

a. I feel unsupported with keeping the house clean, and what I need is for us to talk about how this can be done more consistently together.

b. I feel hurt when I am spoken to like that, and what I need is to be treated more respectfully.

c. I feel uncared for when my needs aren't considered, and what I need is more communication about what both of us need.

d. I feel disrespected when I am left waiting, and what I need is more attention and consideration for the agreements we make.

Defensiveness

We often get defensive when we feel attacked, so the natural response is to counterattack and verbally hit our partners back where it hurts the most in order to protect ourselves, but this is not a healthy way to deal with situations. If anything, defensiveness only escalates conflict.

Defensiveness is mostly projected in two (2) ways: counterattacking and taking a victim stance.

Example of a counterattack: Your partner says, "You didn't switch the clothes over and now they stink!"

You counterattack with, "Well you should have done the washing yesterday and I wouldn't have had to do it in the first place!"

Example of a victim stance: Your partner says, "The trash bin hasn't been taken out again!"

You reply with, "That's not fair; I only got home 20 minutes ago!"

The antidote: Take responsibility. Acknowledge your part in the situation even if you know that the majority of the blame is on their part, and then show a willingness to find a solution together.

THE FOUR HORSEMEN OF THE RELATIONSHIP APOCALYPSE AND THEIR ANTIDOTES

Examples of the antidote:

a. Your partner says, "You didn't switch the clothes over and now they stink!"
b. You respond, "Oh you are right. I forgot this time. I'm sorry."
c. Or your partner says, "The trash bin hasn't been taken out again!"
d. You respond, "You are right, I haven't quite gotten to it yet, but I will." (said with a cheeky smile)

Contempt

Contempt is the strongest indicator of relationship breakdown. In fact, Gottman was able to predict with 92% accuracy which couples would break up and which would stay together just by measuring how much contempt was used in a 10-minute conflict conversation. He repeated that study seven (7) times!

Contempt is like criticism on steroids. Contempt is generally characterized by actions like eye-rolling, acting superior to your partner, using mean, nasty, or sarcastic comments, and acts of belligerence such as slamming doors, yelling, swearing, etc., e.g., "Oh that's right, you know everything, of course," accompanied with an eyeroll.

The antidote: Describe your feelings and needs. Focus on expressing your feelings and needs directly to your partner without attacking their words or their character. In other words, it should not become a personal attack just because you disagree. Express what you are feeling in the moment and concerning the subject at hand. Don't bring up things your partner did or said in the past.

Example of the antidote:

a. "I am **feeling frustrated** and a bit **hopeless right now** as I listen to you. It sounds like you are making a very firm statement there and I am not convinced that is the only way to go about this. I would really like **us** to **keep an open mind** and **talk through a range of possibilities. Can we please try that**?"

THE CARE METHOD

Stonewalling

Stonewalling generally occurs when you become physiologically aroused and shut down. Gottman discovered that once your heart rate reaches 100 beats per minute, your stress hormones, cortisol and adrenaline, flood the nervous system and compromise the prefrontal cortex of your brain.

At this point, you are not able to rationally or logically think straight. Your ability to problem-solve, think flexibly, process your emotions, or empathize with another is completely compromised. Anything that is said at this point will only be more detrimental to the conversation and relationship.

The antidote: Physiological self-soothing. This is an attempt to calm yourself and may include slowing the conversation down while you both do some deep breathing, agreeing to take a break for 20 to 40 minutes during which you might go for a walk, meditate, or just take some time out to think about what you are really trying to express.

Once you have calmed down, it is important to reconnect with your partner. You do not have to continue the conversation, you just have to reconnect.

Example of the antidote:

a. You might say something like, "Sorry I got a bit hot under the collar, can we try having that conversation again after dinner?"

The key is to reconnect and not to avoid the conversation but indicate your willingness to keep working on it.

THE FOUR HORSEMEN OF THE RELATIONSHIP APOCALYPSE AND THEIR ANTIDOTES

Homework

1. Which Horsemen were you able to relate to (criticism, defensiveness, contempt, stonewalling)?

____

____

____

____

____

2. How do you believe your identified Horsemen have impacted your intimate relationships and how you resolve conflict in your life?

____

____

____

____

____

3. How do you believe the Horseman you related to the most contributes to previous or current abusive behaviors in your relationship(s) and your involvement with domestic violence?

____

____

____

____

____

181

THE CARE METHOD

4. What is your plan to eliminate this way of thinking and acting moving forward?

5. What have you begun to do to eliminate this way of thinking and acting?

16

The Four Styles of Communication

"In any relationship, the way you communicate with each other is more important than the disagreements you have."

—John Gottman

Effective communication is the cornerstone of any relationship, shaping the way individuals connect and interact. In this chapter, clients will delve into the various styles of communication and examine how these patterns impact their relationships. The way individuals express themselves can either foster understanding or build barriers. This chapter encourages clients to reflect on their communication habits, especially their responses during conflicts or emotionally charged situations, to promote healthier, more constructive interactions.

As a counselor, your role is to help clients identify their dominant communication style and the impact it has on their relationships. Passive communication often leads to unmet needs and frustration, as individuals suppress their own feelings to avoid conflict. Aggressive communication, while forceful, tends to alienate others and create hostility. Passive-aggressive communication, with its indirect expression of anger or dissatisfaction, can leave relationships fraught with confusion and resentment. Assertive communication, on the other hand, allows for direct and respectful exchanges, where both parties' needs and boundaries are honored.

This chapter also emphasizes the importance of self-awareness in communication. Encourage clients to reflect on how their communication style has shaped past interactions and contributed to relationship dynamics. You will guide them in examining specific situations where a shift in communication style could have led to a different, more positive outcome. By helping clients develop assertive communication skills, they can begin to express their needs clearly, listen effectively, and reduce misunderstandings.

Throughout this chapter, clients will learn that assertiveness is key to building healthy, respectful relationships. By participating in this exercise and becoming aware of their communication patterns, they are taking important steps toward improving their interpersonal connections. The goal of this chapter is to equip clients with the tools to communicate more effectively, fostering stronger and more supportive relationships moving forward.

Goals of This Chapter

Effective communication can be the key to transforming relationships. Understanding communication styles is crucial for improving interactions, managing conflicts, and fostering healthier relationships. The primary goal is to help clients identify their habitual communication style and recognize how it influences their behavior and the responses they receive from others.

Clients will be encouraged to reflect on past interactions where their communication style may have contributed to misunderstandings, conflicts, or strained relationships. By understanding the differences between passive, aggressive, passive-aggressive, and assertive communication, clients can begin working toward adopting an assertive style—one that is respectful, direct, and fosters open dialogue without infringing on the rights or boundaries of others.

As a counselor, your role is to guide clients through this self-examination, helping them see the advantages of assertive communication. You will support clients in developing assertive communication skills, enabling them to express their needs and boundaries clearly while respecting those of their partners. This shift toward assertiveness will not only enhance their relationships but also contribute to their overall emotional well-being.

Colorado DVOMB Standards Competencies

Chapter 16 aligns with Colorado Domestic Violence Offender Management Board (DVOMB) standards, emphasizing **self-regulation**, **boundaries**, **dynamic DV risk factors**, and **insight and empathy**. It focuses on self-regulation, guiding clients to control their emotional responses, especially in high-stress situations. The DVOMB highlights self-regulation as crucial in preventing impulsive, harmful behaviors. Clients learn strategies like mindfulness and grounding exercises to respond thoughtfully instead of reacting impulsively, reducing the risk of abusive behaviors and improving communication.

Understanding and respecting boundaries is also a key aspect. Clients explore how to establish and maintain personal boundaries, promoting mutual respect and safety in relationships. This chapter differentiates between healthy boundary-setting and controlling behaviors, fostering trust and understanding. Additionally, it addresses dynamic DV risk factors, helping clients identify and manage these evolving factors to minimize potential future violence.

Insight and empathy are integral components, encouraging clients to understand their behaviors' impact on others. By developing empathy, clients can appreciate others' perspectives and feelings, leading to more compassionate interactions. These standards are crucial to the CARE Method, equipping clients with the skills for emotional regulation, boundary-setting, and empathetic understanding, paving the way for healthier, more balanced relationships.

Important Things to Know

Last week, we focused on identifying and addressing the **Four Horsemen of the Relationship Apocalypse** and learning the antidotes for destructive communication patterns like criticism, defensiveness, contempt, and stonewalling. This chapter builds on those concepts by diving deeper into the **four styles of communication—passive, aggressive, passive-aggressive, and assertive**—and exploring how each impacts relationships.

This week, you'll guide clients through identifying their dominant **communication style** and reflecting on how it affects their interactions and conflict resolution. By recognizing the differences between these styles, clients can learn to shift toward assertive communication, which fosters respect, understanding, and clear expression of needs.

Next week, we will shift focus to **responsible parenting**, examining how communication patterns influence relationships with children and how parents can model healthy communication for the next generation.

Key Concepts and Terminology

Passive communication: A style where individuals avoid expressing their needs, desires, or opinions. This often leads to unmet needs, internal resentment, and emotional buildup, which can eventually manifest as frustration or anger. In relationships, passive communication often results in the avoidance of conflicts but can cause long-term issues as feelings are suppressed.

Aggressive communication: This style involves expressing one's needs or desires in a forceful or hostile manner, often at the expense of others. Aggressive communication typically results in conflict and pushes others away, creating an atmosphere of fear or resentment rather than connection.

Passive-aggressive communication: A blend of passive and aggressive communication where individuals avoid direct confrontation but express their frustration indirectly, often through sarcasm, subtle insults, or procrastination. This style leads to confusion and tension in relationships, as the real issue is never openly addressed.

Assertive communication: The healthiest and most balanced communication style, assertive communication allows individuals to express their needs and desires clearly and respectfully, while also considering the needs of others. This style fosters mutual respect, open dialogue, and effective conflict resolution, making it essential for healthy relationships.

Self-regulation: The ability to manage one's emotions and reactions, particularly in stressful or conflict-ridden situations. Self-regulation is a crucial skill for maintaining assertive communication, as it helps individuals stay calm and composed, preventing them from resorting to aggressive or passive-aggressive behaviors.

Pro-social activities: Positive and constructive behaviors that enhance relationships and promote mutual respect. Engaging in pro-social activities involves active listening, empathy, and compromise, all of which support assertive communication and healthy relationship dynamics.

Discussion Prompts

These prompts will help foster meaningful reflection and conversations about how different communication styles affect relationships and personal interactions.

Identifying communication styles:

- Encourage clients to think about the communication styles they tend to use in their relationships and how these styles have impacted their interactions.
- **Discussion prompt**: "When you reflect on your communication style, do you see patterns of passive, aggressive, passive-aggressive, or assertive communication? How do you think these styles have affected your relationships?"

Exploring passive communication:

- Help clients consider how passive communication has affected their ability to express themselves and get their needs met.
- **Discussion prompt**: "Can you recall a time when you stayed quiet about your needs or feelings to avoid conflict? How did that affect the situation, and what would have changed if you communicated more assertively?"

Addressing aggressive communication:

- Invite clients to reflect on the consequences of using aggressive communication in their relationships.
- **Discussion prompt**: "Think of a moment when you communicated aggressively. How did your partner or friend react? What could you have done differently to handle the situation in a healthier way?"

Recognizing passive-aggressive behaviors:

- Encourage clients to explore how passive-aggressive communication has created tension in their relationships.
- **Discussion prompt**: "Have you ever used sarcasm or indirect comments to express your frustration? How did it affect the situation, and how might directly addressing the issue have led to a better outcome?"

Developing assertive communication:

- Guide clients in understanding how assertive communication can improve their relationships and help them express their needs while respecting others.

- **Discussion prompt**: "How would practicing assertive communication—clearly expressing your needs and respecting others—change the way you handle conflicts or daily conversations with your partner or friends?"

Shifting communication patterns:

- Encourage clients to consider how they can start adopting assertive communication more consistently.
- **Discussion prompt**: "What small steps can you take to move from passive, aggressive, or passive-aggressive communication to assertive communication? How can these changes positively impact your relationships?"

Contents

Chapter 16: The Four Styles of Communication
The Four Styles of Communication
Passive Communication
Aggressive Communication
Passive-Aggressive Communication
Assertive Communication
Verbal Versus Nonverbal Aspects of Communication Styles
Homework

16

The Four Styles of Communication

"Communication to a relationship is like oxygen is to life. Without it, it dies."

—Tony A. Gaskins Jr.

One of the major themes of this workbook, especially these last few chapters, has been communication. There is extensive research in various fields about the different facets of communication, like the Four Horsemen of the Relationship Apocalypse that we discussed in the previous chapter. Building on that, we will focus on the four (4) styles of communication in this chapter.

The Four Styles of Communication

Communication is an essential aspect of human interaction because it influences how we interact with other people, and these define our life experiences. In relationships, communication styles influence how we express ourselves, listen to our partners, and handle disagreements, among other things. We all have a natural style of communication that falls within these four (4) categories:

1. Passive
2. Aggressive
3. Passive-Aggressive
4. Assertive

THE CARE METHOD

Passive Communication

Passive communication is when you avoid expressing your opinions or feelings, protecting your rights, and meeting your needs. Instead of speaking up, you keep your thoughts and emotions to yourself.[75] This might seem like a way to avoid conflict, but it often leads to bigger problems. When you don't speak up, you let annoyances build up inside until you can't take it anymore, and then you might explode over something small. After an outburst, you might feel guilty or confused, and you go back to being passive, starting the cycle all over again.

Signs of Passive Communication:

a. Avoiding eye contact
b. Speaking softly or hesitantly
c. Using apologetic or self-deprecating language
d. Always going along with what others want
e. Ignoring your own needs and desires

How Does Passive Communication Affect You and Your Relationships?

- **You feel anxious**: When you don't express your needs or feelings, life can feel out of control. You might constantly worry about things because you're not handling issues as they come up.
- **You feel depressed**: Keeping everything inside can make you feel hopeless and stuck. It's hard to feel happy when you never get to say what you really think or want.
- **You build up resentment**: Even if you're not always aware of it, not getting your needs met can make you feel angry and resentful. This anger builds up over time and can harm your relationships.
- **You feel confused**: Ignoring your own feelings can leave you feeling confused about what you want or need. It's hard to make decisions or feel confident when you're not in touch with your own emotions.
- **You don't grow emotionally**: If you never address real issues, you don't learn how to deal with conflict or express yourself. This keeps you from growing and maturing emotionally.

Example: When a partner asks, "What would you like for dinner?" a passive communicator might simply say, "I don't care, whatever you want is fine." (But secretly, they desire something else.)

---

75. Gillis, K. (2023, August 17). Passive Communication: Definition, Examples, & How to Handle It. Retrieved from *Choosing Therapy*: https://www.choosingtherapy.com/passive-communication/

THE FOUR STYLES OF COMMUNICATION

Aggressive Communication

Aggressive communication is when you express your feelings and opinions and advocate for your needs in a way that violates the rights of others.[76] This can include being verbally or physically abusive. While it might feel like you're getting your point across, it often harms your relationships and makes it hard for others to connect with you.

Signs of Aggressive Communication:

a. Using a loud, demanding, or threatening tone
b. Criticizing, blaming, or insulting others
c. Dominating conversations and not letting others speak
d. Ignoring or dismissing others' feelings and opinions
e. Using intimidating body language, such as standing with crossed arms or glaring

How Does Aggressive Communication Affect You and Your Relationships?

- **You become alienated from others**: When you communicate aggressively, people often feel hurt or afraid, and they may start to avoid you. Over time, this can lead to loneliness and isolation because people don't want to be around you.
- **You alienate others**: Aggressive communication pushes others away. They may feel resentful, scared, or angry. This creates a barrier in relationships, making it difficult to form healthy, supportive connections.
- **You generate fear and hatred**: Your aggressive behavior can cause others to fear or even hate you. This fear can lead to a lack of trust and open communication, further damaging your relationships.
- **You always blame others**: Aggressive communicators often blame others for problems instead of taking responsibility for their actions. This prevents personal growth and maturity because you don't learn from your mistakes or understand how your behavior affects others.

Example: In the same scenario, an aggressive communicator might say, "Why don't you ever ask me what I want? You never consider my needs! You're so inconsiderate!"

76. Wilson, C. (2017, 11 21). Communication Style. Retrieved from *The Better You Institute*: https://thebetteryouinstitute.com/2017/11/21/communication-style-2/

THE CARE METHOD

Passive-Aggressive Communication

Passive-aggressive communication is a style where individuals seem passive on the surface but express anger in subtle, indirect, or behind-the-scenes ways.[77] People who communicate this way often feel powerless, stuck, and resentful. They struggle to deal directly with the source of their resentment and instead choose to undermine others in subtle ways.

Signs of Passive-Aggressive Communication:

a. Using sarcasm or making subtle digs
b. Procrastinating or intentionally being inefficient
c. Giving the silent treatment or sulking
d. Denying anger while acting out
e. Making vague or ambiguous statements that have hidden meanings

How Does Passive-Aggressive Communication Affect You and Your Relationships?

- **You become alienated from others**: Passive-aggressive behavior pushes people away. When you communicate indirectly, it confuses and frustrates others. They may start to avoid interacting with you because they don't know where they stand or how you truly feel.
- **You feel stuck and powerless**: By not addressing issues directly, you remain in a position of powerlessness. Instead of resolving conflicts, you keep them alive, which can make you feel even more stuck and resentful.
- **Resentment builds up**: Passive-aggressive communication allows you to discharge some of your resentment, but it doesn't solve the underlying issues. Because real problems are never addressed, you don't grow or mature emotionally. This keeps you in a cycle of anger and frustration.

Example: The passive-aggressive partner might sigh dramatically and say, "Oh, well, surprise me then," or simply not respond at all, leaving their partner to guess their true feelings.

---

77. Wilson, C. (2017, 11 21). Communication Style. Retrieved from *The Better You Institute*: https://thebetteryouinstitute.com/2017/11/21/communication-style-2/

THE FOUR STYLES OF COMMUNICATION

Assertive Communication

Assertive communication is when you clearly state your opinions and feelings and firmly advocate for your rights and needs without violating the rights of others.[78] Assertive individuals value themselves, their time, and their emotional, spiritual, and physical needs. They are strong advocates for themselves while being very respectful of the rights of others.

Signs of Assertive Communication:

a. Clearly stating needs and wants in a respectful manner
b. Expressing feelings appropriately and respectfully
c. Using "I" statements to convey personal thoughts and feelings
d. Showing respect for others
e. Listening well without interrupting
f. Maintaining good eye contact
g. Speaking in a calm and clear tone
h. Having a relaxed body posture

How Does Assertive Communication Affect You and Your Relationships?

- **You feel connected to others**: When you communicate assertively, you create an open and honest environment. This allows for deeper connections and understanding in your relationships, making you feel more connected to the people around you.
- **You feel in control of your life**: Assertive communication helps you take charge of your life. By expressing your needs and wants clearly, you can navigate situations more effectively and feel more in control.
- **You address issues as they arise**: Being assertive means tackling problems head-on. This approach helps you mature and grow emotionally because you're not avoiding conflicts or letting issues fester. You handle things as they come, which leads to personal growth.

78. Wilson, C. (2017, 11 21). Communication Style. Retrieved from *The Better You Institute*: https://thebetteryouinstitute.com/2017/11/21/communication-style-2/

THE CARE METHOD

- **You create a respectful environment**: Assertive communication fosters a respectful environment where everyone's rights and needs are considered. This respectful atmosphere encourages others to grow and mature as well, leading to healthier and more functional relationships.
- **You create a functional household**: In a household where assertive communication is practiced, everyone feels heard and respected. This leads to a more harmonious and cooperative living environment, where issues are addressed promptly and effectively.

Example: The assertive communicator might say, "I'd love to have Thai food tonight, but I'm open to other suggestions. What are you in the mood for?"

Verbal Versus Nonverbal Aspects of Communication Styles

	Verbal	**Nonverbal**
Passive	• Apologetic or self-deprecating language • Indirect speech • Hesitant	• Avoiding eye contact • Nervous gestures, such as fidgeting • Closed body language, such as crossed arms
Aggressive	• Loud and demanding tone • Use of "you" statements to blame others, like "You always" or "You never" • Harsh, critical, or insulting language	• Intimidating body language • Angry facial expressions, such as scowling or glaring
Passive-aggressive	• Sarcasm or backhanded compliments • Indirect hints rather than direct statements • Negative tone masked by polite words • Ambiguous or evasive responses	• Facial expressions that do not match the words spoken, such as smiling while being upset • Avoiding direct confrontation while subtly undermining others • Rolling eyes or sighing
Assertive	• Clear and direct statements • Use of "I" statements to express feelings and needs, such as "I feel" or "I need" • Respectful and positive language	• Consistent and appropriate eye contact • Relaxed and open posture • Calm and steady tone of voice • Confident body language

THE FOUR STYLES OF COMMUNICATION

Homework

1. At the end of each day over the course of the next week, take an honest assessment (provide examples) of how often you find yourself using each style of communication.

2. Assess the impact each style had on your ability to communicate effectively.

3. Which style did you use most often over the course of the week?

4. As you reflect on these styles of communication, what did you observe about how your use of styles changed throughout the day and the course of the week?

THE CARE METHOD

5. What are you now more aware of about styles of communication and how you use them?

____

____

____

____

____

6. Now that you have observed your patterns, what is your dominant style of communication?

____

____

____

____

____

7. What do you want to change about your style of communication to move you away from abusive ways of communicating?

____

____

____

____

____

17

Responsible Parenting

"Live so that when your children think of fairness,
caring, and integrity, they think of you."

—H. Jackson Brown Jr.

Parenting is a profound responsibility that shapes not only the lives of children but also the dynamics of relationships. In this chapter, clients are introduced to the principles of responsible parenting, exploring how their role as a parent profoundly affects their children and their children's interactions with others. The aim is to encourage clients to reflect on the significance of modeling healthy behaviors and creating a nurturing environment. This chapter also guides clients in recognizing how past abusive or unhealthy patterns may have influenced their parenting approach, offering a pathway toward positive change.

You will guide clients in understanding the long-term effects that abusive or neglectful parenting can have on children, including the potential for perpetuating cycles of trauma and violence. Encourage clients to think critically about the values they want to instill in their children and how their behavior—whether positive or negative—shapes their child's emotional and psychological development.

As a counselor, your role is to support clients as they explore the ways in which their actions, particularly any abusive tendencies, may have impacted their parenting. Help them recognize that change is not only possible but essential for breaking cycles of dysfunction and fostering a healthy, supportive environment for their children. By fostering an open dialogue, you can help clients identify strategies for positive parenting and improving family dynamics.

Encourage full engagement with the exercises in this chapter, which are designed to promote self-awareness and provide practical tools for clients to shift toward more responsible and constructive parenting methods. It is essential to approach this material with empathy and a non-judgmental stance, as clients may feel defensive or ashamed when discussing their parenting. Use this opportunity to cultivate a safe space where clients can reflect honestly on their behaviors and begin making meaningful changes.

Goals of This Chapter

Responsible parenting is the foundation for raising emotionally healthy children. The chapter highlights the importance of creating a safe, nurturing environment for children while emphasizing the responsibilities parents have in fostering their children's emotional and physical well-being.

Clients are encouraged to reflect on their own upbringing and parenting styles, particularly examining how past behaviors—both positive and negative—may have affected their children. The aim is to provide clients with the tools and awareness needed to shift toward healthier parenting practices that promote stability, love, and positive role modeling.

By focusing on support, discipline, involvement, and responsibility, clients are invited to rethink their approach to parenting and assess how their actions influence their children's long-term development. This chapter plays a crucial role in the CARE Method, as it helps clients align their parenting behaviors with core values that prioritize the child's well-being.

Colorado DVOMB Standards Competencies

Chapter 17 aligns with the Colorado Domestic Violence Offender Management Board (DVOMB) standards, emphasizing **parental responsibility**, **accountability for behavior**, and **intergenerational patterns**. It highlights the crucial role clients play as parents and the impact their behaviors have on their children. The DVOMB stresses the importance of creating a safe and nurturing environment, encouraging clients to reflect on how their actions influence their children's development and understanding of relationships. By acknowledging their responsibility, clients can strive to be positive role models, fostering a home environment that prioritizes safety and emotional well-being.

Accountability for behavior is central to this chapter, challenging clients to take full ownership of their actions, especially in their parenting role. Recognizing the negative effects of abusive behaviors on children is crucial in breaking the cycle of violence. By confronting these behaviors and committing to change, clients can make amends and establish healthier patterns that support their children's growth.

Intergenerational patterns are also a key focus, guiding clients to explore how their upbringing has influenced their parenting style and relationship dynamics. Understanding these patterns empowers clients to break the cycle of abuse and dysfunction, creating a legacy of positive, nonviolent interactions for their children. This chapter is fundamental to the CARE Method, equipping clients to foster healthier relationships and create a nurturing environment for their families, ultimately promoting long-term change.

Important Things to Know

Last week, we focused on the **four styles of communication**, helping clients understand how their communication patterns impact their relationships. This week, we shift focus to **responsible parenting**, guiding clients to reflect on the influence their parenting style has on their children's emotional and psychological well-being. Many clients may not fully realize how their actions as parents affect their children, especially in terms of modeling behaviors and setting the foundation for healthy relationships.

In this chapter, you'll encourage clients to think about how their upbringing and past experiences have shaped their parenting approach. Responsible parenting isn't just about providing basic needs—it's about creating a supportive and nurturing environment that helps children thrive. As clients work through this material, they'll explore ways to align their parenting practices with healthier values that promote positive development in their children.

Next week, we'll build on this by moving into **healthy conflict resolution**, helping clients recognize how unresolved conflicts in their relationships can affect both their partners and their children. This chapter on responsible parenting lays the groundwork for clients to reflect on their role in fostering emotional security for their families, leading to more constructive and positive family dynamics.

Key Concepts and Terminology

Responsible parenting: Responsible parenting involves nurturing the healthy development of children both physically and emotionally. It includes creating a safe and supportive environment, providing discipline, and being involved in a child's life. Responsible parenting also emphasizes the growth of the parent, encouraging self-awareness and emotional maturity.

Support: Providing consistent emotional and physical support is essential to helping children reach their full potential. Support involves being present and attentive, and encouraging your child's growth and exploration in a safe environment.

Discipline: Discipline in responsible parenting is about setting clear, consistent boundaries that align with family values. It is not about punishment but guiding children toward positive behavior and self-control.

Involvement: Active participation in a child's life, including attending events, getting to know their friends, and engaging in their interests. Involvement helps parents stay connected to their children's world and provide appropriate guidance.

Adverse childhood experiences (ACEs): ACEs refer to potentially traumatic events during childhood, such as abuse, neglect, or household dysfunction, which can have long-lasting effects on a child's physical and emotional health, and influence their future relationships.

Emotional security: Emotional security refers to a child's feeling of safety and stability within the family environment. It is built through consistent love, support, and healthy communication, which helps children develop self-confidence and a positive self-image.

Positive reinforcement: A key component of responsible parenting is focusing on positive behaviors and encouraging children with praise or rewards. Positive reinforcement helps build self-esteem and motivates children to repeat constructive actions.

Accountability: In the context of parenting, accountability means taking responsibility for one's actions and their effects on the family, especially in terms of how parenting styles affect a child's development.

Discussion Prompts

These prompts will guide thoughtful discussions to encourage self-reflection on the impact of parenting styles and the steps needed for growth.

Exploring parenting styles:

- Ask clients to reflect on how their communication style affects their parenting approach.
- **Discussion prompt**: "How do you think your current communication style influences your parenting? Are there areas where you notice a positive or negative impact on your children?"

Role of past experiences in parenting:

- Encourage clients to consider how their upbringing and past experiences shape their parenting behaviors.
- **Discussion prompt**: "How has your own childhood and the way you were raised influenced the way you parent your children? Are there patterns you recognize that you'd like to change?"

The importance of emotional support:

- Guide a discussion on the importance of providing emotional support and stability for children.
- **Discussion prompt**: "What do you believe are the most important emotional needs of your children? How do you currently meet those needs, and where might you improve?"

Addressing discipline:

- Discuss with clients how they approach discipline in their parenting and whether their methods align with responsible parenting principles.
- **Discussion prompt**: "What is your approach to discipline, and how do you ensure it fosters growth and self-control rather than fear or resentment?"

Breaking cycles of abuse:

- Help clients identify patterns of abusive or neglectful behaviors they might have inherited and wish to change.
- **Discussion prompt**: "Are there any behaviors or patterns from your past that you feel might negatively impact your children? How can you work toward breaking these cycles to foster healthier relationships?"

Modeling positive behaviors:

- Engage clients in a conversation about the importance of being a role model for their children.
- **Discussion prompt**: "What behaviors do you want to model for your children? How do you believe these behaviors will shape their development and relationships?"

Contents

Chapter 17: Responsible Parenting
What Is Responsible Parenting?
What Are Some Elements of Responsible Parenting?
Why Responsible Parenting Matters
How Does DV Impact Your Children?
Long-Term Effects
Can Children Recover from Witnessing IPV?
How Can You Help Your Own Children?
Homework

17

Responsible Parenting

"Neglectful parents can inflict more damage than any external enemy."

—Unknown

In the previous chapter, we discussed different styles of communication, which are very important. What most people don't realize is that their communication style can bleed into their parenting style and affect their children. Let's discuss this.

What Is Responsible Parenting?

Raising a child is an incredible journey. It is a mix of joy, challenges, and unconditional love. But what truly defines responsible parenting? At its core, responsible parenting serves a two-fold purpose. First, it's about nurturing the healthy development of your child, both physically and emotionally. It's providing a safe and supportive environment where they can learn, grow, and explore their potential. Second, responsible parenting is about growing and maturing as a parent. The challenges and rewards of raising a child push us to become more patient, understanding, and emotionally aware. This bond is complicated by its very nature and often reflects the values of previous generations.[79]

79. Lonczak, H.S. (2019, May 8). What is Positive Parenting? 33 Examples and Benefits. Retrieved from *Positive Psychology*: https://positivepsychology.com/positive-parenting/

THE CARE METHOD

What Are Some Elements of Responsible Parenting?

Responsible parenting isn't about achieving perfection. It's about creating a nurturing environment that fosters your child's healthy development and well-being. Here are some key elements that contribute to this foundation:[80]

- Support
- Discipline
- Involvement
- Responsibility
- Positive focus
- Love

Let's look at these elements more closely.

Support

Every child deserves support and attention. As a parent, it's important to be there for your child in various ways to help them reach their full potential. This means creating a safe space for them to share their dreams, their fears, and their emotions, encouraging their interests, and being present in their lives. In other words, it is giving them unwavering support to bring out the best in them.

Discipline

Discipline is an essential element of responsible parenting, but it should be approached thoughtfully. Effective discipline focuses on setting clear and consistent boundaries, ones that align with your family's values. The consequences should be age-appropriate, fair, and implemented consistently. Ultimately, the goal of discipline is to guide your child toward positive behavior and self-control, not to punish them.

Involvement

Being actively involved in your child's life goes beyond simply being physically present. Take a genuine interest in their activities, attend school events, and get to know their friends. Staying informed about their world allows you to offer relevant support and guidance.

80. Lonczak, H.S. (2019, May 8). What is Positive Parenting? 33 Examples and Benefits. Retrieved from *Positive Psychology*: https://positivepsychology.com/positive-parenting/

RESPONSIBLE PARENTING

Responsibility

Assigning age-appropriate chores and tasks is an essential part of responsible parenting. It teaches children valuable life skills like responsibility, time management, and the importance of contributing to the household. This not only helps around the house but also helps prepare children for adulthood and instills a strong work ethic.

Positive Focus

Children thrive on positive reinforcement. Focus on catching them doing good things, and acknowledge their positive behaviors with praise, encouragement, or small rewards. This approach motivates them to repeat positive actions and builds their self-esteem.

Love

Love is the foundation of responsible parenting. It's the driving force behind all the other elements we've discussed above. Parental love is providing unconditional and unwavering support, guidance, and a sense of security, no matter how the child acts. When children feel loved and accepted unconditionally, they develop a healthy sense of self-worth and the confidence to explore the world. Openly expressing love and affection builds emotional security and teaches children to be caring individuals themselves.

Why Responsible Parenting Matters

As a parent, you hold an incredibly important role in your children's lives. You are their most valuable asset, and your good character and generous care are critical to their development. Understanding why responsible parenting matters can help you appreciate the profound impact you have on your child's future. You are the primary influence on your child's development. From teaching them right from wrong to providing emotional support, your actions and interactions shape their character and values. Your child looks to you for guidance, love, and security. By being a responsible parent, you set a positive example and create a stable environment where they can thrive.

There is an important term in psychology called "adverse childhood experiences" (ACEs), which are potentially traumatic events that occur in childhood.[81] These experiences can have a tremendous impact on a child's future health, opportunities, and well-being. ACEs include things like abuse,

81. CDC. (2024, April 9). Adverse Childhood Experiences (ACEs). Retrieved from Centers for Disease Control and Prevention: https://www.cdc.gov/aces/about/index.html

THE CARE METHOD

neglect, and household dysfunction. These negative experiences can leave lasting scars and lead to chronic health conditions, risky behaviors, and difficulties in forming healthy relationships.[82]

The effects of ACEs can vary widely, but there's no doubt that they can have a lasting impact on a child's life. Children who experience abuse or neglect often carry these wounds into adulthood, affecting their mental and physical health.[82] They may struggle with chronic conditions, engage in risky behaviors, or find it hard to connect with others. As a responsible parent, you aim to protect your child from these harmful experiences and provide a safe and nurturing environment.

Responsible parenting isn't about being perfect. You will make mistakes and have regrets—every parent does. The key is to strive to do your best, interact positively with your child, and respond to their daily needs. In other words, you should have your child's best interests at heart and make a genuine effort to support their growth and well-being.

Why do you think responsible parenting is important?

How Does DV Impact Your Children?

Domestic violence (DV) creates a toxic environment that extends far beyond the immediate conflict between partners. Children living in homes with DV are exposed to significant emotional and psychological harm, even if they are not directly involved in the abuse. Here's how DV can impact children at different stages of development:[83]

82. CDC. (2024, April 9). Adverse Childhood Experiences (ACEs). Retrieved from Centers for Disease Control and Prevention: https://www.cdc.gov/aces/about/index.html

83. NCTSN. (2024). Effects. Retrieved from The National Child Traumatic Stress Network: https://www.nctsn.org/what-is-child-trauma/trauma-types/intimate-partner-violence/effects#:~:text=Despite%20the%20high%20occurrence%20of,in%20the%20aftermath%20of%20IPV.

RESPONSIBLE PARENTING

Preschool-Aged Children (Up to 5 Years Old)

- **Regression**: Young children who witness DV might regress in their development, exhibiting behaviors like bedwetting, thumb-sucking, and increased crying.
- **Sleep disturbances**: Difficulty falling asleep, frequent night terrors, and separation anxiety are common.
- **Fear and withdrawal**: They may become withdrawn, exhibit signs of fear like stuttering or hiding, and constantly feel on guard, worrying about the next outburst.

School-Aged Children (6-12 Years Old)

- **Self-blame and guilt**: Children in this age group might develop feelings of guilt and blame themselves for the abuse, believing they caused it in some way.
- **Academic and social struggles**: They may experience difficulty concentrating in school, leading to lower grades and decreased participation in activities. Social interactions might become challenging, leading to fewer friendships and increased isolation.
- **Physical manifestations**: Stress and anxiety from the abusive environment can manifest as frequent headaches and stomachaches.

Teenagers (13-18 Years Old)

- **Acting out**: Teens may express their internal struggles through negative behaviors like fighting with family members, skipping school, or engaging in risky activities.
- **Substance abuse and self-destructive behaviors**: To cope with the trauma, they might turn to alcohol, drugs, or risky sexual behavior.
- **Relationship issues**: Low self-esteem and difficulty trusting others can lead to problems forming healthy relationships, both romantic and platonic. They might become aggressive or withdrawn in social interactions.
- **Increased risk of future violence**: Teens exposed to DV are more likely to become perpetrators or victims of violence in their future relationships.

THE CARE METHOD

What are some ways you think children can react differently to DV? Have you experienced this or do you know of a child who has experienced this?

Long-Term Effects

The impact of domestic violence on children extends far beyond their immediate experiences. With more than 15 million children in the United States living in homes where domestic violence has occurred at least once, the long-term effects are significant and concerning.

Children who grow up witnessing domestic violence are at a greater risk of repeating the cycle of abuse as adults.[84] This can manifest in two (2) ways:

1. **Becoming abusers**: For example, boys who see their mothers being abused are ten (10) times more likely to abuse their own female partners in adulthood.
2. **Becoming victims**: For example, girls who grow up in abusive homes are more than six (6) times as likely to be sexually abused compared to those from non-abusive homes.

Witnessing or being a victim of domestic violence can lead to various mental health problems that persist into adulthood such as depression, anxiety, and PTSD. The stress and trauma can also manifest as physical health problems such as diabetes, obesity, and heart disease, among other things.

84. NCTSN. (2024). Effects. Retrieved from The National Child Traumatic Stress Network: https://www.nctsn.org/what-is-child-trauma/trauma-types/intimate-partner-violence/effects#:~:text=Despite%20the%20high%20occurrence%20of,in%20the%20aftermath%20of%20IPV

RESPONSIBLE PARENTING

Can Children Recover From Witnessing IPV?

Children can recover from witnessing domestic violence (DV) or intimate partner violence (IPV), though it will vary depending on the child and the circumstances.[85] Several factors influence how well a child can recover from witnessing IPV:

- A good support system or good relationships with trusted adults
- An effective mental health professional
- High natural self-esteem
- Healthy friendships

Although children may never forget the violence they witnessed or experienced, they can learn healthy ways to deal with their emotions and memories. With the right support and interventions, children can process their experiences and build coping mechanisms that will serve them well into adulthood.

The sooner a child receives help, the better their chances of recovery. Early intervention can include therapy, counseling, and support groups. These resources can help children understand their emotions, develop healthy coping strategies, and build resilience. Seeking help as soon as possible increases a child's chances of becoming a healthy adult.

How Can You Help Your Own Children?

Help them feel safe. Children who witness or experience domestic violence need to feel safe. Consider whether leaving the abusive relationship might help your child feel safer.[86] Talk to your child about the importance of healthy relationships.

Talk to them about their fears. Let them know that it's not their fault or your fault. You can learn more about how to talk to your child about domestic violence by visiting the National Child Traumatic Stress Network's website.[87]

---

85. NCTSN. (2024). Effects. Retrieved from The National Child Traumatic Stress Network: https://www.nctsn.org/what-is-child-trauma/trauma-types/intimate-partner-violence/effects#:~:text=Despite%20the%20high%20occurrence%20of,in%20the%20aftermath%20of%20IPV

86. Office of the Assistant Secretary for Health (OASH). (2021, February 15). Leaving an abusive relationship. Retrieved from OASH: https://www.womenshealth.gov/relationships-and-safety/domestic-violence/leaving-abusive-relationship

87. NCTSN. (2015). Children and Domestic Violence: Listening and Talking to Your Child About Domestic Violence. Retrieved from The National Child Traumatic Stress Network: https://www.nctsn.org/resources/children-and-domestic-violence-listening-and-talking-your-child-about-domestic-violence

THE CARE METHOD

Talk to them about healthy relationships. Help them learn from the abusive experience by talking about what healthy relationships are and are not. This will help them know what is healthy when they start romantic relationships of their own.

Talk to them about boundaries. Let your child know that no one has the right to touch them or make them feel uncomfortable, including family members, teachers, coaches, or other authority figures. Also, explain to your child that he or she doesn't have the right to touch another person's body, and if someone tells them to stop, they should do so right away.

Help them find a reliable support system. In addition to a parent, this can be a school counselor, a therapist, or another trusted adult who can provide ongoing support. Know that school counselors are required to report domestic violence or abuse if they suspect it.

Get them professional help. Cognitive behavioral therapy (CBT) is a type of talk therapy or counseling that may work best for children who have experienced violence or abuse. CBT is especially helpful for children who have anxiety or other mental health problems as a result of the trauma.[88] During CBT, a therapist will work with your child to turn negative thoughts into more positive ones. The therapist can also help your child learn healthy ways to cope with stress.[88]

88. Office of the Assistant Secretary for Health (OASH). (2021, February 15). Effects of domestic violence on children. Retrieved from OASH: https://www.womenshealth.gov/relationships-and-safety/domestic-violence/effects-domestic-violence-children

RESPONSIBLE PARENTING

Homework

1. Based on what you learned in this chapter, if you are a father, stepfather, or guardian, identify and explain your **strengths and weaknesses** as a parent.

____

____

____

____

____

2. Explain your **challenges** and **successes** with co-parenting.

____

____

____

____

____

3. In what ways have your own patterns of abusive behaviors affected the children in your life?

____

____

____

____

____

____

THE CARE METHOD

4. What is your plan to end the cycle of violence for your children's generation?

5. As you reflect on your own upbringing, what were some of the things your parents struggled with when raising you?

6. How do you feel the adverse experiences you endured as a child contributed to your attachment style in intimate relationships?

18

Healthy Conflict Resolution

"The aim of argument, or of discussion, should not be victory, but progress."

—Joseph Joubert

Conflict is an unavoidable aspect of human relationships, but how it is handled can make all the difference. In this chapter, clients are introduced to the principles of healthy conflict resolution, a crucial skill for nurturing both intimate relationships and responsible parenting. This chapter aims to convey that while disagreements are inevitable, the approach to resolving them can either fortify or undermine the connections we value most.

You will guide clients in recognizing that conflict goes beyond simple disagreements—it stems from deeper clashes of values, needs, or perspectives. When unresolved, these conflicts can lead to negative emotional patterns, communication breakdowns, and even the potential for intimate partner violence (IPV). Clients will learn that avoiding conflict can be as harmful as engaging in it destructively, as both behaviors contribute to unresolved tensions and resentment.

As a counselor, your role is to help clients explore their conflict resolution styles and reflect on how these approaches have impacted their relationships in the past. Some clients may tend to avoid conflict entirely, while others may engage in competitive, win-lose dynamics. It is essential to provide space for clients to examine these patterns and encourage them to adopt healthier strategies, such as collaboration and compromise.

Encourage full participation in the exercises, which will focus on skills like active listening, using "I" statements, and setting boundaries during disagreements. This chapter is designed to promote emotional self-regulation and to teach clients the value of resolving conflicts in a manner that fosters mutual understanding rather than resentment or escalation.

As you facilitate, be mindful of clients' potential resistance, particularly those who may struggle with the idea of vulnerability in conflict. Foster an empathetic and supportive environment, helping clients see that healthy conflict resolution is not about winning or losing but about maintaining respect and empathy within their relationships.

Goals of This Chapter

Healthy conflict resolution can be the key to stronger, more balanced relationships. While conflict is inevitable in any relationship, the way it is handled can significantly affect relationship dynamics, emotional well-being, and the potential for violence. This chapter emphasizes the importance of effective communication, empathy, and compromise as essential components in resolving disagreements without resorting to abusive or harmful behaviors.

Clients are encouraged to reflect on their past experiences with conflict, examining how their conflict resolution styles—whether avoidance, aggression, or manipulation—may have contributed to negative outcomes in their relationships. The aim of this chapter is to help clients replace these destructive patterns with healthier methods of managing disagreements and fostering mutual respect, understanding, and growth in their relationships.

By focusing on communication strategies, boundary-setting, and emotional regulation, clients are invited to rethink how they approach conflict and how they can use it as an opportunity for strengthening their relationships rather than weakening them. This chapter is essential to the CARE Method, as it helps clients develop skills that promote healthier relationships and prevent the escalation of conflict into abusive situations.

Colorado DVOMB Standards Competencies

Chapter 18 aligns with the Colorado Domestic Violence Offender Management Board (DVOMB) standards, emphasizing **accountability/responsibility** and **insight and empathy**. This chapter underscores the importance of taking full responsibility for one's actions and understanding their impact on others. Clients are encouraged to confront their behaviors directly, acknowledging the harm caused without resorting to denial or excuses. By taking ownership, they can begin making amends and lay the foundation for genuine change.

Insight and empathy are also central themes. Clients are guided to view their actions from the perspective of those they have affected, cultivating a deeper understanding of the emotional and psychological impact of their behavior. This shift fosters more compassionate and respectful interactions, motivating clients to change in ways that promote healing and nonviolence.

These standards are vital to the CARE Method's therapeutic goals, ensuring clients not only take responsibility for their actions but also develop the empathy necessary for meaningful change. By fostering insight into the effects of their behaviors and committing to accountability, clients can work toward healthier, more empathetic relationships.

Important Things to Know

Last week, we explored the concept of **responsible parenting**, helping clients reflect on their role as parents and the impact their behaviors have on their children. This week, we focus on **healthy conflict resolution**, a vital skill that affects both intimate partner relationships and parenting. How clients handle conflict not only influences their relationships with partners but also sets an example for their children, impacting future generations.

In this chapter, you'll help clients understand the different conflict styles and how unresolved conflicts can lead to destructive patterns in relationships. Many clients may have avoided conflict in the past, or they might have resorted to aggressive communication. The goal is to guide them toward healthier conflict resolution strategies that prioritize communication, empathy, and mutual respect.

Next week, we will dive deeper into **neuroplasticity and relationships**, helping clients understand how their brain's ability to form new pathways can aid in creating healthier relationships. This chapter on healthy conflict resolution sets the foundation for clients to understand that conflict, when handled constructively, can lead to personal growth and stronger, more respectful relationships.

Key Concepts and Terminology

Conflict: Conflict refers to a clash of needs, values, or perspectives that can lead to frustration, anger, or resentment. It can be expressed verbally or nonverbally and can be open or passive. In relationships, conflict is inevitable, but when handled constructively, it can lead to personal growth and a deeper understanding between partners.

Conflict avoidance: A conflict style where individuals prefer to avoid engaging in conflicts, often leading to unresolved issues that can build resentment and weaken relationships over time.

Conflict styles: The different approaches people use to handle conflict. These include competing, avoiding, compromising, accommodating, and collaborating. Each style reflects a different way of addressing or avoiding disagreements, and understanding these can help individuals navigate conflict more effectively.

Emotional reactivity: The tendency to respond emotionally during conflicts, which can cloud judgment and lead to unproductive conversations. Managing emotional reactivity is key to resolving conflict constructively.

Healthy conflict resolution: The process of resolving disagreements in a way that fosters mutual respect, communication, and understanding. Healthy conflict resolution reduces stress, strengthens relationships, and prevents resentment.

Power imbalances: A situation in which one partner holds more control or authority in a relationship, which can exacerbate conflicts and lead to unhealthy dynamics.

Active listening: A communication skill where individuals fully concentrate, understand, and respond thoughtfully during conversations, especially in conflicts. Active listening ensures that all parties feel heard and understood.

Discussion Prompts

These prompts will facilitate deep reflection and thoughtful discussion, encouraging clients to examine their conflict styles and how they approach disagreements in relationships.

Understanding conflict:

- Help clients define what conflict means to them and how they typically respond to disagreements.
- **Discussion prompt**: "How do you typically react when conflict arises in your relationships? What emotions do you experience during these conflicts?"

Conflict styles:

- Encourage clients to reflect on their conflict resolution styles and how these impact their relationships.
- **Discussion prompt**: "What is your conflict style? Do you tend to avoid conflict, become aggressive, or seek compromise? How has this affected your relationships?"

The role of unresolved conflict:

- Discuss with clients the impact unresolved conflicts can have on their relationships and emotional well-being.
- **Discussion prompt**: "Think about a time when a conflict in your relationship was left unresolved. How did it affect your connection with the other person, and what were the long-term consequences?"

Healthy conflict resolution techniques:

- Explore healthy ways to resolve conflicts and the importance of mutual respect and communication.
- **Discussion prompt**: "What strategies can you use to approach conflict in a healthy way? How do you think these strategies could improve your relationships moving forward?"

Modeling conflict resolution for children:

- Guide clients in thinking about how their approach to conflict affects their children.
- **Discussion prompt**: "How do you think your children view conflict, based on what they see in your relationships? What behaviors would you like to model for them in terms of handling disagreements?"

Overcoming barriers to conflict resolution:

- Help clients identify barriers to resolving conflicts, such as pride, emotional reactivity, or fear of vulnerability.
- **Discussion prompt**: "What personal barriers do you face when trying to resolve conflicts? How can you work on overcoming these barriers to promote healthier communication?"

Contents

Chapter 18: Healthy Conflict Resolution
What Is Conflict?
The Impact of Conflict on Relationships
Common Conflict Styles
Why Healthy Conflict Resolution Matters
Strategies for Healthy Conflict Resolution
Barriers That Hinder Healthy Conflict Resolution
Homework

18

Healthy Conflict Resolution

"Conflict forces us to be fully present because it shatters our ego—stripping away all hope of escape or sugarcoating. It removes everything that is nonessential to our authentic being; it removes all superficial layers.

—Alison Hutchinson

We covered responsible parenting in chapter 16, and something we touched on but didn't go into detail about is how to handle conflict as partners. Healthy conflict resolution is a big part of responsible parenting because what you model for your kids is what they will eventually model for future generations. However, it is also vital for your relationship as partners.

What Is Conflict?

Conflict goes beyond simple disagreements. It's the clash of underlying needs, values, or perspectives that can lead to frustration, anger, or resentment. It can be verbal or nonverbal, expressed openly or passively. While conflict can be unpleasant, it doesn't have to be destructive. In fact, when handled constructively, conflict can lead to a stronger relationship, personal growth, and generally a better understanding of each other as partners.[89]

89. Sutton, J. (2021, November 9). Conflict Resolution in Relationships & Couples: 5 Strategies. Retrieved from *Positive Psychology*: https://positivepsychology.com/conflict-resolution-relationships/

THE CARE METHOD

The Impact of Unresolved Conflict on Relationships

Unresolved conflict can be detrimental to your relationships because it is a breeding ground for negativity. Rather than addressing issues constructively, unresolved conflicts tend to perpetuate destructive patterns of behavior and communication. These patterns become ingrained in the relationship, making it increasingly difficult to break free from negative cycles. It is sort of like slow poison. It can easily be forgotten as you ingest it in small quantities until it eventually builds up. Over time, this buildup of negativity can escalate into larger conflicts that eventually destroy the relationship.

Unresolved conflict is most often a result of conflict avoidance, which can impact a relationship in many ways including:[90]

- Stir up negative emotions such as resentment, anger, and frustration
- Cause a communication breakdown between you and your partner
- Damage trust and intimacy
- Create power imbalances
- Heighten stress and anxiety
- Result in intimate partner violence (IPV) (worst case scenario)

Reflect on a time you and your partner had an unresolved conflict. How did it affect you personally?

90. Wright, S.A. (2022, March 11). How Conflict Avoidance Can Impact a Relationship. Retrieved from *Psych Central*: https://psychcentral.com/blog/how-conflict-avoidance-can-impact-a-relationship

HEALTHY CONFLICT RESOLUTION

How did it affect your relationship?

Common Conflict Styles

Just as people have unique personalities, they also have preferred styles for dealing with disagreements. Understanding these common styles can help you navigate conflict more effectively with your partner. There are five (5) types of conflict styles that are defined in the Thomas Kilmann Conflict Mode Instrument (TKI) assessment, namely (USCG, 2020):[91]

1. **Competing**: This person takes a "win-lose" approach. They prioritize their needs and desires above their partner's and may use assertive or even aggressive communication to get their way.
2. **Avoiding**: This person dislikes conflict and may withdraw from arguments or shut down communication entirely. They might try to downplay the issue or change the subject.
3. **Compromising**: This person seeks a middle ground, willing to concede some points to reach a solution that satisfies both parties to some degree.
4. **Accommodating**: This person prioritizes harmony and may sacrifice their own needs to keep the peace. They might readily agree with their partner to avoid conflict.
5. **Collaborating**: This person seeks a win-win solution. They value open communication and work with their partner to understand each other's needs and find a solution that works for both.

91. United States Coast Guard (USCG). (2020, January 16). 5 Types of Conflict Styles. Retrieved from United States Coast Guard: https://www.uscg.mil/Portals/0/seniorleadership/chaplain/5%20Types%20of%20Conflict%20Styles.pdf?ver=2020-01-16-150312-237

THE CARE METHOD

What is your conflict style and how does this style help or hinder progress when it comes to conflict resolution in your relationships?

Why Healthy Conflict Resolution Matters

Effective conflict resolution is important in every relationship for several reasons, such as the following:

- Strengthens relationships
- Improves effective communication
- Reduces stress
- Builds trust
- Prevents resentment

Strategies for Healthy Conflict Resolution

Effective conflict resolution requires a combination of skills and strategies.[92] Here are some practical steps to resolve conflicts in a healthy and constructive manner:[93]

- **Pick your battles**: Not every disagreement needs to be a full-blown argument. Learn to identify issues worth addressing and let go of minor ones.

92. Gillette, H. (2022, March 29). 6 Conflict Resolution Tips for Couples. Retrieved from *Psych Central*: https://psychcentral.com/relationships/conflict-resolution-in-relationships

93. Pace, R. (2023, June 14). Types of Conflict in Relationships and How to Deal With Them. Retrieved from *Marriage.com*: https://www.marriage.com/advice/relationship/types-of-conflict/

HEALTHY CONFLICT RESOLUTION

- **Stay calm and collected**: Emotions can run high during conflicts which makes it difficult to think clearly and communicate effectively. Taking a moment to breathe and calm down can help prevent the situation from escalating any further. If necessary, take a break and return to the conversation when both of you are more composed.
- **Active listening**: Active listening involves fully concentrating on what the other person is saying, without interrupting or planning your response while they are speaking. Show that you are listening by nodding, maintaining eye contact, and summarizing what you've heard. For example, "It sounds like you're upset because I forgot our plans."
- **Use "I" statements**: Express your feelings and needs using "I" statements. This helps avoid accusatory language and keeps the focus on how the situation affects you (e.g., "I feel hurt when you . . . " instead of, "You always . . . ").
- **Focus on the issue, not the person**: It's important to separate the person from the problem. Avoid personal attacks, bringing up the past, and name-calling. Stay focused on the specific issue at hand and what needs to be resolved.
- **Set boundaries and ground rules**: Establishing boundaries and ground rules for discussing conflicts can prevent conversations from becoming hostile. Agree on basic rules such as no yelling, no interrupting, and taking breaks if emotions run too high. You should tailor these ground rules to what works best for you and your partner.
- **Seek common ground**: Identify areas that you both agree on and build on them. Finding common ground can create a sense of shared purpose and make it easier to work toward a solution. For example, "We both want what's best for our child, so let's discuss how we can co-parent effectively."
- **Agree to disagree**: Sometimes, it may not be possible to reach a complete agreement. In such cases, it's okay to agree to disagree and respect each other's viewpoints. The key is to maintain respect and continue to work together constructively. This will often lead to the last point below.
- **Seek mediation or professional help**: When you cannot arrive at a common ground, professional help from a mediator or therapist is always the best way to go. A professional will guide you to a resolution by offering a different perspective and strategies that you can employ to arrive at this resolution.

THE CARE METHOD

Barriers That Hinder Healthy Conflict Resolution

Even if you have the best intentions, navigating conflict can be tricky. While healthy conflict resolution is crucial for maintaining strong and positive relationships, various barriers can hinder this process. These barriers can stem from personal habits, emotional responses, communication styles, and external factors. Understanding these barriers is the first step toward overcoming them and improving how you handle conflicts.

Let's look at some common barriers that can hinder healthy conflict resolution:[94]

- **Emotional reactivity**: When emotions run high, it's easy to get defensive, blameful, or even shut down. This can cloud our judgment and make it difficult to have a rational conversation.
- **Poor communication skills**: Lack of active listening, unclear communication, and resorting to accusatory language can all derail a productive discussion.
- **Focus on winning**: If one or both partners see conflict as a competition to be "right," it becomes harder to find solutions that benefit everyone. This win-lose mentality can lead to resentment and further conflict.
- **Unidentified underlying issues**: Conflict often stems from deeper issues that haven't been addressed. Ignoring these underlying issues, like unmet needs or past hurts, can prevent a true resolution from occurring.
- **External pressures**: External factors like stress, financial problems, or family issues can exacerbate conflict and make it harder to focus on resolving the issue at hand.
- **Unwillingness to compromise**: Sometimes, both partners are unwilling to budge from their positions. This rigidity makes it difficult to find solutions that address everyone's needs.

94. Crestcom. (2020, May 13). 6 Conflict Resolution Barriers. Retrieved from *Crestcom*: https://crestcom.com/blog/2020/05/13/6-conflict-resolution-barriers-2/

HEALTHY CONFLICT RESOLUTION

Homework

1. Think about a recent conflict you experienced in a relationship. Did it go unresolved? What was the impact this had on you and your partner?

2. What would you say is your predominant conflict style? How can you improve it?

THE CARE METHOD

3. Reflect on your own emotional state during the conflict. Did your emotions hinder your ability to communicate effectively? How could you have managed your emotions differently?

4. What strategies can you use moving forward to resolve conflict in a healthier way?

19

Neuroplasticity and Relationships

"The brain is the most flexible thing in the universe. Neuroplasticity proves that we are not hardwired; we can change our minds and, by doing so, change our lives."

—Dr. Joe Dispenza

The brain's incredible ability to adapt and reshape itself lies at the heart of healing and growth. In this chapter, clients will delve into the concept of neuroplasticity—the brain's capacity to form new neural pathways in response to experiences. This chapter focuses on how the brain can change, particularly in the aftermath of trauma, and the profound impact these changes can have on relationships. Clients will discover that while past experiences, including abuse and violence, have the power to shape behavior, neuroplasticity offers a hopeful path for transformation and recovery, enabling the formation of healthier, more supportive relationship patterns.

As a counselor, you will guide clients through the concept that repeated behaviors, whether positive or negative, form strong neural pathways in the brain. For clients who have engaged in harmful or abusive behaviors, the goal is to help them understand that these patterns can be altered over time with effort and consistent practice of healthier behaviors.

Encourage clients to reflect on past behaviors that have caused harm in their relationships and explore how these may have been ingrained through neuroplasticity. Your role is to help them recognize that while certain reactions may feel automatic or difficult to change, the brain is capable of creating new pathways that support healthier responses, such as emotional regulation and empathy. This chapter will also help clients see the connection between trauma and their current relationship patterns, offering tools to begin the process of change.

Through exercises and discussions, support clients in identifying specific behaviors they wish to change. Highlight the importance of consistency and mindfulness in rewiring the brain toward more constructive and empathetic responses. Encourage clients to engage with the material fully, reinforcing the idea that change is both possible and empowering.

As you facilitate the sessions for this chapter, it's essential to create an open and non-judgmental environment where clients feel safe discussing their struggles with past behaviors. Help them see that, although challenging, they have the power to reshape their future relationships by rewiring their brain through neuroplasticity.

Goals of This Chapter

The brain's ability to change and adapt can be a powerful tool for personal growth. Understanding neuroplasticity empowers clients to realize that past behaviors and reactions—especially those rooted in trauma—are not permanent. With effort, clients have the potential to change, leading to healthier relationships and improved emotional regulation.

Clients are encouraged to reflect on how their brain's wiring may have been shaped by past negative experiences, including abusive or unhealthy relationships. The aim of this chapter is to help clients develop the self-awareness needed to identify ingrained patterns and work on replacing them with healthier, more constructive behaviors. By focusing on the brain's capacity for growth and healing, this chapter offers hope and a clear path toward building healthier relationships.

Through the exploration of neuroplasticity, clients learn that emotional regulation and pro-social activities can strengthen positive neural pathways, reinforcing healthy habits and interpersonal skills. This chapter is crucial to the CARE Method, as it provides clients with the foundational understanding that change is possible at any stage of life, no matter the challenges of the past.

Colorado DVOMB Standards Competencies

Chapter 19 aligns with the Colorado Domestic Violence Offender Management Board (DVOMB) standards on **past experiences/trauma**, **pro-social activities**, and **self-regulation**. The DVOMB emphasizes the importance of addressing the long-term effects of trauma on clients' emotional regulation and relational behaviors. By recognizing the impact of trauma, clients can start to take control of their actions and responses, opening up opportunities for healing and positive change.

The competencies in this chapter focus on helping clients acknowledge how past trauma has shaped their emotional and behavioral responses, particularly in stressful or conflict-driven situations. Encouraging clients to engage in pro-social activities, which promote positive interactions and emotional growth, is another core aspect of this chapter. Additionally, self-regulation is emphasized as an essential skill that clients must develop to break the cycle of violence and create healthier relationships moving forward.

Important Things to Know

Last week, we explored the importance of **healthy conflict resolution**, emphasizing how managing conflicts constructively can prevent escalation and foster more positive relationships. This week, we turn to the fascinating concept of **neuroplasticity and its impact on relationships.** Neuroplasticity refers to the brain's ability to form new neural pathways and change its structure based on experiences, including past trauma. This chapter focuses on helping clients understand that while past negative patterns may feel entrenched, they can be rewired with new, healthier behaviors and thought patterns.

In this chapter, you'll guide clients through understanding how their past experiences, including trauma, have shaped their brain's responses and behaviors, particularly in relationships. The key takeaway for clients is that change is possible through conscious effort, emotional regulation, and the practice of new, constructive relationship patterns.

Next week, we will move into the topic of **accountability**, helping clients recognize how taking responsibility for their actions is crucial for sustainable, positive change. This chapter on neuroplasticity provides the scientific foundation that empowers clients to believe in the possibility of change and begin reshaping their relationships for the better.

Key Concepts and Terminology

Neuroplasticity: The brain's ability to reorganize itself by forming new neural connections throughout life. Neuroplasticity allows individuals to adapt to new situations and recover from past trauma by creating new, healthier neural pathways. This concept is crucial in understanding how individuals can shift away from abusive or destructive relationship patterns and develop healthier behaviors.

Neural pathways: These are the connections between neurons in the brain, formed through repeated behaviors and experiences. When an individual frequently engages in negative behaviors, such as aggression or avoidance, these pathways become reinforced. However, neuroplasticity allows new, positive pathways to be formed by consciously practicing healthier relationship behaviors.

Emotional regulation: This refers to the ability to manage and respond to emotions in a healthy and productive manner. Through neuroplasticity, individuals can learn to regulate their emotions better, replacing reactive and destructive patterns with calmer and more thoughtful responses in relationships.

Cognitive behavioral therapy (CBT): A therapeutic approach that helps individuals identify and modify negative thought patterns. CBT can help rewire the brain by promoting healthier ways of thinking and behaving, which ties into the principles of neuroplasticity by allowing individuals to create new patterns of thought and behavior.

Mental rehearsal: A technique used to create new neural pathways by mentally practicing positive behaviors or responses. For instance, by mentally rehearsing how to respond calmly in a conflict, individuals can help to reinforce those behaviors in real-life situations, facilitating change in relationships.

Discussion Prompts

The following prompts will encourage clients to explore how past behaviors have shaped their neural pathways and what steps they can take to form new, healthier habits.

Understanding neuroplasticity:

- Help clients reflect on how their past behaviors have shaped their brain's responses and relationship dynamics.
- **Discussion prompt**: "How have your past experiences and behaviors shaped your brain's responses in relationships? What patterns have you noticed, and how might neuroplasticity help you change them?"

Rewiring negative patterns:

- Encourage clients to think about the negative relationship habits they've developed and how they can begin to rewire those patterns.

- **Discussion prompt**: "What negative patterns in your relationships would you like to change? How can you use the concept of neuroplasticity to start rewiring these behaviors?"

Building healthy neural pathways:

- Guide clients to consider how practicing new, positive behaviors can create healthier neural connections.
- **Discussion prompt**: "What are some new behaviors you can practice to build healthier relationships? How do you think these new behaviors will strengthen positive neural pathways in your brain?"

Emotional regulation:

- Explore the connection between emotional regulation and neuroplasticity, helping clients understand the role of practicing emotional control.
- **Discussion prompt**: "How has emotional reactivity affected your relationships in the past? What strategies can you implement to regulate your emotions and create new, healthier responses?"

Long-term benefits of change:

- Discuss the long-term benefits of using neuroplasticity to reshape behavior and improve relationships.
- **Discussion prompt**: "What long-term benefits do you anticipate from rewiring your brain for healthier relationships? How do you think these changes will impact your emotional well-being and relationships moving forward?"

Contents

Chapter 19: Neuroplasticity and Relationships
What Is Neuroplasticity?
How Neuroplasticity Affects Emotional Regulation
The Impact of Domestic Violence on the Brain
Rewiring the Brain for Healthy Relationships
The Benefits of Neuroplasticity
Homework

19

Neuroplasticity and Relationships

"Any man could, if he were so inclined, be the sculptor of his own brain."

—Santiago Ramon y Cajal

Learning how to resolve conflict in a healthy manner is a vital skill for any type of relationship, and specifically romantic relationships. However, sometimes the problem isn't the inability to handle conflict in a healthy way but more the repetition of negative reactions and habits due to neural pathways that were formed by traumatic events in your past. Let us dive deeper into this.

What Is Neuroplasticity?

Neuroplasticity is your nervous system's ability to create new neural pathways and modify existing ones throughout your lifetime in response to both positive and negative stimuli.[95] Your brain can change and adapt in response to new experiences, new information, and even after trauma.

This means that the more you engage in any type of behavior, whether positive or negative, the deeper these neural pathways become ingrained into your brain. In other words, just like you can strengthen negative pathways, you can also weaken them and build new, healthier ones.

History

The idea that our brains can change and adapt throughout life is a relatively recent scientific discovery, at least in its current form. In the early 1900s, Santiago Ramón y Cajal, often referred to as the

95. Mateos-Aparicio, P., and Rodríguez-Moreno, A. The Impact of Studying Brain Plasticity. *Frontiers in Cellular Neuroscience, 13:66*, (2019, February 27). https://www.ncbi.nlm.nih.gov/pmc/articles/PMC6400842/; https://doi.org/10.3389/fncel.2019.00066

"father of neuroscience," observed remarkable differences in brain structure based on experience.[96] He saw intricate connections, or synapses, between neurons, suggesting the brain wasn't a static organ. In the mid-20th century, studies on brain injuries and stroke recovery demonstrated the brain's remarkable ability to rewire itself and compensate for lost function after trauma.[96]

The term "neuroplasticity" itself is a relatively recent invention. It's credited to Polish neuroscientist Jerzy Konorski in 1948.[96] Since then, the field of neuroplasticity has exploded. Advanced imaging techniques like MRIs allow us to see the brain actively changing in response to stimuli.[97] Scientists can now observe how the brain physically changes in response to learning, experiences, and even rehabilitation. We can now see evidence of new connections forming and existing ones strengthening with practice.

What all of this means is that neuroplasticity offers us hope and possibility. It shows that no matter what your past looks like, your brain has the capacity to change, and with it, your thoughts, behaviors, and interactions can change too. This means that the patterns of behavior that led to domestic violence can be altered, helping you build a more positive future that will be filled with healthy relationships.

How Neuroplasticity Affects Emotional Regulation

Emotional regulation is your ability to manage and respond to your emotions in a healthy way.[98] Neuroplasticity plays a big role here. Your brain is constantly learning from your experiences and the ways you handle emotions. Back in chapter 5, we talked about how repeated behaviors become ingrained in our brains, thus becoming automatic responses. This is actually neuroplasticity.

This means that when you experience positive interactions and practice healthy emotional responses, your brain strengthens those neural pathways. For example, learning to calm yourself when you feel anxious helps create strong neural pathways that support this behavior in the future.

96. Ackerman, C.E. (2018, July 25). What Is Neuroplasticity? A Psychologist Explains [+14 Tools]. Retrieved from *Positive Psychology*: https://positivepsychology.com/neuroplasticity/

97. Kays, J.L., Hurley, R.A., and Taber, K.H. The Dynamic Brain: Neuroplasticity and Mental Health. *The Journal of Neuropsychiatry and Clinical Neurosciences*, 24:2, 118-124 (2012, April 1). https://psychiatryonline.org/doi/full/10.1176/appi.neuropsych.12050109; https://doi.org/10.1176/appi.neuropsych.12050109

98. Lebow, H.I., and Casablanca, S.S. (2022, April 6). Do You Know How to Manage Your Emotions and Why It Matters? Retrieved from *Psych Central*: https://psychcentral.com/health/emotional-regulation

In the same way, if you've been in an environment where violence and aggression were common occurrences, your brain may have created strong neural pathways for those responses.

Take a moment and reflect on your life. What are some positive and negative neural pathways that have been created in your brain? (Think about your most common behaviors.)

The Impact of Domestic Violence on the Brain

Domestic violence doesn't just affect your relationships, it also has a profound impact on the brain. Throughout this workbook, you have learned that experiencing or witnessing violence can cause the brain to develop unhealthy patterns. This might mean heightened stress responses, difficulties with trusting people, and challenges in your emotional regulation. When the brain is frequently exposed to stress and trauma, it can become more reactive and less flexible to change.[99] This is because the brain's fight-or-flight response is often triggered, leading to a constant state of alertness and anxiety. Over time, this can make it harder to feel calm, think clearly, or react appropriately in stressful situations, which we have discussed in previous chapters.

99. McEwen, B.S. Neurobiological and Systemic Effects of Chronic Stress. *Chronic Stress (Thousand Oaks)*, (2017, Jan.-Dec.). https://pubmed.ncbi.nlm.nih.gov/28856337/; doi: 10.1177/2470547017692328

Rewiring the Brain for Healthy Relationships

Some studies have shown that mental rehearsal can produce new or different neuroplastic changes in your brain.[100118] This means that you can actually rewire your brain by making a conscious effort to remove yourself from negative or toxic habits. Essentially, rewiring your brain for healthy relationships involves creating new neural pathways that support positive interactions and emotional regulation. Here are five (5) things you can implement in your life to rewire your brain:

1. Get physical exercise (be active!)
2. Practice meditation and mindfulness on a regular basis
3. Learn a new language or skill
4. Eat a healthy diet
5. Get adequate sleep

These five (5) things promote what we call "neurogenesis." Neurogenesis is the process of creating new neurons, or nerve cells, in the brain.[100] The concept of neurogenesis aligns beautifully with the idea of a "growth mindset." This mindset emphasizes that our brains are not static, and we can learn and improve throughout our lives. Studies suggest that social interaction and positive experiences can stimulate neurogenesis. This means building healthy relationships can literally create new brain cells.[101]

What are some new practices you can incorporate into your life to potentially rewire your brain for the positive?

100. Kays, J.L., Hurley, R.A., and Taber, K.H. The Dynamic Brain: Neuroplasticity and Mental Health. *The Journal of Neuropsychiatry and Clinical Neurosciences*, 24:2, 118-124 (2012, April 1). https://psychiatryonline.org/doi/full/10.1176/appi.neuropsych.12050109; https://doi.org/10.1176/appi.neuropsych.12050109

101. Lieberwirth, C., and Wang, Z. The Social Environment and Neurogenesis in the Adult Mammalian Brain. *Frontiers in Human Neuroscience*, 8:118 (2012, May 8). doi: 10.3389/fnhum.2012.00118

The Benefits of Neuroplasticity

There are several benefits to neuroplasticity, and as scientists continue to research this field, I believe even more will be discovered. For the sake of this chapter, we will only focus on five (5) benefits, namely:[102]

1. **Enhanced learning and memory**: Neuroplasticity allows your brain to strengthen existing neural pathways and create new ones every time you learn something new. This can significantly improve your ability to acquire new skills, retain information, and adapt to changing environments.
2. **Improved cognitive function**: As we age, our cognitive functions like memory, attention, and problem-solving can decline. However, neuroplasticity offers hope that activities that stimulate the brain, like puzzles, learning new things, or engaging in mentally stimulating conversations, can help strengthen our cognitive pathways and potentially slow down age-related cognitive decline.
3. **Stroke recovery**: After a stroke, which damages brain tissue, neuroplasticity plays a crucial role in recovery. The brain can reroute functions from damaged areas to healthy ones, allowing the patient to regain lost abilities like speech, movement, or coordination. Rehabilitation therapies leverage neuroplasticity to promote this rewiring process and improve functionality.
4. **Addiction treatment**: Addiction hijacks the brain's reward system, creating strong neural pathways associated with substance use. Through therapy and rehabilitation programs that promote healthy behaviors and coping mechanisms, these pathways can weaken, while new, healthier ones associated with positive reinforcement can be strengthened.
5. **Mental health benefits**: Perhaps the most inspiring benefit of neuroplasticity is its role in healing. The brain can rewire itself after injuries, and this has significant implications for conditions like stroke, depression, and even addiction. Therapies like cognitive behavioral therapy (CBT) can help you identify and modify negative thought patterns, potentially leading to positive changes in brain function and improved mental well-being.

---

102. Ackerman, C.E. (2018, July 25). What Is Neuroplasticity? A Psychologist Explains [+14 Tools]. Retrieved from *Positivepsychology.com*: https://positivepsychology.com/neuroplasticity/

Homework

1. Identify a specific behavior you'd like to change to build a healthier relationship.

____

____

____

____

____

2. Reflect on a past relationship where communication or conflict management was a challenge. How might understanding neuroplasticity help you approach similar situations differently in the future?

____

____

____

____

____

3. Identify specific behaviors you often used during past abusive incidents. This could be yelling, name-calling, or controlling behavior. Think about this created neural pathway and try to trace it back to its root.

____

____

____

____

____

20

Becoming Accountable

"The moment you take responsibility for everything in your life
is the moment you can change anything in your life."

—Hal Elrod

Taking responsibility for one's actions is a powerful catalyst for transformation. In this chapter, clients are introduced to the concept of personal accountability, an essential step in creating positive change in both behavior and relationships. The focus here is on recognizing that accountability is not just a pathway to personal growth; it is also vital for strengthening relationships and breaking harmful cycles of abuse. Clients are encouraged to take ownership of their actions and gain a deeper understanding of how these actions impact those around them.

You will guide clients in exploring the barriers to accountability, such as pride, fear, and avoidance, and help them reflect on how these obstacles have influenced their behavior. The goal is to foster self-awareness and create a space where clients can openly discuss their difficulties with being accountable in past situations.

As a counselor, your role is to support clients as they explore the impact of their actions on their relationships, encouraging them to be honest about their mistakes and take responsibility for the outcomes. Help them recognize that accountability is not about blaming oneself but about acknowledging the role they played in unhealthy dynamics and taking proactive steps toward change.

Encourage clients to engage fully with the exercises designed to foster accountability and self-reflection. These exercises will help clients identify areas in which they need to be more responsible and explore ways to make amends for past behaviors. By fostering an empathetic and supportive environment, you can help clients understand that taking responsibility and being accountable are powerful steps toward healing and building healthier relationships in the future.

This chapter is critical in setting the foundation for clients to embrace their role in creating positive changes, both in themselves and in their interactions with others. As they work through this material, ensure that clients feel safe and supported in their journey toward personal accountability.

Goals of This Chapter

Taking responsibility is the foundation for lasting personal change. Accountability requires clients to take ownership of their actions, acknowledge their role in past destructive behaviors, and commit to adopting more positive, responsible approaches in their relationships and daily lives. This chapter encourages clients to deeply reflect on how their choices and behaviors have impacted themselves and others, particularly within intimate partner relationships.

Clients will be guided to explore common barriers to accountability—such as pride, fear of vulnerability, or playing the victim—that may have previously prevented them from fully accepting responsibility for their actions. The goal is to provide clients with the tools to overcome these barriers and begin to hold themselves accountable in constructive ways that promote personal growth and healthier interpersonal dynamics.

By fostering an understanding of how accountability leads to greater self-awareness and emotional maturity, this chapter plays a critical role in the overall CARE Method. It supports clients in their journey toward breaking negative cycles and creating more respectful, nonviolent relationships.

Colorado DVOMB Standards Competencies

Chapter 20 aligns with the Colorado Domestic Violence Offender Management Board (DVOMB) standards, emphasizing **accountability and responsibility for behaviors**, **domestic violence history**, **pro-criminal activities**, and the **history of pro-criminal behaviors**. It highlights the importance of clients recognizing and taking full responsibility for their actions, particularly those tied to patterns of domestic violence and criminal behavior. Clients are encouraged to examine their past behaviors, acknowledge the harm caused, and commit to change, establishing a foundation for nonviolent interactions.

This chapter also explores the client's history of domestic violence and pro-criminal behaviors, guiding them to recognize patterns that have contributed to abusive and unlawful actions. By reflecting on how these behaviors have impacted their relationships and lives, clients gain a deeper understanding of the factors influencing their actions.

Additionally, the chapter addresses the role of pro-criminal attitudes in perpetuating abusive dynamics. Clients are encouraged to identify and challenge these attitudes, understanding how they may have justified harmful actions. By confronting these mindsets and aligning their behaviors with values of respect and nonviolence, clients take proactive steps toward creating a positive future. This approach is fundamental to the CARE Method's therapeutic goals.

Important Things to Know

Last week, we explored the concept of **neuroplasticity** and how the brain can rewire itself to adopt healthier behaviors, especially in relationships. This week, we focus on **accountability**, a key component in creating meaningful and lasting change. Accountability requires clients to take ownership of their past actions and recognize their role in both the harm they may have caused and their ability to change.

In this chapter, you'll help clients understand the barriers to accountability, such as pride, fear, and shame, and guide them in overcoming these obstacles. Many clients may struggle with admitting their mistakes, but this step is crucial for fostering self-awareness and personal growth. Accountability is not about blame; it's about responsibility and committing to doing better moving forward.

Next week, we'll delve into creating a **personal change plan**, where clients will outline concrete steps toward sustaining the positive changes they are beginning to make. This chapter on becoming accountable is critical for laying the foundation of trust, both in their relationships and in themselves, as they continue their journey toward self-improvement.

Key Concepts and Terminology

Accountability: Accountability is the willingness to take responsibility for one's actions, behaviors, and their impact on others. It involves acknowledging mistakes without making excuses and committing to changing behaviors that have caused harm. Accountability is key to personal growth and fostering healthy relationships.

Responsibility for behaviors: This concept emphasizes the importance of recognizing that individuals are responsible for their actions, words, and choices. In relationships, responsibility extends to how those actions affect partners, children, and the broader community. Understanding and accepting responsibility is essential for rebuilding trust and breaking cycles of abuse.

Self-awareness: A key aspect of accountability, self-awareness involves recognizing one's own emotions, thoughts, and behaviors, and understanding how they affect relationships. It is a crucial first step in taking responsibility for past actions and making meaningful changes.

Apologizing sincerely: A genuine apology acknowledges the harm caused by one's actions and expresses a commitment to doing better. It is not about merely saying, "Sorry," but about showing remorse and taking active steps to prevent future harm.

Barriers to accountability: These are the emotional or psychological obstacles that prevent individuals from taking responsibility for their actions. Common barriers include pride, shame, fear of judgment, and the tendency to blame others. Overcoming these barriers is critical to achieving true accountability.

Discussion Prompts

These prompts will help guide clients through discussions that encourage them to reflect on their past actions, acknowledge their role in those actions, and embrace accountability for meaningful growth.

Understanding accountability:

- Encourage clients to explore their understanding of accountability and what it means to them in the context of relationships.
- **Discussion prompt**: "What does personal accountability mean to you? How has being accountable—or not being accountable—impacted your relationships?"

Identifying barriers to accountability:

- Help clients identify emotional or psychological barriers that have prevented them from being accountable in the past.
- **Discussion prompt**: "What barriers have kept you from taking responsibility for your actions in the past? How have these barriers affected your ability to grow and change?"

Impact of accountability:

- Discuss how embracing accountability can lead to healthier relationships and personal growth.
- **Discussion prompt**: "How do you think taking full responsibility for your actions will affect your relationships moving forward? What positive changes can you foresee by embracing accountability?"

Making amends:

- Encourage clients to think about ways to make amends and repair damage caused by past behaviors.
- **Discussion prompt**: "What steps can you take to make amends for any harm your actions may have caused? How can making amends help rebuild trust in your relationships?"

Overcoming pride and shame:

- Discuss the role of pride and shame in preventing accountability and how clients can work through these emotions.
- **Discussion prompt**: "How have pride or shame prevented you from taking responsibility for your actions in the past? What strategies can you use to overcome these feelings and embrace accountability?"

Contents

Chapter 20: Becoming Accountable
What Is Accountability?
What Are the Barriers to Accountability?
How to Respond When Someone in Your Life Avoids Taking Responsibility
How to Hold Yourself Accountable
Homework

20

Becoming Accountable

"Taking personal accountability is a beautiful thing because it gives us complete control of our destinies."

—**Heather Schuck**

We talked about neuroplasticity in the previous chapter, which is the brain's ability to create new neural pathways. Part of creating new, positive habits and responses is to be accountable for your actions. You cannot make any change unless you first acknowledge the role your actions and reactions have played in the choices you've made. If you can embrace accountability, you can change. Let's talk about this in depth.

What Is Accountability?

Accountability is about taking ownership of your actions, as well as their consequences, whether good or bad.[103] It means being responsible for your behavior and being willing to accept the outcomes, whether positive or negative.

103. MindTools. (2024). Developing Personal Accountability. Retrieved from *MindTools*: https://www.mindtools.com/ami110w/developing-personal-accountability

Here are some key aspects of accountability:[104]

- **Ownership**: Accepting responsibility for your actions, even when they are difficult or uncomfortable
- **Transparency**: Being honest and upfront about your thoughts, feelings, and actions
- **Responsibility**: Following through on commitments and promises
- **Amends**: Taking steps to repair any damage caused by your actions

What Are the Barriers to Accountability?

There are five (5) barriers that hinder personal accountability:[105]

1. Pride
2. The blame game
3. Playing the victim
4. Fear
5. Shame

Let's look at these in more detail.

Pride

Pride often stems from deep-seated insecurities or a need for validation. It can be rooted in childhood experiences where self-worth was tied to achievements or external approval.

Pride is associated with some unhealthy and distorted thoughts including but not limited to:

- **Feeling superior**: Believing you're above making mistakes or being wrong
- **Sense of entitlement**: Feeling like you're owed something and don't need to be held accountable
- **Fear of vulnerability**: Avoiding admitting mistakes because it might make you appear weak or flawed

104. Guthrie, G. (2022, October 19). What is personal accountability, and why does it matter in the workplace? Retrieved from *Nulab*: https://nulab.com/learn/collaboration/what-is-personal-accountability-in-the-workplace/

105. Foster, B.J. (2024). 5 Barriers to Taking Responsibility. Retrieved from *All Pro Dad*: https://www.allprodad.com/5-barriers-to-taking-responsibility/

The Blame Game

The "blame game" is a tactic where you focus on the other person's shortcomings while absolving yourself of any responsibility. This behavior stems from unhealthy thought patterns.

The blame game includes some unhealthy thought patterns as well including but not limited to these:

- Believing it's never your fault
- Being constantly on the lookout for other people's errors
- Being able to spot ways people have wronged you with an eagle eye, but when it comes to your own part, being blind or viewing yourself as holy and innocent
- Believing a lie that is not only a barrier to responsibility but ultimately intimacy too

Playing the Victim

This is when you focus on the negative actions of others and frame yourself as the one being wronged. People who play the victim always believe that everyone is out to get them. Playing the victim can stem from past experiences of trauma, neglect, or abuse. This prevents you from taking ownership of your role in a situation.

Fear

We are often afraid of taking accountability for the following reasons:

- **Judgment**: Fear of being seen as less than perfect or being criticized
- **Weakness**: The misconception that admitting mistakes portrays weakness when in reality, it shows strength and character
- **Consequences**: Worrying about potential negative outcomes of taking responsibility
- **Rejection**: Fear that being accountable might lead to rejection by your partner or loved ones

Shame

Shame is a powerful emotion associated with feelings of inadequacy or worthlessness. It can be linked to past experiences where you felt humiliated, unworthy, or exposed. This emotion can be powerful and paralyzing, which makes it hard to take responsibility for your actions.

Remember the chapter on core values? Shame often stems from core beliefs about yourself that may not be accurate when you make decisions that do not align with your core values.

Think back to a time when you might have struggled with accountability. What were the barriers that prevented you from taking accountability for your actions?

How to Respond When Someone in Your Life Avoids Taking Responsibility

Here's how to respond when someone in your life avoids taking responsibility for their actions and the results of their actions:

1. Explain to them why their behavior bothers you
2. Set boundaries
3. Offer help or support

What does this look like?

1. Explain the Behavior That Bothers You

Begin by having a conversation with the person about their behavior and how it affects you. The goal is not to attack or blame them but to express your feelings and frustrations. They might not even realize they are avoiding responsibility, and an honest, open conversation can be enlightening for both of you.

This is how you would do it:

- **"I" statements**: Use "I" statements to express your feelings without resorting to blame. For example, "I feel frustrated when you . . ." instead of "You always make excuses and never take responsibility."
- **Avoid the Four Horsemen**: Remember the Four Horsemen of the Relationship Apocalypse in communication: criticism, contempt, defensiveness, and stonewalling. Avoid these destructive approaches because they shut down communication.
- **Focus on the behavior**: Focus on the specific behavior that bothers you instead of attacking their character.

Effective communication can happen if you can remain calm, avoid destructive ways of speaking, and address the other person's behavior. As an example, you might say, "I feel frustrated when you dismiss my concerns about how we discipline our kids. It makes me feel like my opinion isn't important, and I want us to work together as partners in this relationship."

2. Set Boundaries

Being around someone who avoids responsibility can take a toll on your well-being, so you must set clear boundaries with them. Here is how you would do this:

- **Recognize avoidance**: Learn to identify signs of deflecting blame, making excuses, or playing the victim.
- **Communicate boundaries**: Calmly but firmly communicate that you won't tolerate the particular behavior.
- **Limit exposure**: If needed, limit your interactions with this person until they show a willingness to take accountability for their actions.

You need to know what lines others cannot cross (in different aspects of your life) and make these boundaries clear:

- **Physical boundaries**: You may need physical space from this person after they avoid responsibility because you feel overwhelmed.
- **Emotional boundaries**: These are the things that trigger certain emotions in you. For example, certain topics might trigger stress and anxiety, so you would let your partner know that you will not entertain such topics.

- **Communication boundaries**: You might need to limit communication or clearly state that you won't engage in conversations if they will not communicate in a calm or respectful manner.
- **Financial boundaries**: How finances are managed often makes or breaks a relationship. You need to establish clear agreements on shared expenses and make sure both you and your partner honor this agreement.

Let the person know what your boundaries are and why they are important to you. Be clear and firm but also kind. For instance, you might say, "I need some time alone after work to decompress, and I'd appreciate it if we could respect that."

3. Offer Help or Support

Sometimes, walking away isn't an option, especially with family or coworkers. In such cases, explore solutions that work for both of you. Here's how to offer support without enabling their behavior:

- **Focus on solutions**: Instead of dwelling on blame, suggest solutions that encourage your partner to take ownership of their actions.
- **Offer help**: If appropriate, offer resources or support that might help them address the underlying reasons behind their behavior.
- **Avoid making them feel worse**: The goal is not to make them feel bad but to encourage self-reflection and growth.

The key is to offer suggestions, not orders. Instead of telling them what to do, offer suggestions that open them up to other possibilities and encourage them to find their own solutions. For example, you would say, "What if we tried setting multiple alarms to help you get up early? Do you think that could help?" instead of something like, "Just set an alarm and you'll get up early enough to do XYZ."

Remember not to try to fix them. You can only control your own actions and responses.

How to Hold Yourself Accountable

Building strong relationships requires you not to only hold others accountable but also to hold yourself accountable. You have the responsibility of taking ownership of your actions, words, and choices. Holding yourself accountable in a healthy way is just as important as holding your partner accountable in a healthy way.

BECOMING ACCOUNTABLE

Here are some steps you can implement to hold yourself accountable in your relationships:[106]

1. Be self-aware
2. Communicate openly and honestly
3. Own up to your mistakes
4. Apologize sincerely

Here's what's involved with these steps toward improving your accountability:

1. Be Self-Aware

Ask yourself these questions about interactions you have:

- How do your actions and words affect your partner(s)?
- Do you keep your promises and commitments?
- Do you take responsibility for your mistakes and apologize sincerely?
- Are you a good listener and communicator?

2. Communicate Openly and Honestly

Openly communicate your needs and expectations in the relationship. Share your thoughts and feelings openly, even when it's difficult. It's also important to be honest about what you can and cannot do. If you say you'll do something, follow through on your word.

3. Own Up to Your Mistakes

Recognize and admit your mistakes without making excuses. Accepting that you have made a mistake is the first step toward making things right. Remember, everyone makes mistakes, and what matters is how you handle them.

4. Apologize Sincerely

A genuine apology expresses remorse and a commitment to do better. Focus on how your actions affected your partner, rather than just stating that you're sorry.

106. Pace, R. (2024, April 29). 17 Practical Ways to Practice Accountability in Relationships. Retrieved from *Marriage.com*: https://www.marriage.com/advice/relationship/accountability-in-relationships/

Homework

1. As you reflect on today's topic and the reason why you are seeking help, what are some of the reasons you might have struggled with personal accountability? How has the barrier you identified in this chapter prevented your personal growth in the past or present?

2. Describe the impact of your actions on your partner, former partner, your children, yourself, your co-workers, and the community.

3. What are specific actions you intend to take to hold yourself accountable?

21

My Personal Change Plan

"A goal without a plan is just a wish."

—Antoine de Saint-Exupéry

The journey toward lasting change culminates in this final chapter, where clients embark on creating a personal change plan—a structured framework designed to help set goals, outline strategies, and track progress toward meaningful behavioral change. This chapter serves as a guide for clients to consolidate the insights and skills they've gained throughout the program, integrating them into their daily lives. The aim is to ensure that the pursuit of healthier relationships and personal accountability extends well beyond the Care Method curridulum sessions, providing a road map for ongoing growth and transformation.

You will guide clients in identifying specific areas in their lives where change is necessary, helping them to set realistic and actionable goals. This chapter emphasizes the importance of not only setting goals but also developing a clear road map for achieving them. By outlining strategies for overcoming obstacles and maintaining progress, clients can stay motivated and accountable for their growth.

As a counselor, your role is to provide support and guidance as clients begin to draft their personal change plan. Help them reflect on the behaviors they have worked to change throughout the program, and encourage them to incorporate the principles of personal accountability and self-awareness into their plans. Reinforce the concept that change is an ongoing process, and that setbacks should not be seen as failures but as opportunities for learning and growth.

Encourage clients to engage fully with the exercises in this chapter, which will help them break down their goals into achievable steps and identify the resources and support systems they will need to succeed. This chapter is critical for ensuring that clients leave the program with a concrete plan for continuing their personal development and maintaining the positive changes they have made.

As you facilitate the sessions in this chapter, remind clients of the progress they have already made, and emphasize the importance of ongoing commitment to their personal change plan. By creating a detailed and personalized road map, clients can take control of their future, build healthier relationships, and live in alignment with their values.

Goals of This Chapter

Creating a clear plan is the first step toward lasting change. Clients are encouraged to set clear, realistic goals that will facilitate growth, promote healthier relationships, and sustain positive behavioral shifts. This chapter equips clients with the tools to reflect on their past actions and make concrete plans for improvement, with a focus on strategies that will support their journey toward healthier interactions and personal accountability.

By outlining their goals, strategies, and the resources they need, clients can develop a step-by-step guide to implement long-term changes in their behavior. The chapter also emphasizes the importance of preparing for challenges that might arise, helping clients identify potential barriers, and offering solutions to overcome them. This chapter serves as a critical foundation for creating a safe and accountable future.

Colorado DVOMB Standards Competencies

Chapter 21 aligns with the Colorado Domestic Violence Offender Management Board (DVOMB) standards on **safety plans**, **compliance with supervision**, and **reintegration into the community**. The DVOMB emphasizes the need for creating detailed safety plans that protect clients and others from harm, while also focusing on compliance with the legal and therapeutic frameworks that guide their rehabilitation. Reintegration into the community is a key component, highlighting the importance of clients' roles in fostering safer, more supportive environments as they transition back into society.

The competencies in this chapter guide clients in outlining personal safety plans that address specific risks and behaviors associated with domestic violence. Clients are encouraged to work collaboratively with their counselors and supervisors to develop a personal change plan that is both comprehensive and realistic. Reintegration into the community is included in this process, as clients learn how to rebuild trust and establish healthier patterns of interaction within their communities. This involves understanding the impact of their behavior not only on intimate partners but also on the broader community network.

Adherence to supervision rules is also emphasized, as demonstrating a commitment to change through consistent accountability is crucial. Reintegration efforts involve showing respect for community standards and legal requirements, fostering a sense of responsibility and engagement. By successfully navigating these frameworks, clients work toward creating safer relationships and communities, reflecting their dedication to personal growth and societal well-being.

Important Things to Know

Last week, we focused on becoming accountable, exploring the importance of acknowledging past behaviors and **being accountable**. This week, we transition into crafting **a personal change plan**, a critical tool that encapsulates the commitment to apply the lessons learned and move forward with actionable steps. This chapter is designed to provide clients with a structured framework to outline their goals, the strategies to achieve them, and the resources they might need along the way.

In this chapter, clients should be encouraged to set clear, measurable goals that reflect both their short-term and long-term aspirations for personal growth and relationship improvement. The personal change plan serves as a road map, guiding individuals through self-reflection, goal-setting, and the execution of plans that lead to sustainable change.

Key Concepts and Terminology

Personal change plan: A structured framework designed to help clients set clear, actionable goals related to personal growth and behavior change. The plan outlines strategies and steps to track progress over time, helping individuals take control of their transformation process. This serves as a road map for making sustained changes in relationships and overall behavior.

Goal-setting: The process of identifying specific, measurable, achievable, relevant, and time-bound (SMART) goals that guide clients toward positive change. Goal-setting provides direction and motivation throughout the change process, offering clarity on what needs to be accomplished.

Aftercare plan: A part of the personal change plan that focuses on long-term strategies for maintaining progress after completing formal counseling or intervention. It emphasizes the importance of ongoing support and resources to prevent relapse into negative behaviors.

Self-reflection: A critical aspect of the personal change plan, involving introspection and evaluation of past behaviors. Clients are encouraged to reflect on how their choices have impacted their relationships and what changes are necessary to improve their future actions.

Motivational interviewing (MI): A therapeutic technique that helps clients explore and resolve ambivalence about change. MI is used to encourage individuals to develop their own motivations for altering harmful behaviors.

Cognitive behavioral therapy (CBT): A type of therapy that focuses on identifying and changing negative thought patterns and behaviors. CBT helps clients build new mental frameworks that support positive actions and emotional regulation.

Discussion Prompts

The following prompts will guide clients through the process of setting realistic goals, identifying challenges, and planning for long-term success.

Setting personal goals:

- Encourage clients to reflect on the goals they want to achieve and why those goals are important.
- **Discussion prompt**: "What are the personal goals you want to achieve through your change plan? Why are these goals important to you, and how do you think achieving them will improve your life and relationships?"

Identifying challenges and obstacles:

- Help clients consider the potential challenges that might arise and how they can address them.

- **Discussion prompt**: "What obstacles do you anticipate as you work toward your goals? What strategies can you use to overcome these challenges and stay on track?"

Creating an action plan:

- Guide clients in creating a concrete action plan (their personal change plan) that outlines the steps they will take to achieve their goals.
- **Discussion prompt**: "What specific actions will you take to achieve your goals? How will you ensure that these steps are realistic and achievable?"

Long-term accountability:

- Discuss with clients the importance of maintaining accountability for their change plan over the long term.
- **Discussion prompt**: "How will you hold yourself accountable for following through on your personal change plan? What support systems can you put in place to help you stay committed?"

Measuring success:

- Encourage clients to think about how they will measure their progress and know when they are succeeding.
- **Discussion prompt**: "How will you know that you are succeeding in your change plan? What are the indicators or milestones you will look for to track your progress?"

Contents

Chapter 21: My Personal Change Plan
What Is a Personal Change Plan?
The Importance of a Personal Change Plan
Personal Change Plan Template
Resources

21

My Personal Change Plan

"A goal without a plan is just a wish."

—Antoine de Saint-Exupéry

What Is a Personal Change Plan?

A personal change plan is a structured framework designed to help individuals set goals, outline strategies, and track progress toward personal growth and behavior change. It serves as a roadmap for individuals undergoing a transformative journey, guiding them through the process of self-reflection, goal setting, and implementation of strategies aimed at achieving positive outcomes.

The Importance of a Personal Change Plan

1. Creating a personal change plan is a crucial step toward achieving lasting transformation and improving your relationships. It serves as a roadmap that guides your journey from self-awareness to positive action. By outlining clear goals, strategies, and timelines, you empower yourself to take proactive steps toward personal growth and behavior change.
2. In the context of *The Care Method*, the personal change plan helps you reflect on past behaviors, identify triggers, and develop healthier coping mechanisms. This plan is not just about setting goals—it's about fostering a commitment to accountability, self-improvement, and building respectful relationships.
3. As you embark on this journey, remember that change is a process. Your personal change plan should evolve with you, adapting to new insights and experiences along the way.

By investing in your personal growth and committing to positive change, you not only enhance your own well-being but also contribute to healthier, safer communities.

4. This template provides a structured approach to creating a personal change plan tailored to your individual needs and circumstances. Use it as a tool to empower yourself and take meaningful steps toward a future free from violence and filled with healthy, fulfilling relationships.

Personal Change Plan Template

Goals

List specific goals you want to achieve related to personal growth, relationship improvement, and behavior change.

1. ____________________

2. ____________________

3. ____________________

4. ____________________

5. ____________________

Reasons Why I Want to Make This Change

Describe why each goal is important to you. Reflect on how achieving these goals will enhance your life and relationships.

1. ____________________

2. ____________________

3. ____________________

4. ____________________

5. ____________________

MY PERSONAL CHANGE PLAN

Strategies

Outline the strategies or actions you will take to achieve each goal. Include steps that are realistic and achievable.

1. ______________________________

____

2. ______________________________

____

3. ______________________________

____

4. ______________________________

____

5. ______________________________

____

Resources Needed

Identify any resources, support systems, or tools you will use to help you achieve your goals (e.g., counseling, support groups, etc.).

____

____

____

____

____

____

____

How Will I Know That I Am Succeeding?

Define specific indicators or milestones that will show your progress toward each goal. Consider measurable outcomes or changes in behavior.

1. ______________________________

2. ______________________________

3. ______________________________

4. ______________________________

5. ______________________________

Barriers and Challenges

Anticipate potential obstacles that may hinder your progress. Outline strategies to overcome these challenges.

____

____

____

____

____

____

____

____

____

____

____

____

How Others Can Help Me in Achieving These Goals

Specify ways in which friends, family, or professionals can support you in reaching your goals. This may include encouragement, accountability, or practical assistance.

1. ____

____

2. ____

____

3. ____

____

4. ____

____

5. ____

____

Resources

1. The Arbor Behavioral Healthcare. (2022, January 14). What Is an Aftercare Plan for Addiction Recovery? Retrieved from *The Arbor Behavioral Healthcare*: https://thearbor.com/blog/what-is-an-aftercare-plan-for-addiction-recovery/
2. Wurzburg, S. (2024). Relapse Prevention Plans. Retrieved from The Council of State Governments Justice Center: https://csgjusticecenter.org/publications/collaborative-comprehensive-case-plans/relapse-prevention-plans/

Start Date: __/__/____ My Recovery Goals:	PERSONAL CHANGE PLAN
My Triggers	**My Emergency Plan**
Short-Term Goals	**Long-Term Goals**
❒ ______________	❒ ______________
❒ ______________	❒ ______________
❒ ______________	❒ ______________
❒ ______________	❒ ______________
❒ ______________	❒ ______________
❒ ______________	❒ ______________
❒ ______________	❒ ______________
My Coping Strategies	**My Self-Care Practices**

MY SUPPORT SYSTEM

Primary Therapist/Counselor	
Full Name	
Contact Number	
Email	

Trusted Friend/Family Member	
Full Name	
Relationship	
Contact Number	
Alternate Number	
Email Address	

Second Trusted Friend/Family Member	
Full Name	
Relationship	
Contact Number	
Alternate Number	
Email Address	

Support Group Details

Appendix A

Required Presentations

General Instructions

Upon receiving your first treatment plan review (TPR), you will be asked to complete the following individual presentations. These presentations are essential components of your treatment, and while completing them does not signify the end of your treatment, failure to complete them may impede your eligibility for treatment discharge.

The purpose of these presentations is to gauge your individual progress. You should expect additional questions from the DV counselor and your peers at the end of each presentation.

*For examples of the following presentations, go to CareMethodBook.com/resources

Presentation List

1. Financial Accountability Presentation (Appendix B)

- Review the template provided by your DV counselor (Appendix B).
- Reflect on financially abusive behaviors and identify any you've engaged in.
- Answer reflection questions with specific examples.
- Admit to any financial infidelity and its impact on your relationships.
- Outline steps to change these behaviors and prevent future abuse.
- Present your findings on paper, on poster board, or digitally.
- Give a 10–15-minute presentation, including answering questions.
- Ensure both you and your counselor sign the completed template.

2. Genogram Presentation (Appendix C)

- A genogram provides insight into your family dynamics and struggles, such as divorce, death, and broken relationships. It helps identify patterns of behavior, especially those you wish to change like abuse, conflict, legal problems, or addiction. See Appendix C for the template.
- Include at least three (3) generations: grandparents, parents, and yourself.
- Indicate any significant events, relationships, or patterns that have influenced family dynamics.
- Present your genogram on a poster board, PowerPoint, or dry-erase board. If using a dry-erase board, arrive early to draw your genogram before the group session.
- Give a 10–15-minute presentation about your genogram, including answering questions and discussing patterns you've identified.

3. Timeout Contract Presentation (Appendix D)

- If you are in a relationship, explain to your partner that this activity is designed to prevent future episodes of violence and encourage their participation without pressure. Ensure they understand this is a collaborative effort for healthier communication.
- If you are not currently in a relationship, complete only the section regarding your triggers and the five (5) expectations on the last page.
- Do not fill out sections meant for a partner's input to avoid assumptions.
- Answer the following questions before presenting to the group:
  - How did you approach your partner, and what was their response?
  - What was it like to discuss the expectations for your relationship moving forward?
- Prepare a 10–15-minute presentation of your completed Timeout Contract, including time for group feedback and questions.
- Be prepared to discuss the process and any insights or challenges you encountered while working on this contract with your partner.

4. Develop and Present Your Own Cycle of Abuse (Appendix E)

- Describe the honeymoon, tension-building, and explosion phases with personal examples of yourself as an aggressor, using a diagram or bullet points and arrows.

- Explain how long you have engaged in these forms of abuse.
- Discuss the impact of your abusive behaviors on your victims.
- Presentation must be on a poster board, PowerPoint, or dry-erase board, including a drawn-out circle.
- Use "I" statements throughout the presentation.
- This is the most important presentation in your treatment. If you are not 100% accountable (using "I" statements), you may be asked to redo it.
- Presentation should be 10–15-minutes, including feedback.

5. Letter of Apology to Your Children (Appendix F)

- Write a one-to-two (1–2) page letter of apology to your children regarding any domestic violence incidents.
- Start by expressing what you love most about your children.
- Take full accountability for your actions and assure your children they are not to blame.
- Avoid making promises; instead, commit to actions you will take to prevent future incidents of domestic violence.
- Share the letter with the group.

The following tasks will be given to you upon completion of all required Treatment Plan Reviews (TPR) and agreement by the Multidisciplinary Treatment Team (MTT) for your successful discharge from treatment:

A. Final Personal Change Plan Template

B. Letter of Accountability to the Victim Template

C. Discharge Packet

Appendix B

Financial Accountability Presentation

This presentation is designed to help you identify and understand any financially abusive behaviors you've engaged in within relationships. Recognizing these patterns is a vital step toward accountability and change. By reflecting on the impact of these actions, you can work toward establishing healthier financial boundaries and more respectful, equitable relationships. This process will guide you in taking concrete steps to prevent financial abuse in the future.

Instructions

1. **Preparation**: On a sheet of paper or poster board, write down the answers to the following sections by utilizing the template provided to you.
2. **Self-assessment**: Carefully read the list of financially abusive behaviors provided below. Reflect on your past and current relationships and identify any patterns of behavior you have engaged in that match these descriptions.
3. **Reflection questions**: Answer the reflection questions thoroughly. If you identify any of the listed behaviors in your past or present relationships, explore the thoughts and emotions you experience as you take responsibility for them. If none of the behaviors apply to you, proceed to the next section.
4. **Financial infidelity**: Reflect on your past actions in relationships and describe any behaviors that could be considered financial infidelity. Be honest and specific about how these behaviors have affected your relationships.

5. **Action steps**: Based on what you have learned from this exercise, outline specific steps you plan to take to change or eliminate these behaviors in the future. Consider how you can set healthier financial boundaries and promote equality in relationships.
6. **Preventing financial abuse**: Reflect on how you have (or have not) set financial boundaries with partners in the past. Describe the impact of these actions on your relationships and how DV treatment has influenced your awareness.

Self-Assessment

According to research, the following behaviors indicate the presence of financial abuse in a relationship. As you read this list, identify and describe patterns of financially abusive behaviors you may have engaged in throughout the history of all your adult relationships:

1. Stealing money from your partner or their family.
2. Forcing your partner to give you access to their bank accounts to make transactions without their input.
3. Making your partner feel as though they do not have a right to know any details about money or household resources.
4. Putting your partner on an allowance, even if they object.
5. Forcing your partner to account for all money they spend, for example, by asking for receipts.
6. Overusing your partner's credit cards or refusing to pay the bills, thereby ruining their credit.
7. Preventing your partner from working or attending school or skill-training sessions.
8. Withholding physical resources from your partner, including food, clothes, necessary medications, or shelter.
9. Forcing your partner to turn over their paychecks or public benefit payments.
10. Forcing your partner to cash in, sell, or sign over any financial assets they own (e.g., bonds, stock, or property).
11. Forcing your partner to agree to a power of attorney that would enable you to legally sign documents without their knowledge or consent.
12. Forcing your partner to work in a family business for little or no pay.
13. Preventing your partner from obtaining or using credit cards or bank cards.

14. Refusing to work to help support the family.
15. Sabotaging your partner's employment opportunities by refusing to provide transportation, hiding keys, or creating unnecessary conflict before important work events.
16. Interfering with your partner's performance at work by calling nonstop, visiting their workplace unannounced, etc.
17. Threatening to falsely report your partner for cheating on their public benefits so they will be cut off.
18. Forcing your partner to cash in, sell, or sign over any inheritance they own.

Reflection Questions

1. If you identified any of the above behaviors, what new thoughts or emotions did you experience while taking responsibility for these behaviors? (If you did not identify any of the above behaviors, skip this question and proceed to the next section of this assignment.)
2. Describe in detail the impact your previous or current patterns of abusive behaviors have had on your partner or family members.
3. Describe how your own patterns of financially abusive behaviors interfere with your ability to have healthier relationships. In what ways does this also affect you?

Financial Infidelity

Financial infidelity covers a wide range of behaviors. It could be something as seemingly trivial as not informing your partner about small purchases, like after-work happy hours with colleagues. It could also be something more serious, such as siphoning money from shared accounts, lying about your income or debts, lending large amounts without consent, making extravagant purchases without permission, or keeping bank accounts or credit cards secret. This also includes using marital or conjugal income to pay for porn subscriptions, prostitutes/escorts, drugs, etc.

1. Describe any and all types of behaviors you have engaged in that would be considered "financial infidelity" and the effects these behaviors have had on your relationships.
2. Based on what you have learned regarding financial abuse, what specific steps do you plan on taking to eliminate or change these patterns of behavior?

Preventing Financial Abuse

1. Describe how you have set financial boundaries with current or previous partners (e.g., did you discuss sharing household bills before moving in together?). If you did not have financial discussions, describe how you made the decision to move in together with previous or current partners and who pays which bills.
2. If you have not set financial boundaries in previous relationships, what impact did this have on your relationship (e.g., fighting over finances, financial arguments leading to more severe consequences like an arrest or involvement from the Department of Human Services)?
3. Describe how domestic violence (DV) treatment has helped increase your awareness of the need to set financial boundaries in the future. What specifically has been most helpful to you in increasing your knowledge of financial abuse?

Signatures

Client signature: ______________________________

Print name: ______________________________

Counselor signature: ______________________________

Appendix C

Genogram

Creating a genogram is an important step in understanding your own behavioral patterns and how they're connected to your family history. By mapping out your family relationships and histories, you can see how certain behaviors and emotional responses have been passed down through generations. This visual tool helps you pinpoint recurring themes in your family, such as conflict resolution styles or coping mechanisms, and understand how these patterns influence your own actions and relationships today. In your journey through domestic violence treatment, building a genogram allows you to explore these connections more deeply, helping you to recognize and break unhealthy cycles. By gaining this insight, you can start to make positive changes and develop healthier relationships.

Instructions

To create your genogram, you can use a poster board or a dry-erase board. Start by mapping out your family relationships beginning with your grandparents. Take note of key issues or events you have been told about or witnessed. Spend 10-15-minutes presenting this activity, including time for feedback from your group peers. This brief presentation will help you and your peers better understand the connections between family patterns and your own behaviors.

Example of a real client genogram:

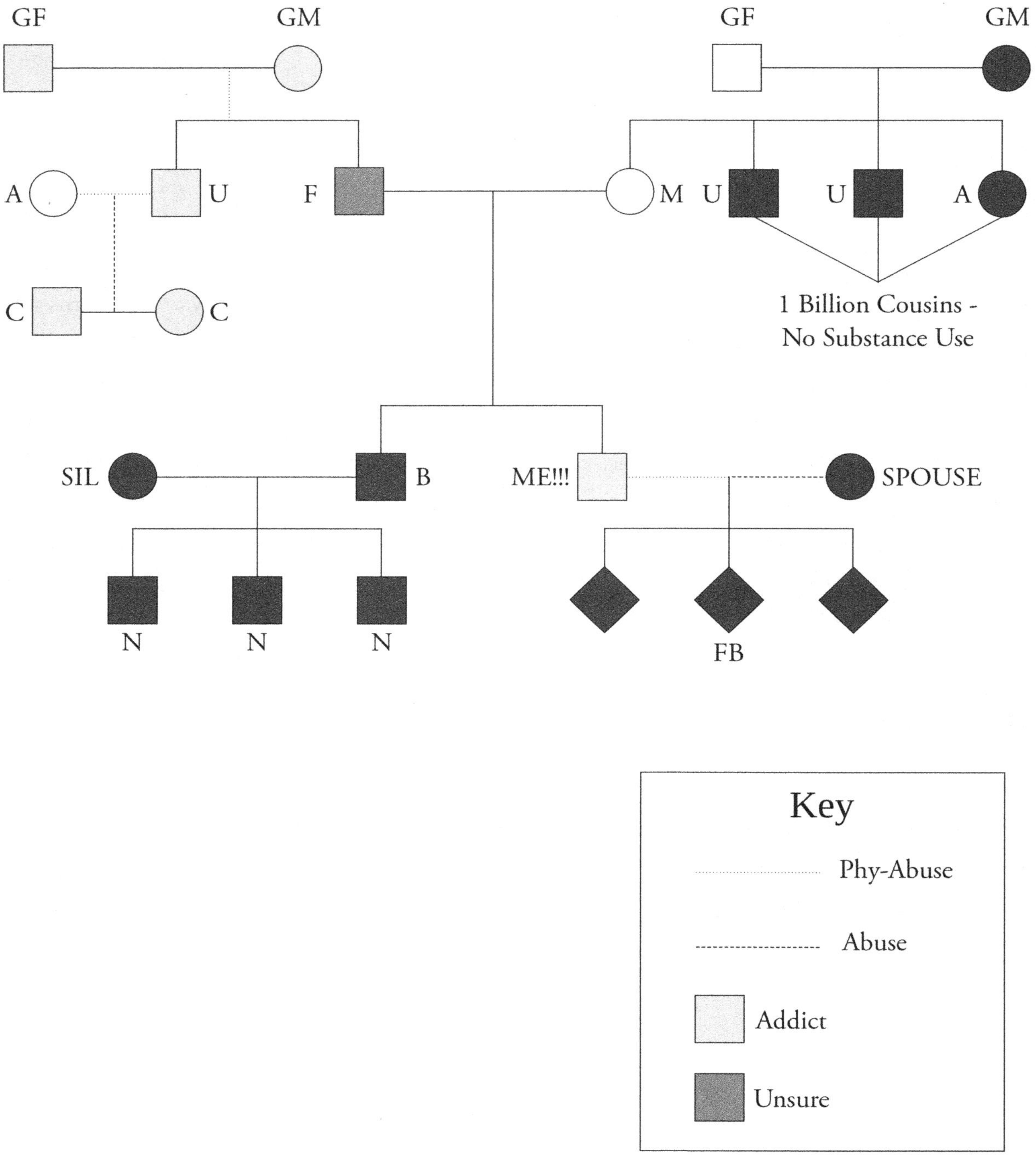

GF
GM
GF
GM
A
U
F
M
U
U
A
C
C
1 Billion Cousins -
No Substance Use
SIL
B
ME!!!
SPOUSE
N
N
N
FB
Key
Phy-Abuse
Abuse
Addict
Unsure

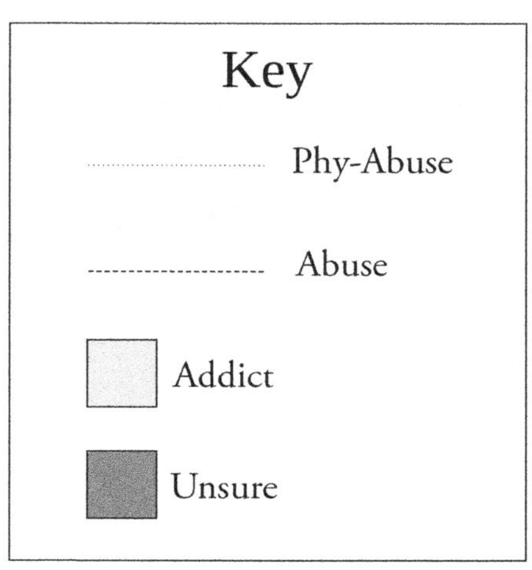

Appendix D

Time-Out Contract

A time-out contract is a vital tool in reducing violence and preventing escalation during conflicts in a relationship. It establishes clear guidelines and boundaries for both partners, providing a structured approach to de-escalation and conflict resolution. By mutually agreeing on how to take a break during heated moments, both parties can prevent situations from spiraling out of control, ultimately fostering a healthier and more respectful relationship.

Time-Out Contract

This contract is to be completed by both partners in a relationship. Its purpose is to establish a mutual understanding and agreement on how to handle conflicts and take time-outs when necessary.

Partner 1: Name: ________________________ Signature: ______________________________

Partner 2: Name: ________________________ Signature: ______________________________

Date: ___________________

1. Identifying Triggers

Your triggers:

____

____

Partner's triggers:

____

____

2. Requesting a Time-Out

When one partner feels overwhelmed or triggered, they will use the agreed-upon phrase to request a time-out. The phrase can be:

- "I need a break."
- "Time-out, please."
- "Let's take a pause."

Create your own safety-neutral, non-blaming word:

---

3. Where to Go During a Time-Out

Each partner will agree on a specific location where they will go to calm down and reflect during a time-out.

Your location safe place:

Partner location safe place:

---

4. Duration of the Time-Out

The agreed-upon duration for a time-out is (e.g., 15 minutes, 30 minutes, 1 hour):

If either partner needs more time, they will communicate this to the other and mutually agree on an extended time-out.

5. Rules During the Time-Out

While the time-out is in effect, both partners agree to follow these rules to ensure the time-out is used constructively:

- No playing video games
- No driving

- No getting on social media
- No calling friends or family to discuss the conflict
- No consuming alcohol or drugs
- No engaging in any form of retaliation or negative behavior

List any additional agreed-upon rules:

____

____

____

6. Reconnecting After a Time-Out

Once the time-out is over, both partners will come back together to discuss the issue calmly and respectfully. They will use the following steps to resolve the conflict:

Step 1. Acknowledge feelings:
You: "I felt [emotion] when [trigger] happened because [reason]."

____

____

Partner: "I felt [emotion] when [trigger] happened because [reason]."

____

____

Step 2. Active listening:

- Each partner will listen without interrupting, repeating back what they heard to ensure understanding.

Step 3. Problem-solving:

- Discuss possible solutions and compromises that address both partners' needs and concerns.

Step 4. Agreement:

- Agree on a solution and how to implement it. Both partners will commit to the agreed-upon changes and check in regularly on progress.

7. Commitment to Nonviolence

Both partners agree to the following:

- To refrain from any form of physical, verbal, or emotional abuse
- To respect each other's need for space and time during a time-out
- To work collaboratively toward resolving conflicts in a healthy and constructive manner

8. Expectations Moving Forward

List five (5) things that each partner will do differently moving forward to maintain a healthy relationship.

Your expectations/commitment:

1. ______________________________

2. ______________________________

3. ______________________________

4. ______________________________

5. ______________________________

Partner expectations/commitment:

1. ______________________________

2. ______________________________

3. ______________________________

4. ______________________________

5. ______________________________

Appendix E

Cycle of Abuse Presentation

Understanding and presenting your own cycle of abuse is a crucial step in your journey toward change and accountability. This exercise allows you to identify and acknowledge the specific patterns of behavior that have contributed to abusive dynamics in your relationships. By breaking down the cycle into the honeymoon, tension-building, and explosion phases, you gain insight into how these patterns develop and perpetuate harm.

Instructions

Develop and present your own cycle of abuse:

- Describe the honeymoon, tension-building, and explosion phases with personal examples of yourself as an aggressor.
- Explain how long you have engaged in these forms of abuse.
- Discuss the impact of your abusive behaviors on your victims.
- Presentation must be on a poster board, PowerPoint, or dry-erase board, including a drawn-out circle.
- Use "I" statements throughout the presentation.
- This is the most important presentation in your treatment. If you are not 100% accountable (using "I" statements), you may be asked to redo it.
- This presentation should be 10–15-minutes and include time for feedback.

Actual Client Presentation:

Honeymoon

- Love bombing
- Being sorrowful
- Reassuring safety and security
- Giving absolute time and attention
- Gaslighting

Explosion Phase

- Yelling
- Verbal abuse
- Belittling/ emotional abuse
- Threats of violence
- Intimidation
- Isolation

Tension Building

- Avoidance
- Projection
- Denial
- Compensating with alcohol
- Contemptuous attitude
- Gaslighting
- Stonewalling
- Walking on eggshells

Appendix F

Apology Letter to My Child(ren) Template

Writing an apology letter to your child(ren) is a crucial step in acknowledging the impact of your actions on their lives. It's important because it helps you take responsibility for the harm caused and opens the door for healing and rebuilding trust. This letter is an opportunity to express empathy, demonstrate a commitment to change, and set a foundation for a healthier relationship with your child(ren). By clearly communicating your intentions and the steps you're taking to become a better parent, you are showing your child(ren) that they are valued, loved, and deserving of a safe and supportive environment. This exercise not only fosters personal accountability but also contributes to breaking the cycle of violence for future generations.

Instructions

On a blank piece of paper, write a letter to your child(ren) and include the following:

1. Acknowledgment of domestic violence incidents:

Instructions

- Address the incidents of domestic violence that occurred, even if the children were sleeping or unaware.
- Apologize for any distress or fear these incidents may have caused your child(ren).

2. Expressing empathy for the impact on the child(ren):

Instructions

- Express understanding of how these incidents might have affected your child(ren) emotionally, financially, psychologically, etc.

- Acknowledge the pain your child(ren) may have felt when you were taken away and couldn't return home.
- Reassure them that these situations are not your child(ren)'s fault.

3. Commitment to change without making promises:

Instructions

- Explain the steps you are taking to change and become a healthier father/stepfather/guardian and person.
- Acknowledge that change takes time and effort, and that you are committed to doing your best.
- Avoid making specific promises that may not be possible to guarantee.

4. Ending the cycle of violence:

Instructions

- Express a firm commitment to breaking the cycle of violence for your children and their generation.
- Discuss seeking help, counseling, or programs to learn healthy ways to handle emotions and conflicts.
- Emphasize that violence is never acceptable and that it ends with you.

5. Understanding healthy relationships and protecting your child's future:

Instructions

- Describe what a healthy relationship looks like, emphasizing respect, kindness, and safety.
- Reiterate that you never want them to experience an abusive relationship.
- Emphasize your commitment to ensuring their safety and well-being.

End the letter with expressing your love and commitment to change. Speak from your heart and use your own words. Share it with the group.

Example:

Dear [Child's Name],

I want to talk to you about some important things. I know there were times when you heard yelling or saw me lose my temper, and I am so sorry for the fear and confusion that caused you. Even if you were sleeping or didn't know what was happening, it's important for me to apologize because none of it was your fault.

I understand that seeing or hearing those incidents may have made you feel scared or worried about me and our family. You might have felt unsure about what was going to happen next, and for that, I am deeply sorry. When I was taken away that night and couldn't come back home right away, I know that must have been really hard for you. I want you to know that you did nothing wrong, and it was my actions that caused this pain.

I am working hard to change and become a better person and a healthier parent. I'm learning how to manage my emotions in a positive way, and I am committed to this process. For example, I've started going to counseling to understand my behavior and to make sure this never happens again. Change takes time, but I promise to keep doing my best each day.

It's important to me to break this cycle of violence. I want you to see that I am learning healthier ways to handle my feelings and conflicts. I am committed to creating a peaceful and safe home for you, where you can feel secure and loved.

A healthy relationship is based on respect, kindness, and safety. I want to be a role model for you, showing you what that looks like. You deserve to feel safe and never have to worry about being in an abusive relationship. I am dedicated to ensuring you grow up in an environment where you can see and learn what a loving, supportive relationship is.

I love you more than anything, and I am determined to make things better. If you ever want to talk about this or anything else, I am here for you. You deserve a safe and happy home, and I am committed to providing that for you.

With all my love,
[Your Name]

The Evaluation and Intake Process

When I embarked on developing the CARE Method, my initial focus was on its potential impact for domestic violence counselors within the state of Colorado. My aim was to share my insights on client evaluation, group facilitation, and overcoming common challenges. However, as I progressed with writing, I began to consider the broader applicability of this approach to clients and counselors in other states, where regulatory boards for court-mandated domestic violence treatment might not be present.

Below, you will find a comprehensive overview of our interview and evaluation process in the state of Colorado, used prior to placing a client into treatment. I want to emphasize that regardless of whether your state adheres to this specific framework, it is crucial to conduct thorough evaluations and collaboratively develop treatment plans with your clients. This approach ensures a tailored and effective treatment process, irrespective of regional variations in treatment standards.

Colorado DVOMB Standards Requirements

Section 5.0 1.03 General Overview of the Evaluation and Treatment Process, Colorado Domestic Violence Offender Management Board Standards and Guidelines for Domestic Violence Offenders

I. Upon order by the Court or Parole Board, an offender is required by statute to receive an evaluation and attend treatment as recommended. The offender evaluation will result in treatment recommendations that assess the offender's need for treatment, determine what type of treatment is needed, and identify the initial risk level and any additional needs the offender may have related to containment, stabilization, and safety (Section 4.0). Please refer to the Figure 1 below for a visual depiction of this process.

1. Referral — Offender is referred to a DVOMB Approved Provider

2. Offender Evaluation

Pre- and/or Post-Sentence Offender Evaluation

- Determines offender's need for treatment
- Determines what type of treatment is needed
- Identifies and recommends the initial risk level based on any additional needs

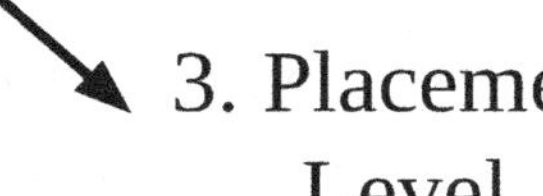

3. Placement Level — MTT Reaches Consensus on Initial Treatment Level

4. Treatment

Level A	Level B	Level C
A minimum of two required Treatment Plan Reviews and additional reviews as deemed necessary by the MTT.	A minimum of three required Treatment Plan Reviews and additional reviews as deemed necessary by the MTT.	A minimum of three required Treatment Plan Reviews and additional reviews as deemed necessary by the MTT.

5. Discharge — Eligibility for discharge shall not occur until all Treatment Plan Reviews have been completed AND competencies have been demonstrated by the offender AND there is MTT consensus for discharge

II. Treatment is the comprehensive set of planned therapeutic experiences and interventions designed to assist the offender in changing any power and control dynamics, abusive thoughts, and behaviors (Section 5.0). Treatment requires the offender to attend in-person group or individual sessions at a minimum of once a week or more depending on the offender's treatment level (Section 5.05). Treatment is individualized and progress is assessed during a Treatment Plan Review (TPR), which occurs every two to three months (Section 5.06). The degree to which an offender progresses in treatment and remains compliant is based on meeting goals associated with the core competencies rather than the passage of a specific amount of time or sessions (Section 5.07).

III. Progress through treatment and victim safety is monitored by the Multi-Disciplinary Treatment Team (MTT), consisting of the Approved Provider, the supervising officer, a Treatment Victim Advocate (Section 7.0), and any other adjunct member of the MTT (Section 5.02). The MTT communicates regularly and shares information about the offender during the course of treatment in order to mitigate risks, support accountability, and improve victim safety. At the conclusion of treatment and as required by the Standards, an offender can be discharged as complete, unsuccessful, or administratively (Section 5.09).

As you read this counselor manual for the CARE Method curriculum, I want to acknowledge that each state has its own rules and procedures for domestic violence offender treatment. However, I cannot stress enough how remarkably effective the process outlined in Colorado's DVOMB Standards has been for my clients. The thorough evaluation, personalized treatment plans, and diligent monitoring by the Multi-Disciplinary Treatment Team consistently led to significant progress and heightened victim safety. If you are interested in adopting best practices like the Domestic Violence Risk Needs Assessment (DVRNA), I strongly encourage you to reach out to our board staff for appropriate training on the DVRNA.

About the Colorado DVOMB

Domestic violence offenders were treated on a voluntary basis prior to 1979, as no formal court referral system existed. In 1979, the Jefferson County District Attorney's Office in conjunction with Women in Crisis began a domestic violence program for individuals who had been criminally charged. The following year, Alternatives to Family Violence, an Adams County treatment program, assisted in the development of a referral system for offenders from municipal court; however, there were no formal standards governing the treatment of those who were referred.

Like many other states, Colorado passed legislation (§16-11.8-103, C.R.S.) in 2001 that created the Domestic Violence Offender Management Board (DVOMB) in an effort to create consistency for DV criminal cases and "so that such offenders will be less likely to offend again and the protection of victims and potential victims will be enhanced" (C.R.S. 16-11.8-101). Of its many statutory functions, the DVOMB is primarily a policy board mandated to develop state standards for the evaluation, treatment, and monitoring of DV offenders. In alignment with the fidelity principle, the DVOMB is mandated to periodically review, revise, and approve the standards in response to emerging research, best practices, implementation challenges, or recent case law.[2] During the last significant revision, the DVOMB considered a broad spectrum of modalities and interventions designed to address intimate partner violence. The conclusion of these revisions produced standards that embraced a PEI (principles of effective intervention) framework emphasizing research support. Further, the DVOMB is charged with managing the regulatory process by which someone is deemed eligible to work with DV offenders. Only those who are identified and listed as DVOMB Approved Providers (hereafter Providers) are eligible to receive referrals for

---

2. Tunstall, A.M., Weible, C.M., Tomsich, E.A., and Gover, A.R. Understanding policy reform in Colorado's domestic violence offender treatment standards. *Social Policy & Administration*, 50(5), 580–598 (2016). https://doi.org/10.1111/spol.12136

DV offender services. The purview of the DVOMB extends to offenders who have received a conviction, deferred sentence, plea deal, or an underlying factual basis of DV found by the presiding court, including offenders placed on probation, private probation, and community corrections, as well as those ordered by the Colorado Parole Board. Social services cases are generally referred to providers approved by the DVOMB; however, the DVOMB maintains no purview in those cases and the standards are used as a guideline, as providers may choose how and to what extent the standards for criminal cases should be used in conjunction with their professional and ethical judgment. The DVOMB has sought to review and incorporate empirical research when revisions to the standards were explored. This reliance on research was pivotal in the adoption and integration of the RNR principles in 2010, which eliminated the previous minimum length of 36 weeks for all offenders. The rationale for this change was prompted by mounting concerns that the time-driven model was inadequate for addressing the diversity of criminological, pathological, and typological profiles and characteristics of DV offenders.[3,4] Drawing upon the RNR research with general offenders, the DVOMB designed a differentiated and risk-informed model[5] that emphasizes meeting individualized goals rather than the passage of time over a predetermined number of sessions.[6]

2023 Annual Legislative Report

The most recent annual legislative report prepared by the Office of Domestic Violence and Sex Offender Management; the Domestic Violence Offender Management Board Program; Jesse Hansen, Manager, Statistical Analyst; and Dr. Rachael Collie states:

> "To identify the most current research- and evidence-based practices to date within the field of domestic violence offender treatment and management, the DVOMB conducted a literature review in support of ongoing committee work and the development of this report. Travers et al. (2021) conducted the most recent, comprehensive meta-analysis of domestic

3. Fowler, D.R., Cantos, A.L., and Miller, S.A. Exposure to violence, typology, and recidivism in a probation sample of domestic violence perpetrators. *Child Abuse & Neglect*, 59, 66–77 (2016). https://doi.org/10.1016/j.chiabu.2016.07.007

4. Johnson, R.R., and Goodlin-Fahncke, W. Exploring the effect of arrest across a domestic batterer typology. *Juvenile & Family Court Journal*, 66:1, 15–30 (2015). https://doi.org/10.1111/jfcj.12024

5. Radatz, D.L, Hansen, J., and Thomason, C. Domestic Violence Treatment in Colorado: An Overview of an Evidence-Based Approach. *Partner Abuse*, 11:3, 268-291 (2020). https://www.innovatingjustice.org/sites/default/files/media/document/2021/Radatz%20et%20al%20%282020%29%20DV%20treatment%20in%20CO.pdf

6. Gover, A.R., Richards, T.N., and Tomsich, E.A. Colorado's innovative response to domestic violence offender treatment: Current achievements and recommendations for the future. Denver, CO. Buechner Institute for Governance (2015).

violence treatment and the only one to date that examined adherence to the RNR model as a moderator of treatment outcome (recidivism rates following treatment).[7]

Travers et al. focused on more recent contemporary treatment approaches that were published from 2008 onward. Overall, the domestic violence treatments produced a positive treatment effect compared to no treatment, but one that was clearly moderated by degree of adherence to the RNR principles. Programs that fully adhered to the model had the greatest reductions in recidivism rate at two years follow-up, with a 7.0% recidivism rate for treated individuals versus 19.6% for untreated comparisons (k=2, n=479; OR=.30). For programs that partially adhered, the recidivism rate was 23.0% for treated individuals compared to 33.5% for untreated comparisons (k=3, n=8,851; OR=.58). There were few programs that were fully 'one-size-fits-all' (i.e., did not adhere) and these did not produce significant treatment effects."

7. Travers, A., McDonagh, T., Cunningham, T., and Armour, C. The effectiveness of interventions to prevent recidivism in perpetrators of intimate partner violence: A systematic review and meta-analysis. *Clinical Psychology Review*, 84:10, 101974 (2021, January). https://www.researchgate.net/publication/348497785_The_effectiveness_of_interventions_to_prevent_recidivism_in_perpetrators_of_intimate_partner_violence_A_systematic_review_and_meta-analysis; doi:10.1016/j.cpr.2021.101974

Acknowledgments

Writing *The CARE Method* has been one of the most rewarding and humbling experiences of my career. I am deeply grateful to the many individuals who have supported and encouraged me throughout this journey and especially for this second book for counselors.

First and foremost, I want to thank my clients. Your resilience, honesty, and courage have inspired me to create this method. I have learned so much from you, and I am honored to have walked alongside you on your path to healing and growth.

To my incredible husband, Casey Buckley, thank you for being my rock. Your unwavering support and love, along with the way you embrace fatherhood, have meant the world to me. I couldn't have done this without you. To my husband's family, thank you for your encouragement and for welcoming me so warmly into your lives. Your support has been invaluable.

To my family of origin, thank you for shaping the person I am today. To my late father, Pedro Chaves, whose poetic spirit still inspires me, and my mother, Eunice Lima Pacheco Silva, who sacrificed so much to ensure I received an education—your love and support have been the foundation of my journey.

To my staff at Vivus Counseling Services, your dedication and commitment to our work inspire me daily. You are not just my colleagues, but also the heartbeat of what we do. Thank you for your continued passion and collaboration in creating a safe and supportive space for our clients.

A special thanks to the Domestic Violence Offender Management Board (DVOMB), whose approval enabled me to begin this important work. Your guidance and standards have allowed me to grow as a professional and create *The CARE Method*.

To my friends, who have been there every step of the way, your constant encouragement and belief in me have kept me grounded and focused. Whether I should mention names here or not, you know who you are, and I am forever grateful for your presence in my life.

A heartfelt thank you to Maryanna Young, Heather Goetter, and the entire team at Aloha Publishing, who believed in my vision and helped turn *The CARE Method* book into reality. Your faith in this project has been invaluable, and I'm grateful for your support throughout this journey.

Lastly, thank you to every reader who picks up this book. My hope is that *The CARE Method* provides you with the tools, support, and encouragement to create meaningful change in your life or in the lives of those you work with.

Additional Resources

Resistance to treatment:

- **Citation**: Miller, W.R., and Rollnick, S. *Motivational Interviewing: Helping People Change* (3rd ed.). Guilford Press (2013).
    - **Summary**: This book discusses how motivational interviewing can help overcome client resistance and enhance engagement by focusing on clients' intrinsic motivations.

Extrinsic motivation:

- **Citation**: Deci, E.L., and Ryan, R.M. The "What" and "Why" of Goal Pursuits: Human Needs and the Self-Determination of Behavior. *Psychological Inquiry*, 11:4, 227-268 (2000).
    - **Summary**: This article explores the impact of extrinsic versus intrinsic motivation on behavior and engagement, relevant to understanding motivation in court-mandated clients.

Stigma and shame:

- **Citation**: Corrigan, P.W., and Kleinlein, P. "The Impact of Mental Illness Stigma," in P. Corrigan (Ed.), *On the Stigma of Mental Illness: Practical Strategies for Research and Social Change* (pp. 11-44). American Psychological Association (2005).
    - **Summary**: This book chapter addresses how stigma and shame affect individuals with mental illness, including how these factors can impede treatment and recovery.

Building trust and rapport:

- **Citation**: Rogers, C.R. *Client-Centered Therapy: Its Current Practice, Implications, and Theory*. Houghton Mifflin (1951).

- **Summary:** Rogers' foundational text on person-centered therapy emphasizes the importance of building trust and rapport in effective therapeutic relationships.

Complex legal and social issues:

- **Citation**: Hanser, R.D., and Toumbourou, J.W. "Understanding the Challenges of Working with Court-Mandated Clients," in *Handbook of Community-Based Clinical Practice* (pp. 233-249). Routledge (2016).
    - **Summary**: This handbook chapter discusses the complexities and challenges of working with court-mandated clients, including legal and social issues, and the need for a comprehensive approach.

Notes

Notes

Made in the USA
Monee, IL
05 October 2024

66619623R00221